# THE FARM BY LOUGH GUR

*D. Bradley.*

# MARY CARBERY

# *THE FARM*
## *BY*
# *LOUGH GUR*

### THE STORY OF MARY FOGARTY
### (SISSY O'BRIEN)

*With an Introduction by*
*SHANE LESLIE*

*and decorations by*
*ELIZABETH CORSELLIS*

## MERCIER PRESS

MERCIER PRESS
P.O. Box 5, 5 French Church Street, Cork
16 Hume Street, Dublin 2


First published by Longmans, Green and Co. Ltd. in 1937.
The Mercier Press edition was first published in 1973.


ISBN 0 85342 770 4


15    14    13    12    11    10    9    8    7    6

*A CIP catalogue for this book is available from the British Library.*

*This book is sold subject to the condition that it shall not, by way of trade
or otherwise, be lent, resold, hired out or otherwise circulated without the
publisher's prior consent in any form of binding or cover other than that in
which it is published and without a similar condition including this
condition being imposed on the subsequent purchaser.*

*Printed in Ireland by Colour Books Ltd.*

FOR THE DESCENDANTS
OF
JOHN AND ANNE O'BRIEN
OF HAPPY MEMORY

# AUTHOR'S MESSAGE

In the summer of 1904 I was in the county Limerick seeking the words of a lost song. In the little town of Bruff, where the song was born, Mrs. Fogarty welcomed me to her home on the bank of the lovely river Dawn, or Morning Star. I found in her an enthusiast for the old stories and legends of Bruff and Lough Gur. She told me about the notable banshee Ainë and her brother Fer Fi, the dwarf; of fairies in the hollow hills; of a drowned city in the Enchanted Lake; of giants and ghosts, saints' wells and fairy thorns. She had even in her youth heard the lost song sung. It was not, however, until many years later that she told me about her own people and of her happy childhood spent at the farm beside Lough Gur.

It was a story, I felt, that should be shared with others, and in 1935 I asked Mrs. Fogarty if she would write her recollections of those days.

At first she feared that she had forgotten more than she remembered; she considered the task beyond the power of a woman of her years. Still the idea remained in her mind and by long thinking and dwelling on the past, by talking and by answering questions put to her, the mist cleared, and her awakened memory gave back in startling clarity scenes from the past—places, people and events, even fragments of conversation. She saw with the eyes of her mind her parents in their vigour, her nurse, the dairymaids, farm labourers, horses and dogs; once more she worked and played with her sisters, was dutiful to visiting aunts, answered the greetings of wayfarers who came to the door and received their blessings when they passed on their way.

## Author's Message

While Mrs. Fogarty, in Ireland, was remembering and making notes of what she 'saw' and 'heard'—no easy task, yet admirably and faithfully fulfilled—I, in England, was trying to weave the notes, as I received them, into a continuous narrative, here and there filling inevitable gaps and supplying from history, folklore and other sources, certain passages which memory gave in shadowy form, or withheld.

In this way Mary Fogarty's story came to be written, with her and for her, by her friend

MARY CARBERY

St. Patrick's Day, 1937

**REFERENCE**

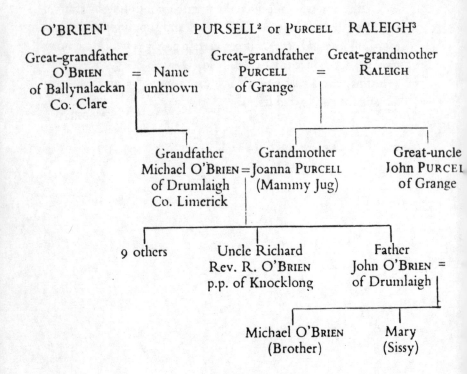

O'BRIEN[1]    PURSELL[2] or Purcell    RALEIGH[3]

Great-grandfather     Great-grandfather   Great-grandmother
    O'BRIEN    = Name        PURCELL    =    RALEIGH
of Ballynalackan | unknown    of Grange
   Co. Clare

        Grandfather    Grandmother        Great-uncle
    Michael O'BRIEN = Joanna PURCELL      John PURCEL
      of Drumlaigh  |   (Mammy Jug)         of Grange
      Co. Limerick  |

  9 others    Uncle Richard         Father
           Rev. R. O'BRIEN     John O'BRIEN =
           p.p. of Knocklong    of Drumlaigh |

            Michael O'BRIEN        Mary
              (Brother)           (Sissy)

1 Of Clare.
2 Descended from David Purcell, of Ballycalhane,
      Co. Limerick, executed as a rebel 1581.
3 Raleigh of Releighstown, descended from Walter Raleigh.
4 Of Clare.

# CHART

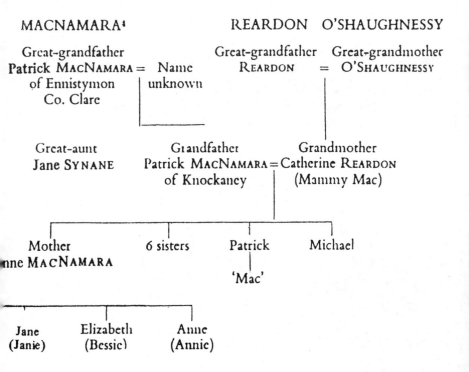

MACNAMARA[1]

Great-grandfather
Patrick MacNamara = Name
of Ennistymon | unknown
Co. Clare

REARDON   O'SHAUGHNESSY

Great-grandfather   Great-grandmother
REARDON   =   O'SHAUGHNESSY

Great-aunt
Jane SYNANE

Grandfather
Patrick MacNamara = Catherine REARDON
of Knockaney   (Mammy Mac)

Grandmother

Mother
Anne MacNamara

6 sisters

Patrick

Michael

'Mac'

Jane
(Janie)

Elizabeth
(Bessie)

Anne
(Annie)

## ACKNOWLEDGMENT

Thanks are due to Messrs. Constable and Co. Ltd., for permission to quote the lines on page 4 from Dr. Robin Flower's *Hymen and other Poems*.

# CONTENTS

# Contents

# INTRODUCTION

This book carries all the mists and memories, all the scent and sting of the Irish countryside. It is not a novel nor an agricultural tract nor a collection of folklore, but it possesses all their several interests without their fatigue. The story is told by an old Irish woman and roughly carries the reader through the nineteenth century. Her father was born in the year after Waterloo and the family lived and farmed under the Counts de Salis, who were good and considerate landlords. But the links with the past stretch even further back. Her mother remembers an old Miss Baily, who must have been the oldest of old maids, for she was born in the same year as the great Napoleon and the Duke of Wellington whom she called 'Arthur Wesley' because she had known him by that name when they were children!

A more wonderful link with other days was an old woman called Moll Ryall, who remembered her father and the neighbours cheering for the death of William of Orange. There are memories of Parnell and of the Great Famine and of the Fenians and the bitter political days. It is noticeable how little of Irish and the Irish literature entered the family life before the days of the Gaelic League. The love and interest in the English Classics is far greater than would be shown in any corresponding English homestead.

Dickens and Thackeray are spread galore, while the practice of reading aloud endeared authors to memory and appreciation in a manner that would else be impossible. It was a generation of readers, for whom there was no wireless and for whom the newspapers were chiefly bearers of political warfare. Not that books were thoroughly approved by all, for Cousin Julia exclaimed, 'Books are the invention of sinful men! If Almighty God had approved of books He would not have created worms to destroy them.'

What is lacking in Irish literature is made up by the amount of folklore and charms and legends which made the weird background of the 'strong farmer's' life. Cows and sheep, milking and pig-killing and harvests and poultry seem materialist enough but it is the suspicion of another intervening world that makes agriculture fascinating in a Celtic country compared to the aridness of farm life on the American prairies and to the dullness in the English Counties, where they have forgotten the traditions of Merry England and the host of fairy beings of whom Shakespeare was so well informed.

Lough Gur lies like a mirror under these lives. An Irish lake is a living creature, not a reservoir or a fishing preserve: 'Lough Gur dominates the scene. It was to us a personality loved, but also feared. Every seven years, so it is said, Gur demands the heart of a human being.'

Wonderful are the ghosts and banshees. There is the wizard, Lord Desmond, who tries to enveigle old Moll.

'Why is Lord Desmond being punished?'

'Because he was a magician. He made wicked spells and frightened people.'

'So now he has to be punished till the silver shoes of his horse are worn away.'

The great unsolved question was always whether fairies could be prayed for. 'Mebbe they wouldn't wish it at all! . . . If any good would come out of praying for them wouldn't the Holy Father in Rome long since have given the word?' And what a wonderful Encyclical it would have been.

As for the country folk, '*God be between us and harm*, was for ever on their lips—if a red-haired stranger came to the door: if a cock crowed during the day: if a heedless girl swept the floor towards the door: if she lit a candle without first crossing herself or forgot to nip the cake.'

Even at Easter the old Pagan rites were fulfilled. The children poured water into a flat pan and made the sun dance on the ceiling just as sun-worshippers did before the coming of Patrick.

And there were strange ancient games which were played at the Wakes: Shuffle the Brogue and the Rope Game and the Horse Fair 'and a very wicked one called the Mock Marriage'. But every half hour the gamesters pray for the soul of the dead. We can understand that it is 'the live wakes', when the young are leaving for America, that are so sorrowful.

Most weird of all was 'the cry of the Ould Kings', which was the sound of the dead encouraging the living to fight the battles of Ireland. 'It came rolling like thunder over the mountains from south to north, from sea to sea. Up the Shannon it came, along the valley and over Lough Gur, loud as Judgment Day, so everyone living and dead must hear the cry of the Ould Kings.'

The labourers were ill paid with a shilling a day but they were content and to live on the countryside without famine was happiness. Pathetic was the struggle of the family to keep alive their labourers in the 'Forties without taking from the children's food. There is little sign of trouble save when a Fenian agent slips in, while the family are saying the Rosary, and borrows the gun from the fireplace without saying a word.

Romance there is little, for without the professional matchmaker there would never be a wedding at all. There is a delightful account of an elopement when the lovers were caught in the floods on their way to a priest.

'Is it the will of God that I take you home to your father?' asks the alarmed swain, but the girl answers pluckily: 'It is not the will of God, John, until the water is higher than my heart.'

The clash of the antiquaries and excavators with the old-fashioned peasants is typical of modern Ireland, which has reluctantly surrendered haunted sites and Giants' Graves to be inspected and desecrated by men of science. When cows are milked by electricity one feels that there will be no fairies left to demand their tiny share of the milk. The cows themselves must miss the musical accompaniment of the milkers, for 'sorra a drop would the cows let down and we cheating them of their song'.

Simply told and without plot or stratagem, what is the charm and value of this book?

We have reached a time when the living and traditional country life of Ireland or England is as valuable as any propaganda of state or philosophy of living, now that the planning of suburbs and the arterialisation of roads threaten to creep into so much of our rural life. It is not so much the trees and hedges, which disappear, or the old homesteads, which are being obliterated. It is the folklore, the traditions of agriculture, the old knowledge about animals and plants, which is none the less practical for being mixed up with fragments of paganism and the moss and lichen of faith which mark the continuity of national life. Even if England became a macadamised garden city she would not have kept her soul. Ireland relinquishing her old ways in the farm and on the roadside will lose something that no new constitutions can possibly give her.

All who hold for the countryside will welcome this accurate and mellifluous record of what rural life was in Ireland when, strange to say, people could be equally poor and happy. The modern city can never give peace. There will likely be a reaction and a return to the land, when the value of such books will be appreciated. Apart from the old-fashioned sentiment, it is realised that great cities without a right proportion of countryside behind them are vulnerable in many ways. Any book is valuable which recalls the secrets and sanctities of rural life from the past as well as the common horse-sense which peasants and farmers have preserved from the time of Piers the Ploughman.

This book will reveal to the exiled Irish in the towns what their country life was like and to the English reader what England might have been before the fairies were expelled and the parsons ceased from conjuring.

SHANE LESLIE

## 1: I AND THE OTHERS

There is a hill in the county Limerick called Knockfennel whose
southern slopes fall steeply into Lough Gur. On a green ridge
above the lake stands an old farmhouse where I was born on
the twenty-ninth of May, 1858.

For many months I was, like other babies, merely a part of
my home, as unconscious of being as is the fire on the hearth or
the window which lets in the light. I knew my father and
mother, big brother and the maids, and Dooley who came
every day from the cottage at our gate to take care of me. Myself I did not know until one morning when I was set down on
my grandmother's bed while Dooley brought in her breakfast-
tray. Mammy Mac was mother's mother. She had a white face
and long black hair and because she was ill she stayed in bed.
On the tray was a boiled egg; she struck off the top and gave it
to me saying, 'Aren't you a bold[1] girl?' In this way I was made
known to myself and because Mammy Mac called me a bold
girl when I was good, I cried until Dooley came to remove me.

Mammy Mac died. Mother and Dooley cried and I was carried across the fields to the cottage of 'the lord' and 'the lady'

[1]Bold, meaning naughty.

who were cousins of father's, where I sat on a settle beside a cat and her kittens until I was carried home at night. Grandmother had gone but I did not forget her.

There were four of us then in the house besides the servants, father and mother, myself and brother, who was many years older than I was, therefore no playmate. He was kind and carried me on his back about the fields; sometimes he took me to the lake to show me coot and wild duck, and when, in winter's dusk, the wild geese flew over our heads, brother told me that the strongest gander flies first to break the air for the rest, and when he tires another takes his place as leader while he falls back to the end of the V. Brother called me little sister, or Sissy, although my name was Mary.

By and by my playmates came, three little sisters, Janie, Bessie, and Annie who I believed was brought in a bag by the fat, kind woman who nursed my mother. I was six when this baby came, and although I was timid by nature and unassertive, I felt a superiority over my sisters because I was the eldest daughter and could remember farther back than they could.

My earliest remembrance of my father and mother is of people who worked while we little girls played, who were a part of us and to whom we ran for help when we fell down and cut our knees. They were the people who made us feel safe, who loved us and helped us to be good, and occasionally punished us when we squabbled or were disobedient. A word of disapproval from my mother distressed me beyond measure, as when I cut off Janie's lovely hair to turn her into a boy. 'Oh dear,' my mother cried when she saw Janie's shorn and jagged head, 'my pretty child! my pretty one! How could you do it?'

Her pretty one! What then was I? A plain—perhaps even an ugly child! I had not thought of my appearance until that moment. I was humiliated, and miserable because I had grieved my mother for I loved her very much, so much indeed that half my love was pain. I was afraid of losing her. At night I used to steal down the steep and narrow stairs to stand and listen at her bedroom door—the door which was always ajar—to hear her quiet breathing and to re-assure myself before I went back to my cot. Sometimes I crept into bed beside her; she never turned me away.

I suffered from many fears; one was that the devil might come into our bedroom at night. I and my sisters used to say fervent prayers, making a special appeal to our angel-guardians for protection; we tried while we were undressing to do our part by making a great racket to scare the evil one away. None of us liked to be alone upstairs. There were noises, strange creaking of boughs, knocking and taps from an oak which grew across the window, the ping of acorns and the squeak of wet leaves on the pane, besides the whining of wind from a grating in the floor through which water was poured for father's shower-bath.

It happened one day that I had a punishment for some naughtiness—punishment was a slap on the hand, after a little lecture from my mother, and being sent upstairs earlier than usual. I was alone with the noises, lying in bed, sorrowful and a little disheartened, when between waking and sleeping I had a vision. There was an altar in the room and on it a small painted statue of the Blessed Virgin wrapped in a blue veil. I saw the statue move, grow larger and come down; I saw the veil drawn back and the Blessed Mother coming towards me with her arms open and her face shining. As I started up to meet her the vision faded, leaving me full of wonder and joy and completely comforted.

Another fear was of thunderstorms, a dread which was shared by my father who was in all other respects a brave man. A thunderbolt which fell in a neighbour's garden, making a hole in the ground, increased my fear. We used to pray for protection and were taught the Irish prayer of Ruman Mac-Colmain, a poet of the seventh century, which has been translated by Robin Flower:

> *Son of God, great Lord of wonder,*
> *Save me from the ravening thunder.*
> *By the Feast before Thy dying*
> *Save me from the tempest crying,*
> *And from hell, tempestuous under.*

Some of the stories which Dooley told us were frightening, about the *Little People* who live in hollow hills and at times make their fires in ancient raths, who come to farms on May-eve, busying themselves about the cows *and for no good*. This we knew must be true for on May-eve our head dairywoman would go into the cowsheds, yard and fields, sprinkling holy water which she had brought in bottles from the chapel after the priest had blessed it. Dooley called fairies the *Good People* because you never know when they will not be listening behind the door. The word fairy must never cross the lips, the risk of their revengeful malice is too great.

The stories were bearable, even enjoyable, in daytime, but at night one began to wonder if *they* would get into the house by a keyhole and come whistling upstairs! Ellie, a young and lively maid, helped to scare away my fears. 'Sure then, never a one will come near ye this night,' she would say, 'never a one but Murnane's ass with the red apple.' Sure enough, a red apple would be under my pillow when I woke in the morning, and I was never quite certain in my young mind whether Ellie hid it there or if the humble shabby ass of Murnane, our carpenter, really climbed the stairs on his small hoofs carrying my apple in his long yellow teeth.

There were so many delightful happenings and distractions on the farm that there seemed to be no time for lessons. I have heard that I did not know the alphabet until I was seven, when my mother engaged a small girl, Moll Hickey, not much older than I was but much more responsible, who went with us early every morning over the hills to the National School at Grange, where she became a scholar like ourselves.

Our school-day was a long one. We worked from ten o'clock to twelve; we had an hour's recreation when we ate the luncheon we brought from home; lessons followed from one to three-thirty when we left for the return walk which we lengthened by gambols in which Moll joined. On wet days we were sent to school and brought home by jaunting-car.

Fortunately for us there was an excellent teacher who saw that we had a thorough knowledge of the subjects taught in those days in National Schools, an advantage which we realised when we went later to boarding school and found ourselves at the head of the class term after term. I was considered a credit to Grange National School and was commended for attention and perseverance by the Dean at the annual prize-giving.

Every three months an inspector came to examine the scholars, and once a week a priest came from Bruff to give religious instruction. We were all Roman Catholics except two little girls, daughters of a gardener at Grange, who were shut out of the schoolroom while we others were taught our religion. Our only trouble at this time was having to wear frocks of dark green homespun which seemed to us very inferior to the flimsier stuffs worn by our school-fellows.

## 2: FATHER, MOTHER, MAMMY JUG

When a child is very young, its parents are taken for granted and it is only later, when it is perhaps five or six, that they become interesting as individuals. A child's instinct leads it to see beauty where kindness lights up a plain face, rather than in regularity of features and fine colouring.

My father had both kinds of good looks. He was of medium height, well made, with slender limbs, a fine forehead, kind and humorous brown eyes, and black hair. He was strong and a noted handball player, and thought nothing of walking seven Irish miles to Kilfinane to the ball-playing and seven miles home again. Unlike most Irishmen, he took little interest in horses, and was no judge of their points. Fox-hunting he left to brother; he had no time for sport and seemed always to be working or supervising the work of his men. He never went away for a holiday. Perhaps it was because of the hardship of his early days that he was so sympathetic to those who worked for him. 'He have the great heart for us all,' they used to say of him; there was no trouble that he did not share. He would not sadden our young hearts by talking of the grief and bitter trials through which Catholics passed in 'the bad old days', but when

6

we were older he told us a little about his childhood and his parents.

Great-grandfather O'Brien was one of the great clan of that name in the county Clare. He came from a place called Bally-nalackan, where his ancestors had lived for generations. His family remained faithful to the Catholic Church when the head of the clan and other members of it became Protestants. Life for those who held fast to the old faith was made intoler-able, and in the end great-grandfather O'Brien was burnt out of county Clare. We never knew what this meant; it sounded dreadful enough without details.

Great-grandfather's son was called Michael. He must have had some means for he bought the interest of the land which was known as Drumlaigh[1] and built the little house where his children and all of us were born, and which he left to father.

I cannot remember more than this about father's father, who died very suddenly after a dispute with a relation about some land, except hearing that grandfather O'Brien was afraid of the wind. On stormy nights when the tempest lashed Lough Gur into waves and came roaring and shrieking round the homestead, he would put the night-bolt on the door and shout to the wind without: 'There you are! Blow away with you to the devil!'

It was otherwise with father's mother, 'Mammy Jug', whose memory was kept alive by those who loved her, so that even to us children, born long after her death, she was so real that none of us would have been astonished to see her sitting in her rocking chair, telling her beads. 'Mammy Jug' was given that pet name by her children on account of her fancy for collecting jugs, large and small, pretty and ugly, of varied shape and every colour. Mammy liked them all for being jugs. She was charit-able, we were told, and in every one she saw the good, and to

[1]Pronounced Drumlay, 'the ridge of grey land.'

the bad in them she turned a blind eye. The old people on the farm still spoke of her with affection, calling her 'Mammy Jug', who had been invariably spoken of as 'the misthress' in her lifetime.

Mammy Jug, with six sons and four daughters, had a hard struggle to bring them all up, but nothing daunted or dismayed her. She managed the farm, making her daughters work as hard as she did. Her sons she sent to a hedge-school, for no self-respecting parent, and certainly not Mammy Jug, would let her children go to the Charter School provided by the government for Catholic children, where all the scholars were compulsorily educated to be Protestants. The hedge-school was held in isolated houses or barns or out of doors in lonely and well-screened places where the risk of discovery and interruption was small and the meeting place could if necessary be changed from day to day. The teachers were outlaws, nominally under the authority of the priest who was sometimes himself an outlaw. At the risk of their lives these masters tried to satisfy the thirst for knowledge which has been characteristic of the Irish from the earliest times. The education they gave was good; they carried many of their scholars from the alphabet to Latin, Greek, mathematics and English literature. Some scholars took orders direct from the hedge-schools, and were known as hedge-priests. What more did the hedge-scholars learn from the outlaw master? To hate England for her persecution of the Catholics, for her attempts to poison the mind and violate the conscience of the children. They taught that Ireland would once more be free if the scholars would be strong to endure and, when the time should come, to fight for their country. Over and above this, the masters comforted them, as they must often have had to comfort themselves, with poetry. The days of the wandering bards were over, the ballads of the past, the feats of kings and warriors, were heard no more. In their place were born songs of promise for the future, when Ireland, at peace with herself, shall be free.

The little scholars came home from the byways and hedges by cow-time,[1] so that they could help with the milking and carry the pails into the dairy for their mother. One brought in turf for the fire, another drove the cows into the fields, a third fed the pigs and shut them into their styes. After supper the boys and their sisters gathered round the Poor Scholar—a Poor Scholar was to be found in almost every farmhouse—who helped them with their lessons, played to them on the fiddle, taught them the songs which they dared not sing under the hedge, and who led the responses when Mammy Jug said the Rosary at bedtime.

The children grew up. Two of them, Michael and Richard, became priests, two made their living in Limerick, two were farmers, of whom my father was one. Three of their sisters were married, one to a farmer, another to a merchant, the third—who would marry for love alone—to a ne'er-do-well. The fourth became a nun, a rare happening in those days, for there were few religious orders in Ireland in the thirties and few convents to receive girls with vocations.

Mammy Jug lived with my father, who was then unmarried, until she died.

My father, who was born in 1816, farmed about 200 acres of land, rented from Count de Salis. He gave constant employment to a number of men and women, some of whom lived in the four cottages on the farm. There was a potato garden for each cottage, also a goat. The labourers were paid a shilling a day, which was threepence more than the wages usually given in the neighbourhood. Their wives and daughters helped with the milking of our fifty beautiful cows, under the supervision of

[1] 5 p.m.

the head dairywoman, whose wages were thirty pounds a year. Extra men, called *spalpeens*, coming usually from Kerry and Cork, were hired for the potato digging in October. My father's head man, Dick Dooley, used to go to Bruff on a Sunday in late September—if the ground was dry enough then for digging—and after Mass he inspected and engaged the required number of *spalpeens* who were waiting in the street to be hired by the highest bidder. The same *spalpeens* came year after year to our farm: quiet and unobstrusive they were, grateful to my father for giving them work and to my mother for providing abundant nourishing food.

At the annual auction of short leases for tenants of Count de Salis, my father bought the lease of some water-meadows which provided sweet hay for the winter feeding of our cows. These marshy fields fell to my father year after year; they were so inaccessible that there was little competition. I can remember how the horses which drew the carts—each loaded with a ton of hay—struggled and strained over the deep ruts on their way to the paddock where the ricks were built. Each horse brought three loads in the day. We young ones were deeply interested watching the rising of the ricks under the direction of Johnny Heffernan, who came year after year to build and thatch so as 'to keep out the drop', that is to say, the rain. There were no hay-barns, no elevators in those days; the men handed up the grey-green grass on long forks.

My father was a successful and progressive farmer who believed in giving his attention to the small matters on the farm as well as to the larger. In fact, his attention to detail and finish gave rise to the local saying, 'The harvest is not over till John O'Brien has brushed and combed his ricks.' He tried, too, to simplify work and installed a machine, turned by a pony, to lessen the labour of churning.

And here I must tell of my dearly loved mother. She was

born in 1819 at Knockaney, not far from Lough Gur. Her
father, Patrick MacNamara, was a farmer. He, like great-grandfather O'Brien, came from the county Clare. He was a fine
horseman and followed the hounds while his wife, Mammy
Mac, managed the farm. She was clever and industrious and
was described as a 'dutiful homekeeper'. Mammy Mac's name
was Catherine Reardon. Her mother was an only child, her
name was O'Shaughnessy. She was a cousin and ward of Mr.
Barry of Sandville. Mother told us that we had gentle blood in
our veins on both sides.

Mammy Mac's farming must have been profitable, for she
had the means as well as the wisdom to give my mother an
exceptionally good education. She was sent for some years to a
boarding-school kept by a gentlewoman from whom she learnt
to appreciate good music, well-written books, poetry, nature
and all beautiful things. She was taught to speak well and to
write delightful letters, and her simple, natural manners were
left unspoilt.

I remember my mother with fair hair and wistful blue eyes,
she was fairly tall and had a fragile appearance which may have
been due to the active life she led. She liked all kinds of work,
whether in the kitchen, dairy or garden. I can see her now, sitting
quietly at her sewing after a strenuous morning, or arranging
flowers on a small altar in 'the children's' bedroom, sitting beside a dying person in a poor cabin, binding up the broken leg
of a lamb that had fallen from the rocks.

## 3: THE MAGIC LAKE

When I think of home I see first Lough Gur, lying in summer sunshine like a bright mirror in which are reflected blue sky, bare hills, precipitous grey rocks and green pastures dotted with cattle and sheep; then a small, white house, half-hiding the fine farm buildings behind it, and four little girls playing ring-o'-roses before the door of their home, or touch-wood on the lawn,[1] darting from the old oak before the house to the copper-beech, from the weeping-ash to the two rings of trees planted by our mother when she came to the farm as a bride.

Lough Gur dominates the scene. It was to us a personality loved, but also feared. Every seven years, so it is said, Gur demands the heart of a human being. Drownings were not infrequent and, as the bodies of the drowned were sometimes not recovered, Gur was said by some to be a bottomless lough.

In the lake is Knockadoon hill, joined to the land by a causeway built on the isthmus, once guarded by two fortresses where now only one, the ruined Black Castle, remains. Sometimes we children climbed by a steep and stony way to the summit of

[1]In Ireland a field near a house, grazed by sheep or cattle.

Knockadoon, where, when father was a boy, eagles made their nests and flew about the hills searching for leverets and new-born lambs to feed their young. From the top of Knockadoon we could see Garret Island, interesting for its prehistoric re-mains which were visited from time to time by antiquaries who gave my mother curious implements of the stone age in return for her hospitality.

Lough Gur has been called the Enchanted Lake; some say that in ancient days there was a city where the lake is now, be-fore an earthquake threw up the hills and filled the hollow with water so that the city was submerged. Even now, the peasants say, when the surface of the lake is smooth one may see from a boat, far down and down again, the drowned city, its walls and castle, houses and church, perfect and intact, waiting for the Day of Resurrection. And on Christmas eve, a dark night without moon and stars, if one looks down and down again, one may see lights in the windows, and listening with the ears of the mind, hear the muffled chiming of church bells.

The hills round Gur are bare of trees, but once they were covered with forest. Great giants, who were among Ireland's first people, hunted in the woods; they hunted deer, wild pigs and wild horses. The bones they picked and gnawed with their strong teeth are brought up from the floor of the lake to this day, with the fossil bones of polar bears and some say of rhino-ceros.

On Baile-na-Cailleach hill one of these giants lies buried in a stone coffin with a long gold sword beside him. The stones of a cromlech stand over the grave, which is called the Pig's Bed or Leaba-na-muice.

Old people who lived on the shore believed that giants built the stone circles which stand near the lake, for who but giants could move such great stones? They were heathen, these giants.

Their god was Bel, and a mighty one he was, as the god of giants should be. Wasn't the curse of Bel a dread and a danger to this day? Wasn't it to please Bel, to get on the right side of him, that the people lit Bel-fires on the hills? Bel could be kind; his blessing was good and lucky, but his brother, the Thunder God, was a Fright and a Spit-Fire—if he spared you to-day he would take you to-morrow. So the old people said. They knew little more than we children did of the gentle moon-worshippers of old who burnt the fire of Samhuin on the night of November the first, and on the sixth night of every moon brought their sick into the moonlight to be healed. The old folk had heard that night called All-Heal. They knew that if a sick person was not better by the eighth or ninth day of the moon he would hear *Ceolsidhe*, the fairy music with which Ainë the Banshee, Spirit of Lough Gur, comforts the dying. He would fall asleep to *Suantraighe*, the whispering song of sleep which Fer Fi[1] plays on a three-stringed harp.

No wonder that they who travelled the roads, the wandering beggars, pipers and harpers, story-tellers, Poor Scholars, drovers and tinkers, all feared to be benighted within a mile of Gur's enchanted waters, feared even to fall asleep in broad daylight, so great was the magic in the air.

We children knew nothing of this dread. The only story we half-believed was of one of the Desmonds, Garret the Earl,[2] who was doomed to gallop once in seven years over the surface of the water and around the lake. He rides on a milk-white horse, shod with silver shoes, and must ride until the silver shoes are worn out. Then he will be loosed from the enchant-

[1]Fer Fi is Ainë's brother, a kindly red-haired dwarf who plays only three tunes, Wail, Sleep, Laughter. It is lucky to hear Fer Fi laughing.

[2]Garret FitzGerald, Earl of Desmond, was the unfortunate leader who fought against the forces of Elizabeth.

ment which binds him and will live, a man among men, for he has never died.

We were afraid to go near the lake alone at twilight lest we should meet him; we wondered why he was cursed and what he sought on his wild ride. Often we prayed that he might find peace.

My father's land came down to the lake on the slope of the hill called the Carrigeen, which lay at the foot of Knock-fennel. The Carrigeen was well fenced to keep in the year-ling bulls which grazed there. Within this enclosure was a smaller one with high stone walls on three sides where dwelt our great bull; on the fourth side was the lake. We were thank-ful that father kept him safely shut up, for at that time many farmers let their bulls range the fields with other cattle and many were the stories we heard of people being chased and gored.

Carrigeen hill is said to be hollow like Tory hill and so many more. The stream flowing from the lake which we called the eel-stream, disappears into Carrigeen close to the eel-weir where there is a large light cave with a small opening at the back of it. It was said that anyone who had the courage to squeeze through the hole would find himself in the hollow heart of the hill.

One day when I was watching old Paddy taking eels, two of the antiquaries who were often rummaging about came by and stopped to talk. They sometimes got clues, mother said, from people like Paddy. Now they wanted a clue about that open-ing.

'Has anyone ever been through the hole?' the old antiquary asked in a loud Sassenach voice.

'Foxes, mebbe,' grunted Paddy.

'I mean, has any person to your knowledge explored beyond the opening in this cave?'

'No, then,' said Paddy, 'no one would be so bould.'

'Do you think I could get through?' the old antiquary who was fat said to the young antiquary who was thin.

'No chance, neither of us could get in.'

The old antiquary growled a good deal as he scrambled into the big open cave and began peering into the hole by the light of a candle-end.

'You won't let him send you in there, will you?' I asked the young one who said his name was Peter. 'There's no need, because everyone knows all the hills about here are hollow and very dangerous inside.'

'You frighten me,' said Peter, 'is it because of . . . you know?'

I nodded.

'I know a lot about *them*,' he said mysteriously. 'If a mortal man gets in . . . you won't be frightened if I tell you?'

'Oh no!' I was trembling already inside.

'Well, he stands there looking round and getting used to the strange green light that shines round him, and suddenly, all in a flash, *they* are all round him, like a cloud of butterflies. . . . Oh! how they tickle! and see! there are two of them scattering fern-seed in his eyes and a few more are plugging his ears with elder-pith so that he will not be able to see or hear with human eyes and ears again. Magic eyes and ears will be more useful where he is now. See, here come a lot of little cooks in white aprons tied behind under their wings . . . they are bringing swallow-meat . . . now others are making the poor mortal eat! It tastes all right but you know, I daresay, that every swallow has three drops of devil's blood in its veins. Now he is properly be-witched and . . .'

'There's worse to it than that,' Paddy interrupted. He had left off taking eels so that he could hear better.

'You can go on now,' said Peter politely.

'When the poor fella have the swallow-meat ate he is done for entirely; he can't confess his sins, he can't go to Mass, and try as he may he can't die.'

'But wouldn't that be nice, Paddy, not to die?' I asked.

'Under them circumstances ye'd sooner be dead,' Paddy said grimly.

'Can nothing save him?' I cried wildly, feeling that the mortal might be father or brother.

'Nothin',' grunted Paddy, as he scraped away the green water-weed which clung round his fingers, using a flint scraper.

'You're wrong there,' said Peter. 'It's possible that after they had him bewitched he could not save himself, but if he had his pipe on him and if directly he was inside the hill he got it going, they would shoot him out through the little hole in the wink of an eye. They can't stand tobacco! Do you mind if I smoke, Miss . . .?'

'Sissy. Yes, do smoke!'

'I think so too. It's safer when we've been talking about *them*. Have some?' He held out his pouch to Paddy.

'God bless your honour kindly,' said Paddy, taking a pipeful.

'But, Peter . . .'

'Go on, Sissy.'

'If the mortal had been bewitched all through, could anything save him?'

'He could be saved by a good little girl like you. She would blow the fern-seed from his eyes—he would see. She would take the elder-pith from his ears—he would hear . . .'

'But . . . but . . . the swallow-meat?'

Paddy had to have the last word. 'Ye'd get Mrs. Dooley to mix a glass o' salt and warm water, strong, and then, after he had it drunk . . '

'Yes, Paddy?'

Paddy chuckled. 'Bein' a y'ung lady, I'd say ye'd make off wid yerself.'

Our gate was close to the lake. Dooley's cottage stood near by, neat and tidy in its garden where marigolds flowered all the year round and the paths were edged with smooth white stones from the lake shore.

Dooley was as neat and sweet as a double daisy; she had a face wrinkled and rosy as a russet apple, a broad smile and large kind hands; she wore a snow-white apron over her blue dress, a small three-cornered plaid shawl over her shoulders and on her head a white frilled cap which hid her hair and which she washed and goffered with a tally (Italian) iron. She came out of her house to make sure that the antiquaries were fit company for me and to enquire if they would like some tea.

'You can have the fat one, darling Dooley,' I whispered, 'and I will take the thin one to tea with mother.'

The old antiquary was just then worrying old Paddy about the flake scraper in his hand and asking where he had found it. Paddy said he had had it in his pocket for twenty years and had come by it honest, and the gentleman needn't be suspicioning him about it. Dooley stepped in to say that she knew of a place where them things were lying in heaps, and handfuls could be gathered by any who wanted them, which diverted the Sassenach from Paddy. The old man was very angry, not only about his flake, but because the eels were slithering over the grass towards the weir.

The road to our house led past the orchard which father let to old Malachy for a very small rent. We bought all the apples, and it would have been cheaper to keep the orchard, but when one day someone who thought himself very clever, suggested that to mother, father answered, 'You may be right; it would be cheaper for us, but for Malachy it would be starvation.'

Malachy was deaf, his sight was getting scattered, and he relied on his old dog to tell him when thieving boys were climbing into the orchard. 'Bite 'em, good fella, bite 'em,' he shouted, waving his blackthorn. If they weren't quick in escaping, old Barker gave them a nip.

Beyond the orchard was a place we called the alley, where there was a small cowshed and a haystack within the crumbled walls of a ruin. When we had passed that and the dangerous sandpit and mother's trees, we arrived at our house.

## 4: THE LONG DAY'S WORK

Our farm was like a little colony, self-contained, where everyone worked hard and all were contented and happy. Besides
the fields, the farmhouse and its good out-buildings, there was a
a quarry, a kiln for burning lime, a sandpit, a turf bog and the
productive eel-weir. Eels were sent direct to Limerick market
or taken by Meggy-the-Eels who came from Bruff to buy 'the
take', which she peddled from house to house in the little town.
Everything we ate and drank came from the farm except tea
and coffee and *J.J.* (John Jameson's whisky), which was kept
for visitors and for medicine. We lived by a strict routine, a
necessity on a farm if it is to prosper, and all the indoor work
took place in the two dairies and the large stone-paved kitchen
which was about twenty-eight feet square and well-lighted
by a large window overlooking the lake. On the opposite
wall was the great hearth, the light and glory of the house,
where a huge fire of turf, wood and coke burnt all day and
smouldered all night, to be roused before dawn into flame by
a few strokes of the well-built bellows. On the third wall
hung a fine array of brass and copper saucepans with the old

mincer[1] on a bracket next to the great dresser, gay with willow-pattern plates, with dishes of various shapes and colours and here and there a jug, left over from Mammy Jug's days. In the lower part of the dresser, instead of cupboards was a long coop in which were sitting hens; it seems to me now that they sat there perpetually except when two geese took their place in early spring. A third goose and many more hens were put to sit in the barn, while the gander, our terror, patrolled the yard, refusing to leave it till his proud wives returned to him, leading their lovely goslings, small moving balls of yellow fluff. It was ear-splitting to hear the gander's welcome to his mates when they came from the nesting.

In the centre of the kitchen was a long oak table at which the ploughman and farmboys had their meals, sitting on forms. For breakfast they had maizemeal stir-about with plenty of milk, sometimes potatoes; in later years home-made bread was added. Dinner was at 12.30, consisting of milk in 'piggins',[2] potatoes and 'dip' (a make-up of gravy and bread); bacon was given twice a week, but later on every day. The men's tea was taken out to them at four o'clock, with bread and butter in great slices. The maids had the same food, but at a different time, and for supper at 7.30 bread and milk, hot or cold, or porridge with plenty of sweet milk. On this simple fare maids and men throve; they were all healthy, hearty and good-tempered.

Opening out of the kitchen was a passage leading to the front door, our parent's bedroom and the little room where after our four o'clock dinner we sat to read or sew or learn our lessons. Upstairs were the spare room and two other bedrooms

[1] This famous old mincer now ninety years old, is still in use and is more efficient than any modern mincing machine.

[2] A round wooden vessel with a high wooden stave for a handle. It held 1½ pints.

for ourselves and the maids, besides a storeroom where mother
kept her dovetailed chest, books, linen, spinning wheels and
many other things. The farmboys had a room in the yard,
fitted with good beds and chairs; except for meals and prayers
they were not allowed inside the house, nor was any sort of
friendship allowed between them and the maids, who were
ever under the watchful eye of 'the misthress'.

This was the farm routine. All hands rose at 4.30 a.m., the
fire was blown up until it blazed, turf and coke were piled on
and an immense iron pot of water suspended from a crane was
moved by a lever to hang directly over the flames to boil for
the feeding of the calves. Outside, one of the boys lit a furnace
in the yard over which was a boiler for more hot water. This
was set close to the pump.

At seven, when the milking was over, my mother came from
her room to receive the milk in the upper or lower dairy according to the season; the lower one, which was reached from
the upper by stone steps, was cooler and used in summer. On
the stone shelves were rows of flat earthen and glass pans; all
was spotlessly clean and fragrant, in fact visitors who came to
Lough Gur seldom left without visiting 'Mrs. O'Brien's show
dairy'. Here entered in a long file, the head dairywoman and
her maids, carrying milk pails on their heads; lowering them
carefully, they poured the milk through strainers into huge lead
cisterns where the cream for butter-making was to rise, the re-
mainder being strained into flat pans on the shelves. A lovely,
homely sight: rich, ivory milk, golden cream—all to be hand
skimmed—firm one-pound pats of perfectly made butter ready
to be sent off to special customers in Dublin and London; other
great pats for home consumption—we children did not spare it
—and the bulk of the butter in firkins, each containing seventy
pounds, set aside for the butter buyer to take to market.

At nine we had our breakfast: two boiled duck eggs every

day for our father, a hen's egg for mother, for us children stir-about, home-made bread, and butter and milk.

Breakfast for all was over by 9.30 when we children and Moll set off across the hills to school. The men had gone to the fields, the women dispersed—some to feeding numerous turkeys, geese, hens, ducks, others to wash the dairy and scrub and scald pails, pans, strainers and churns; one to do housework and another to prepare the men's mid-day meal and perhaps set a great batch of dough to rise in the warmth of the hearth while the brick oven was being heated by burning bundles of furze and sticks. Our dinner was at four o'clock. The evening milking was from five to seven. The morning routine of straining and scalding was repeated. Milking was something of a mystery to us children, as our father forbade us to enter the byres, but from the outside we heard the rythmical swish of milk falling into pails and the dairymaids singing or crooning, each to her cow.

'Why do you sing as you milk?' I once asked Ellie, she who arranged with Murnane's ass to bring me the red apple.

'Sing, is it? And why wouldn't I sing?' she answered, 'Sorra a drop would the cows let down and we cheating them of their song! What's more they milk aisy for the *Wearin' of the Green* and *She's far from the land*, but if ye try them with *The Shan Van Voght* ye'll repent it.'

'Why should I repent it, Ellie?'

'The most of them would be that excited they'd have the milk swep' out of the pail with their tails on the first note, and then what would the misthress say?'

At seven o'clock we sat down for a happy time round the table in the little room, a bright, shaded reading lamp in the middle, and while the rest sewed, one of us or our mother read aloud books suited to our years, such as *Little Women*, which we loved and knew almost by heart, *The Wide, Wide World*, which made us weep over the griefs of pious Ellen Montgomery and shocked us with the irreligion of her Aunt Fortune, *Scottish Chiefs, Masterman Ready, Robinson Crusoe*, and many other children's books.

My father meanwhile sat contentedly with his pipe in an uncomfortable armchair, reading the paper and sipping a glass of fresh spring water. He was very abstemious and had nothing but this between his four o'clock dinner and breakfast next day.

All hands were called to say the Rosary at 9 p.m., mother giving it out, the rest responding. She ended with a fine generous prayer beginning thus: *Bless, O Lord, the repose we are about to take, so that by renewing our bodily strength we may be better able to serve Thee.* The prayer was for those in authority over us, for the poor, sick and sorrowful, for unbelievers and for the dead. One of the farmboys was always the last to answer the call to prayers; my father reproved him, saying, 'It's for only ten minutes, Mike, ten minutes given to Almighty God.' 'Faix, sir,' Mike replied, 'they are the longest ten minutes of the day.'

At 9.30 the long day's work was over.

## 5: SUNDAYS AND SAINTS' DAYS

On Sundays and saints' days, which we called holy days, only necessary work was done. The household rose an hour earlier than usual, breakfast was earlier; the maids went to twelve o'clock Mass at Grange; we went to our parish church, St. Patrick's Well, where Mass was at ten o'clock. Old Paddy brought the side-car to the door; father took the reins to drive us. He was very punctual himself and was greatly tried by us when we were late.

'Mass will not wait for you,' he said and when one or other of us jumped off the car, making excuses, 'I've dropped my beads,' or 'I've dropped my handkerchief,' he used to say, 'What do you mean by *dropped*? Be honest, child! In plain language, isn't it I've forgotten my beads? I didn't get ready in time? I didn't put out my handkerchief? Speak the truth, child.'

St. Patrick's Well was a poor plain little chapel. There was an altar with a large crude statue of the Blessed Virgin on it and two vases for flowers. There was a gallery round the walls and on either side of the aisle little enclosed pews to hold two. We had the two front pews on both sides, close to the altar steps.

There was no singing, no incense, no candles, no pictures nor stations of the cross. The congregation was mostly made up of very poor people, illiterate, ignorant, over-worked and under-fed, who had few joys in their lives. They came to church, or chapel as it was called to distinguish it from Protestant churches, because it was their first duty, because it was their one escape from the hard material life of everyday.

The clerk was a source of constant interest to us children. He was a little youngish-old man with a small, clean-shaven, womanish face and a long unruly lock of black hair which kept falling over his forehead. After every response that he made, Billy-the-Clerk would look proudly round our pews, as if to say, 'Did ye hear me sayin' the Latin?' and twitch his lock back into place. His sister, Joanny, used to steal out during the sermon to get the priest's breakfast of tea, bread and butter and eggs which he ate in the vestry. However carefully we watched Father Ryan, we never discovered whether he gave Joanny a signal, or if she went when she thought he had preached long enough and might as well begin to wind up. We were glad to hear her tiptoeing out for we found sermons very dry.

There were one or two funny old priests near Lough Gur who spoke their minds very freely. I remember hearing one reading a list of his dues,[1] who ended with the name of a well-to-do parishioner. 'There's a true Christian woman for ye to follow! Wasn't she the only one in the parish to remember that I am *entitled* to a good dinner at Christmas and that I enjoy a turkey as well as any man!'

After Mass we all went upstairs to take off our hats and put away our beads. Mother laid her cloak and bonnet on the white counterpane in the spare bedroom; it was little Janie's duty to brush and put them away. Then she would give a glance at the

---

[1] Contributions made by parishioners to the parish priest.

dairy and go with father to look at a new calf or foal or consult over an ailing cow. In springtime, the season which she loved best, they would potter together among the trees she and he had planted in the first year of their marriage and examine the fence which kept the cows from injuring them. She would sometimes call to us to look at the swelling buds in their wrappings, so soon to be discarded, and to show us inside the strong and supple cover, the silken lining, soft to the infant leaves packed tightly within. Sometimes only one of us would answer her call, usually Bessie. 'I'm sorry, but Sissy and Janie are busy with the dinner. They can't leave the pops[1] till they've done getting them into the basket.' In the absence of the maids at Mass, Janie and I took the opportunity of showing what we could do. We sometimes put the potatoes before they were properly cooked into the long oval basket in which they were drained before being served, and we heard of it from Ellie, who would return the whole boiling to the pot. One or other of the maids and all the dairywomen went to their homes after Mass on Sunday, but all had to be back by cow-time.

Now and then our parents went to spend Sunday with Uncle Richard at Knocklong, where he was the parish priest, but as a rule they stayed at home with us.

There were a few small farmers whose land bounded ours who came every Sunday after Mass to hear what was going on in the world from *Freeman's Journal* which my father took in as well as the weekly Limerick paper. Few if any of them could read or write. Father was their link with Ireland outside the county of Limerick, with England, with the nebulous Beyond called Europe whose single familiar point was Rome, and Rome but the dwelling of the Holy Father and the site of the Holy Catholic Church. They set great store by this chance of

[1]We called potatoes, pops or patoes.

enlightenment and believed that what father said could be taken as the truth, all the more so because he was no politician.

The first to arrive was James Regan, a tall, thin man who wore a very tall hat and smooth black clothes. Perhaps it was because of his dark clothes and long sad face that some said he was a spoiled priest.[1] He had no apparent reason for looking dejected for he had a good-looking wife and plenty of sons and daughters. The other farmers I can see before my eyes in corduroy knee-breeches, bright waistcoats and sledge-hammer coats: tall John Heffernan, Jack Donovan, bent almost double with rheumatism; Twomey, whose wife was said to beat him on Sunday night in return for the beating he gave her on Saturday; and old Malachy, he who rented our orchard and was too deaf to hear a word of the reading but enjoyed it all the same.

Each one came in with the greeting, in English or in Irish, 'God save all here,' to which those within responded heartily, 'And you too.' Pipes were lighted and my father proceeded to read the newspaper, his audience commenting in low tones until the close, when one and another would give his opinion while my father listened.

They talked the politics of the day and of the neighbourhood, railing against all landlords and agents except their own landlord, Count de Salis, and his agent. They agreed that most agents deserved to be shot. The Count was humane; he understood the difficulties of the tenants. No one wished to hurt or harm him; he gave timber and slate to build or improve the farms or cottages and although the rents were considered to be too high, the best and most friendly feelings existed between the de Salis family and their tenants. Our landlord understood how great was the small farmer's struggle to make two ends

[1] A man who, having been educated for the priesthood, refused to receive holy orders, or was dismissed for bad conduct or for some other reason.

meet, to pay the rent and bring up his generally large family decently.

Unfortunately there were other landlords who were overbearing and tyrannical, who mocked at any attempt on the part of farmers and their families to improve their position by education other than that of the national school, or by wearing boots and stockings and aiming at a better standard of living. These landlords were hated and despised. The railing of the farmers and others against them was the measure of the wounds they inflicted on the feelings of a sensitive people.

My father thought it good for his visitors to let off steam and he usually calmed them down before they left, for he was a man of peace and justice, giving honour where honour was due. 'You may talk against landlords but there isn't an Irishman who wouldn't be a landowner if he had the chance and a landlord at that.' They would all laugh heartily, slap their knees and agree.

'Faix! Ye've said it! Misther O'Brien have the nail hit on the head!'

Unwelcome visitors who came occasionally on a Sunday, hoping to catch father between Mass and dinner, were political people from Limerick or Cork. They came hoping to persuade him into joining one party or another and sat sipping *J.J.* and gushing with arguments while father stood gravely against the doorpost waiting for the glass to be drained, the flow of words to run dry. Then he explained quietly that he was no politician and that his time was more than taken up on the farm. He would never be drawn into a discussion, but he was kind to the disappointed agents and sorry that their time had been wasted. As they went dolefully away they would cast their eyes over the barns and byres, the fields dotted with grazing cattle, the poultry, the fat ricks.

'Small blame to ye, Mr. O'Brien, 'tis you are the lucky man to be living like a king on the fat of the land!' And according to their natures, they would sigh, wishing themselves farmers and politics at the devil, or they would laugh and smack their lips, dwelling on father's hospitality and the fine taste of *J.J.*

Perhaps it was because father kept out of politics that successful farmers like himself came privately by one and one to ask how he managed to keep clear and how he dealt with those who preached and practised fenianism[1] and especially those who maintained that killing is no murder.

'My religion', father told these enquirers, 'teaches me that all murder is a mortal sin. God says, Thou shalt not kill. Those who kill are breaking the law of God. Leaders who order a man to kill a landlord or an agent are sending that man's soul to hell. That's the truth and that is the answer I give.'

It was the answer he gave one Sunday morning to smaller men who were bewildered by the talk that was going round; having given it he pushed back his chair and being deeply moved went out into the air. After further discussion among themselves the men followed him to thank him for his 'good sensible words'. 'Ye have us strengthened, sir,' said great John Heffernan, 'and by the help of God, not one of us who've heard ye speak will sin his soul[2] to please the fenians.'

---

[1]The Fenian movement began about 1858. Country people had less to do with it than townsfolk. The oath which had to be taken by its members was this:

I, A. B. in the presence of Almighty God, do solemnly swear allegiance to the Irish Republic now virtually established, and that I will do my very utmost, at every risk, while life lasts, to defend its independence and integrity; and finally that I will yield implicit obedience in all things *not contrary to the law of God* to the commands of my superior officers. So help me God.

Catholic priests preached against the movement and threatened excommunication to those who used physical force.

[2]Commit a mortal sin.

Fenianism therefore had no place in our home, yet twice unpleasant things that had to do with it happened there. One night, when father was out and mother was saying the Rosary with children, maids and farmboys kneeling round her, the door opened quietly and a stranger stole into the room, took the gun from over the fireplace and went away as stealthily as he came. No one appeared to notice. Mother's voice did not falter and she went on with the prayer. In the morning the gun was found on the doorstep; we never heard for what purpose it had been borrowed.

The second trouble was when two young nephews of mother's came to the farm after dark, imploring her to hide them from the police who were searching for them round their home. Nothing but father's great love for mother could have made him agree to their staying in the house. The little room off the kitchen was given up to them; the maids were not supposed to know that it was occupied; they looked the other way when mother or Dooley went in with food for the fugitives. After two weeks they left, stealing away without a word to anyone.[1]

We always had dinner at one o'clock on Sundays instead of at four as on weekdays. In fine weather, relations sometimes came to spend the day. There were the aunts, mother's sisters, and their children from round about Knockaney, and cousin Julia, who was good-tempered except when heated from walking, cousin Tom Raleigh and cousin James Barry and father's Uncle John and Aunt Jane Purcell from Grange, a spruce and jaunty couple who were so old that they walked and stood arm in arm to prop one another up. In spite of totters

[1]We heard afterwards that these cousins got safely to America and some years later that they both had got on in life; the elder brother had risen to be head of the police in one of the largest cities.

they were gay and kind and were never tired of telling us stories of old times, when Uncle John was the little brother of Mammy Jug his grown-up sister. 'Tell us how you ran away to be married!' we begged, although we knew by heart that Aunt Jane was a squire's daughter and Uncle John a farmer, and if it hadn't been for the help of the parish priest, young John would never have waited behind the ricks in Mr. Synane's rickyard one stormy daybreak until young Jane, creeping through the laurels, joined him for their elopement. They went by the fields so that no early labourers should see them, not knowing that all night the River Maigue had been over-running its banks and that the path was covered by swirling water. Still the turf-walls and the Holy Thorn were standing out, and the nervous cows had not yet begun to swim. 'Is it the will of God that I take you home to your father?' asked John. 'It is not the will of God, John,' answered Jane, 'until the water is higher than my heart!' So John took her up pick-a-back and they splashed over the drowned fields until they came to dry land. Two wetter people never knocked on a priest's door! 'Well, well,' said the priest, ''tis a true saying that *Many waters cannot quench love, neither can the flood drown it!*' Within an hour he had married them, young John in his reverence's best suit which he kept to wear before the bishop, and young Jane in the fine clothes which the priest's housekeeper had set aside for her own burial.

'Please, Aunt Jane, what did the squire say then?'

'Words, my dears, which I should blush to repeat! But later on, when he knew that John was descended from the famous David Purcell of Ballycalhane, who, being in rebellion, was executed in Limerick in 1581, he grew more friendly, and at last he came to like his son-in-law for himself, for being...'

'*Uncle John*,' we said, while Aunt Jane bowed to us, as she always did, feeling a compliment was intended.

We children were still quite young when Uncle John and

Aunt Jane died. Two aunts followed them. Uncle Michael O'Brien, a priest, went too. There were cousins who took their places, but we were not great friends with any except Millie Purcell, who often came from Limerick. She was a tall, lovely young creature; we little girls adored her and were proud of being in her confidence. Millie was in love with a good-looking man, Alfie Beamish, who often managed to be fishing on Lough Gur on the Sundays when Millie came to see us. When we all went in a pack for a walk to visit the great bull and to saunter by the lake, father would say to mother, 'I believe I see young Beamish fishing from O'Herlihy's boat! Shall we ask him to tea?' Mother would say, 'Certainly, John.' We all shouted at the top of our voices, and Alfie would reel in his line and hurry ashore! Unfortunately, though he loved Millie, they could not be married because he was a Protestant and Millie was a very strong Catholic. 'No, Alfie, no,' she said over and over, 'I won't marry a Protestant!' At last Alfie gave in and was received into our church, so that they were married and lived happily for a time on the bank of the Shannon.

The visitor who spoilt Sunday for us children was Mac, mother's nephew, who teased and ridiculed us, not caring how much he wounded our feelings. He used to call me Ugly Duckling, which hurt me, and one day I escaped and ran to Dooley for comfort. She saw tears on my cheeks and asked the reason.

'Sure ye're never cryin' about the face that Almighty God chose for ye! Whatever will they be thinkin' of ye up above? Haven't ye the fine white skin when there's many a one born black as our ould turkey and blacker! Haven't ye soft brown hair and a fine pair of eyes when there's them that's born white-headed with eyes as red as a pet rabbit's? And haven't ye a mouthful of strong teeth when ye might have them black and crumblin' like Casey's youngest, her with the hump and the squinny eyes, God help her?'

'I know, darling Dooley, I may have all you say and still be ugly.'

'God help me! I'll be losin' me patience! Have ye ten fingers and ten toes and a pair of straight legs, and a back as straight as a bulrush?'

'No, I haven't got a straight back! Mother says I poke and at school the mistress said I hang my head when I walk, like a hen looking for worms.'

'The wumman! and she settin' up to teach manners, to be speakin' so coarse to one of our childer'. That'll pass, my doty child, when Mr. Lavery have ye taught to dance and to hold your head up with the rest of them. Did I ever tell ye the tale of the farmer's son who got sot on a poor lovely young girl? I didn't? Well, he said to her, "I'll marry ye, poor as ye are, if ye'll promise me ye'll hold up your head and not care a tinker's curse what anyone says to cheapen ye." "I will," says she, "I will hold up me head." And what'd she do but go into the bohereen (little lane) and cut a twig o' furze and pin it in her dress so that every time she hung her face the furze druv it up with its sharp spikes and by the next day she held her head as high as the Queen of England.'

'So were they married?'

'Sure were they, be the help of God, and through finding the crock of gold at the foot of the rainbow. 'Twas the poor girl struck it, digging pitaties, an old crock full of things like bits of dirty brass, and be the goodness of God there was passing that way a gentleman that was an honest man. "Och, me God!" says he, "Ye've got there a king's treasure. Rings and pins and brooches and crowns and collars . . . and all of pure gold! It's you are the rich young girl!"'

'What did the farmer's son say?'

'I'm thinkin' he was disappointed at first, being a romantic young fella and proud of not standing out for money and hens and feather beds. "Musha," says he, "it's you are the rich young girl and it's a lord ye will be marryin' with." "If ye think that," says the young girl, "ye're mistook, and if 'tis them ould bits that stands between us, let you bury them where they lay before." But by that time the honest gentleman had them safe in Dublin and the money paid to the bank. And before the match-makers heard a word of it the two were married.'

A week or two later Mr. Lavery arrived, He came once a week from Bruff to give me, Janie and Bessie lessons in dancing and deportment. He was thin with a small pale wrinkled face and light blue eyes, He wore for the occasion a coat and knee-breeches of black velvet, black thread stockings, and shoes with steel buckles which he brought in a bag and put on before the lesson. I can see him, his fiddle tucked under his pointed chin, wrinkling his anxious little face. 'One two, one two, *hold up the head,* Miss Bessie, keep the chin in; one two, one two, not so stiff, Miss Janie; Miss Sissy is the best stepper of you all!'

We liked dancing and practised vigorously between the lessons, often imitating Lavery and reminding one another to keep the chin in and hold up the head. My timidity grew less, dancing, and dancing well, so Lavery said, gave me confidence.

Mother provided a good dinner for the little dancing-master, who looked more than half starved. Before he came as our teacher his wife was often at the door begging for food or old clothes; after our lessons began her visits ceased. It must have been difficult for him in his poverty to dress as he did and to look so spick and span.

## 6: A WALK WITH FATHER

Our brother, called Michael after grandfather O'Brien, had gone to Australia to make his fortune! Lough Gur was too small for him although he loved it; he liked roaming about with his gun, or galloping after hounds on the hunter that father kept for him. Perhaps he was too masterful to work with our masterful father! So he went, tearing himself with difficulty from mother whom he adored, whose one child he had been for so many years before we four little girls joined the family. Perhaps it was parting from Michael that made mother's eyes so sad.

I think my father must often have missed brother. A farmer particularly needs a son to talk to and consult with and to share his work. Sometimes he would look at his four little girls, perhaps wishing one or two of us had been born boys; now and then he would say as he got up from dinner, 'Who'll be a man and come round the fields with me? What about you, Sis?' and I would jump up with alacrity, for a walk with father was a treat at any time. Perhaps we were bound for the garden of oats, oats being grown for the sake of straw-bedding for the animals in winter as well as for the grain; or to inspect the turnips for fly, the mangolds, or the great potato field which was talked about even in Limerick city for the fine 'praties' grown there. Often we went to look at the green crops and admire the exquisite blue of flowering flax—a new venture and a success, my father winning a prize for his first crop and commendation from Dublin. There would be many halts on the way for short chats about the work in hand with Dick Dooley, old Paddy and—until they went to America—with Dooley's sons, with Four-Tooth, one of Heffernan's sons, and Me-John, so called because Biddy, his mother, spoke of him that way.

Sometimes we went to see how the ploughing was getting on. The ploughman, Con Brian, was tall, thin and lanky; with his long legs he used at one time to get over the ground very fast behind the plough and the two strong horses. Mother thought he looked delicate and underfed, so when he came to meals, which he had at different times from the other men, she provided something extra nourishing for him. He worked hard and father said he was quiet and dependable, his favourite words of praise. A great misfortune befell him. Dooley told us, for our parents never spoke before us children of the failings of the workpeople.

One day Con went to market to sell pigs; he returned to his home late—and drunk. He spent the night beside the kitchen fire, lost to the world, while a spark from the blazing turf smouldered on his corduroy trousers until morning when he woke to the biting pain of a deep burn. He had a bad leg for ever after.

'God bless you,' we said loudly as Con and his plough passed us on the outward furrow. It was the custom to bless all workmen so as to avert accidents. Con took no notice. To have replied by a word or a glance would have been unlucky for him and the horses. Not until he had reached the end of the field and turned plough and horses to face in our direction, could he answer 'And you too'.

Father was watching Con as he limped at the tail of the plough, with such a fatherly, kind, sad face that I asked him if going slow or fast mattered to the ploughing. Father said he wasn't thinking of poor Con's loss of speed as a ploughman, but of the loss of power to do what other young men could do, dance, play games or run with the harriers or . . .

'. . . escape from an angry bull?' I suggested.

Father nodded, but he said no more; when he turned away from the plough-land he was whistling softly. It was a sorrowful air; I think it was 'Like Hares on the Mountain'.

Father felt the troubles of his workpeople as if they were his own and often on our walks together we stopped to ask after the sick and sorrowful in the cabins on or near our land. One of these was Mrs. Heffernan, the wife of Heffernan, the rick-builder, who farmed his own small-holding.

'How are you getting on?' father asked the delicate little creature one day, leaning on the half-door. He never went into a cottage unless invited to do so.

'Musha! a bad day and a good day, thanks be to God,' she answered cheerfully; she had grown used to ill-health.

So long as their sons stayed at home most of the mothers were happy, but from every house, sooner or later, they went away. Their sisters went too; bad as it was to lose the girls, it was parting from her sons that broke the mother's heart.

Old Biddy was one of the lonesome mothers. Me-John was the only one of her six children left at home, the youngest and best loved. I can remember a day in summer when he came to my father to say he had had his passage sent him and was following his brothers to America. We were not surprised, for Dooley had heard him boasting to the maids of the amount of

beef he would eat on the other side of the water. All the farmboys talked like that when they were going away. Biddy was
the widow of a thatcher who had died of consumption. She
lived in a wretched two-roomed cabin in great poverty; there
the sick father and herself, four hefty sons and two daughters
had spent twenty or more years, crowded together. Until Me-
John was grown-up Biddy could not go to chapel for want of
suitable clothes; if she was given a dress, she would chop and
cobble it into a coat and trousers for one or other of the boys.
She never wore boots or stockings or put a cap on her tousled
head. When her children clubbed together and gave her a
cloak, she went to chapel, but she had forgotten how to behave;
unable to control her emotions, she would cry out with joy or
grief at any moment. She was dazed when news came from
Chicago that red-haired Pat, her second child, had been killed
in a street brawl. When Me-John showed her his passage-pass
and told her that he was leaving in two days, she would not believe him, and after he had gone she was like a dog that has lost
its master, roaming about the fields where he had worked,
looking into the sheds, asking all whom she met, 'Have ye seen
Me-John anywhere?'

Father never passed Biddy's cabin without saying a few
cheering words, promising her that John would come back
with a fortune one of these days, and that meanwhile she must
take care of herself and keep her love warm against his return.

One day when father was encouraging Biddy in this way I
caught sight of Meggy-the-Eels—the little old fish pedlar—
and ran on ahead to the eel-weir, where Paddy was counting
the take into Meggy's basket. The eels were sold at sixpence or
eightpence the dozen; when one dozen had been counted,
Paddy began again at one for the second dozen, neither he nor
Meggy being very sure of themselves in counting above
twelve. Just after father had come up behind them, walking on

the grass, I saw Paddy pick out a great eel which he slid behind
him, intending to sell it or eat it himself. Thump! came father's
stick on the ground.

'What, Paddy! Aren't you selling by the dozen to this poor
woman? That big eel is the seventh in the count. Put five more
to it and leave her her luck.'

Paddy replaced the eel quickly. 'Begor, sir, and she's welcome to it!' he said, while old Meggy thanked my father for
his justice. Later on I heard her telling the maids about the
transaction.

"'Twas that fella Paddy was sold instead of me great eel, and
him wid a great wish for it! Ye should have heard the masther
pull me buachail[1] up. "Leave the poor woman her luck," says
he, may the Lord reward him,' adding fervently, 'may the
Lord make every eel in the weir as fleshy as me seventh one!'

[1]Boy, a word of contempt.

## 7: THE GROGANS. MAIDS AND MATCHMAKERS

Father had a surprise for us! He had bought the adjoining property known as the Castle farm.[1] There was a fine house on it with large rooms and big windows looking out on a fruit and vegetable garden. We were delighted and begged him to let us move into our grand new house at once. He and mother looked at one another. It seemed they had talked over the advantage of greater space for 'the children', as he always called us, but in the end they decided that the little farmhouse where we and he were born was too dear a home to leave. The big house, he told us, would be for brother when he might choose to come home from Australia to marry and settle down in the old country. In the meantime a tenant would live there to keep it warm for Michael. This puzzled us! Could we not keep it warm as well or better than anyone else?

'Ye'll never get anyone to live in that great lonely house,' father's friends told him. 'Nobody but a hermit would live there unless it was some Sassenach hiding from the police over

[1]This farm was offered to father in the famine year without premium and at a nominal rent. When eventually father bought it it cost him a thousand pounds.

in England.' Mother laughed at them and said they were as
dismal as the friends of Job.

It was not long before a family, father, mother and child,
came to live there, paying a rent of twenty pounds a year,
which Bessie thought a bad bargain for such a good house—
almost a little mansion! Mr. and Mrs. Grogan were kind,
friendly people; they often invited us to tea with their son,
Purcell, a sandy-haired, freckled boy about eight years old.
They played games with us after tea, darting about in blind-
man's-buff or sitting on the floor to play hunt-the-slipper. Mrs.
Grogan was fair and fragile, gentle and undecided in manner
with a confidential way of talking. 'Sissy,' she whispered one
day, 'don't be afraid to cross your t's with a firm straight stroke.
It's only Germans who don't,' or, 'Sissy, don't look anxious
when you dance, look happy.' When she was going to a party
she wore a mauve silk dress with a bonnet to match and a grey
lace shawl. She looked lovely and was as happy as a child. At
one time we used to go in turn for music lessons from Mrs.
Grogan and it wasn't long before our father was persuaded to
buy us an Erard piano to practise on. Mr. Grogan interested us,
particularly as he had never had a hair on him, neither on his
head, nor his face—not even one eyelash. He was as smooth as
a horse-chestnut. He wore a very nice shiny brown wig, and on
windy days he jammed a cap hard on his head for fear of losing
his wig, or he may even have worn his cap and left his nice
little wig at home. He was very fond of sailing, especially when
he felt lively after a sip of J.J. They were not well-off, though
gentlefolk, but they lived well on rabbits and wildfowl and the
jack and roach which Mr. Grogan caught in the lough. That
was before it was stocked with trout. They had a maid, a short,
fat little girl who spent the greater part of her time skinning
rabbits, plucking wild fowl and gutting fish brought in by her
master, who encouraged her in her gory occupation by allow-

ing her to sell skins and feathers. Eggshells she had to wash and send in for her master's consumption. Sometimes when we were having tea with the Grogans, Mr. Grogan would crunch and swallow half-a-dozen shells, an astonishing sight which compelled us to work our jaws as if our mouths were full of grit. After tea he would catch his son firmly by the hair and scalp, and lift him up for our amusement. Purcell, who was very good-tempered, would draw up his legs and grin feebly until his mother rescued him and gently removed the father's smooth, white hand! Mr. Grogan was uncanny though kind. He once insisted on taking my sisters and me in his boat for a sail on the lough; all went well, we were enjoying ourselves and laughing at Mr. Grogan's lively talk, taking no heed of the weather until the sky darkened and a squall made the boat heel over and water began to splash in. Mr. Grogan, who did not seem quite himself and must have felt seasick, tried to take down the sail but fell flat in the bottom of the boat and lay there. Fortunately for us there was another boat on the lake, and the owner, seeing our plight, came alongside; he took the three of us into his boat and so to safety and our anxious mother. Our deliverer then rowed back through rough water and rescued Mr. Grogan. That was our first and last boating expedition!

I think our parents were not sorry when the long summer holidays were over and we returned to school, even though they kept us occupied in one way or another. We were delighted when we could earn a little money by weeding or by killing the great blue-bottle flies, called meat-flies in those days, which abounded in August and September and now and then got into the dairy. We waged war against these pests and were paid a penny-ha'penny a dozen for their corpses. There were no such things as sticky fly-papers or fly-traps. The thought of cruelty was far from us; we killed quickly and outright; flies, like vermin, had to be kept down. Perhaps living on a farm one learnt early that suffering is sometimes necessary, as when a bull has a ring put in his nose, or pigs are likewise treated, or in a lesser degree when sheep are washed. The noise, father said, could not be taken as the measure of the pain inflicted, for some animals are great screamers. He always arranged for pig-killing to take place when we were at school. Six pigs of about two hundredweight were killed in the year for the use of the house; the curing and smoking were supervised by my mother whose secret recipe resulted in delicious ham and bacon. From pigs' heads she made brawn or collared head, and from the cheeks came what we called French hams which, cured and smoked, were good to eat with chicken. We little girls helped—or hindered—her as she went about her preparations. We—and mother—made collared head by boiling part of the head almost to a jelly, then chopped the meat very small and spiced it with pepper, allspice and finely ground nutmeg. After that we put it in a mould which opened on a hinge and was kept shut with a skewer. When it was set and turned out of the shape it made a dish fit for a king!

Another famous recipe, of mother's own invention, we children were allowed to use when cream-cheese was needed for the house. We took thick cream which was just on the turn, mixed with it a pinch of salt and a little dry mustard, and put it into a jelly bag hung between two chairs, with a basin underneath to catch the drip-drops. After twenty-four hours in the cool of the dairy, by which time the cream was solid, it was turned into a mould and pressed under a butter-weight for a short time. Then one of the three carried it to the table for our father to cut.

'Well, Anne,' he would say to mother, 'this is one of the best cheeses you have ever made!'

"I didn't make it!' answered mother.

'You didn't! Surely you don't tell me *the children* made such a perfect cheese? . . .'

'We did, father, we did!' we shouted, jumping up and down for delight and pride.

The maids praised us too. 'Sure the misthress have no need of dairymaids, seein' how clever ye do be growin'! Would there be a taste of the cheese left over for us? What! The masther have it all ate? Heaven preserve us!'

The maids were an interest in our lives: we liked to hear what they did when they were little girls, and what they learnt at school. They taught us many Irish songs, of which we liked best the sorrowful, in minor keys, learning as we sang the joy of mourning griefs not our own. We copied the maids' every gesture, the way they wrung their hands, turned up their eyes, heaved deep sighs and smote their breasts. In broad brogues we *wished we were on yonder hill*—our lovely Knockfennel we imagined—we drooped with the emigrant on his stile, exhorted the *little birds* to *sing less merrily* and *languished* with great effect to *Moyle's winter-wave weeping*. Bessie occasionally shed real tears over Erin's wrongs; Janie, ever sensible, knew songs to be songs, with or without orgies; I knew we were making ourselves ridiculous, wanted to laugh but dared not.

These emotional concerts came to an end, when one afternoon father, coming in from a wet world outside, stood in astonishment while rills of rain poured from his coat and ran about the stone-flagged floor. Then he and I and Janie began to laugh, Bessie joined in and baby-sister with her delightful hiccuppy cackle. Mother came from her room.

'Professional mourners, love,' father gasped, waving towards the hearth, whereupon we laughed still more while Ellie and Bridgie got up in high dudgeon and went about their work.

We heard from the maids and Peg Quirke strange legends of our country, of saints, kings and queens, witches, banshees, merrows, leprechauns, pucas, monsters, serpents and great wurr'ms imprisoned in deep lakes, who rise to ask, in Irish, *Is it to-morrow?* and are for ever doomed to disappointment. To hear these entrancing stories we had to follow the narrator as she went about her work, perching on an ironing table, or the edge of a wash-tub, or an inverted bucket. Dooley would often call us away. She liked to be the only troubadour in the family and did not realise that as we got bigger we found *The Four Little Pigs* trivial and the same old fairy tales dull after the thrilling story-telling of younger people.

All the maids worked hard, following the example of 'the misthress', and except for short runs to their homes now and again they had little respite from labour, nor did they expect it. I remember once seeing a number of girls and boys dancing at the cross-roads on a summer Sunday, but this diversion was strictly forbidden by priests and parents, who had a great dread of young people falling in love. Archbishop Croke was the first, as far as I know, to encourage football, hurling and other games for boys and young men; no entertainment was considered necessary for girls. But for the matchmaker there would have been no marriages.

We had a pretty maid with dark eyes and pink cheeks who wore a little cherry-coloured shawl when she went out. We called her Rosy-posy. She was a trouble to my mother because she would not go to Grange with the other maids on Sunday but chose another Mass where she could meet her sweetheart. One day the sweetheart dared to walk back with her to the very

door. I thought him an ugly old fellow for Rosy-posy—he may
have been twenty-five—and told her so. My mother was
shocked by their effrontery in appearing at the door together,
for 'keeping company' was strictly forbidden. She reprimanded
Rosy, who sulked for a week; the priest spoke to her as well
and made her cry. Then Dooley talked kindly to her one morning and to the sweetheart in the afternoon, and in the evening
she went to see their fathers and mothers who called in a matchmaker and the marriage was arranged, quite nicely and quite
soon. That was the only marriage for love and by the lovers'
own choice that I can remember.

In those days young girls had nothing to look forward to but
a loveless marriage, hard work, poverty, a large family and
often a husband who drank. Small wonder that when they
could they escaped to America. One of our maids, Nancy
Brian, Con the ploughman's sister, a fair, tall girl of seventeen,
gentle and childlike, left us to go to her relations in New York;
she never reached them, and in spite of every effort made to
trace her she was never heard of again. There was consternation
in many little homes when time went on and nothing more was
learnt of Nancy Brian. Mothers tried to keep their daughters
in Ireland. The matchmakers backed them up and hastened
to arrange marriages, even with this professional help there
was many a slip 'twixt the cup and the lip. I remember over-
hearing my father enquiring of old Paddy about a projected
match.

'Tell me, Paddy, did Johnnie make the match for his daughter?'

'He did not, sir, though 'twas very near done when they bruk
it clean off.'

'And what broke it?'

''Twas the ass and car that defeated it. Ould Johnnie would-
n't part with the ass, though the ould woman was content to let

it go. So his darter is disapp'inted of a home and young Johnnie is disapp'inted of a wife.'

'I'm sorry,' said my father, who had a kind heart for all young things.

'There's no need,' replied Paddy, 'no need at all. There's more than one fish in Lough Gur, and the matchmaker is on the trail of another for the both of them.'

## 8: THE DOOLEYS

Our Dooley lived in the cottage at the gate with Dick Dooley, her husband, my father's trustworthy head man. They had four sons and one daughter. Mary had black hair, blue eyes and a happy-child face; in her ways she was as sweet as her mother. At seventeen she was the prettiest girl of Lough Gur and the treasure and pride of her parents who would not let her go to work because she was 'a bit young in her mind'.

On morning Dooley arrived white and shaking and hurried to mother's room. We were frightened and could not tell what had happened; later we heard the maids talking and telling how Mary had been 'thrown out' by her father and the door shut on her. Ellie said, 'Shame on him, then, for a harsh old man and no sort of a father,' but Bridgie disagreed. 'Shame on her,' she said, 'bringing disgrace on her good father and mother.' Dooley went about her work as usual, white and tremulous, while we children stared at her, not knowing what to say and not daring to ask questions. Some days later Mary ventured home, but still the door was shut, so she crept into a pig-sty where her mother made up a bed for her. Ellie praised the mother for her love in caring for her, and Bridgie still stood up for the father

who was, in her opinion, very kind to let Mary stay so near
home after what had happened. The baby, she said, had died.
We could not imagine what baby, whose baby, had died. Then
poor Mary developed rheumatic fever from living in the damp
pig-sty, and when for very shame of his own cruelty, Dick
Dooley relented, she hobbled home almost helpless, crippled
for life.

Another trouble was in store for our Dooley. It happened
one afternoon. We had just got home from school and were
talking to father in the yard when we heard a terrible sound, a
shrill and whistling sound, and then a fearful scream.

'My God!' cried father, and rushed into the kitchen for his
gun. A moment later, Mikey, the boy who scared crows, came
running up.

'Oh, sir, Casey (the stallion) have Mr. Dooley down and
he's . . .'

Father pushed us towards the house, telling us to stay inside;
then he ran to the field where the horse was kept; several of the
farm-men were running ahead with sticks and a rope.

We went in and shut the door as father had told us and soon
mother came down to us from the storeroom. She had heard
the scream and though she was shaking she went to the cupboard for soft linen and J.J. in case it was wanted, and then she
asked us who was hurt? We told her it was Dick.

'I must go to Dooley,' she said and went at once by the short
way and was with her to break the dreadful news and when
they carried Dick in and laid him on his bed downstairs.

We did not look out of the window but we could not help
hearing Mikey telling Ellie how Casey went for Dooley in the
field and attacked him, rearing and striking him on the head
and chest and then kicking him as he lay on the ground. It was
dreadful to hear him and I grew faint and sick and had to lie on

the floor while Janie and Bessie and even baby-sister knelt to pray for poor Dick.

Then Ellie fetched us to have tea with her and Bridgie in the kitchen and very sensibly she talked of other things. While we were still sitting up at the table, we heard a chirp and there was a chicken in the coop, just hatched, staring at us from under the hen's chin and it was so nice that we forgot what had happened till mother came back with father and Doctor Gubbins.

That evening mother, thinking I should know something of the sorrow of life, took me with her to Dooley's cottage. Our cousin Mac was with us, then a medical student, in whose care Dr. Gubbins had left poor hurt Dick. I remember standing in the doorway, looking at the prostrate figure on the bed, his face livid, his mouth open, while from his throat came a terrible sound which someone said was the death-rattles. I did not show the horror I felt until walking home between my mother and cousin, I seemed suddenly to hear a great noise as of a stone wall falling. I collapsed and fell and was carried home and put to bed. By Mac's advice no notice was to be taken of what had happened to me and the next morning he set me to run with my sisters to the top of Knockfennel while he and our parents stood at the door to time the race, which I won. This race was repeated every day for a week, surely an original treatment for shock and nerves. At the end of the week my uncle, Father Richard O'Brien, arrived to take me with him and a grown-up niece to Kilkee for sea-bathing. I was still nervous and having moments of panic fear that, like Dooley, I might die a sudden death. So distraught was I by this terror that I ran to Uncle Richard, who was having tea with my mother, and to his great surprise implored him to hear my confession and give me absolution on the spot! Mother took me to her room and soothed me.

I found sea-bathing terrifying; the ocean was so large and I so small a speck in its vast waters. I held on to my cousin's hand, spluttering and gasping until the three-minutes' dip was over. I was about nine years old and perfectly healthy except for nerves. Some one sent a game, battledore and shuttlecock, 'to distract the child's mind'. Everyone was kind, Dooley, believing that I was grieving on her account, soothed and encouraged me. I knew, however, that something had happened which destroyed for ever my feeling of safety, my confidence, something which broke into my happy childhood as the bright surface of a pool is broken by a falling stone. I, who had known only of life, now knew of death.

My father was very observant, and although he seldom commented on our looks and behaviour, he would always pull us up if we spoke ungrammatically or used expressions and phrases which were only heard from the peasantry. Whatever he thought of the English, he treated their language with the utmost respect. If, perhaps, one of us looked worried on our return from school, he would propose a walk or plan a game of croquet for the evening, and if he saw we were beginning a squabble among ourselves, he would repeat, *This is the house that Jack built*, all through and at a great pace, giving us time to lose our ill-temper in our admiration for his memory and clear enunciation. When I think now of the house that Jack built I see vividly our own, dear home, our ratter-cats, the two shaggy old watchdogs Tear'em and Ate-em and the cow with what we called a *crumley* horn, and Ellie beside her. There is a blank for the man all tattered and torn, but the cock is in my picture, an old-fashioned barndoor, all red and gold pride, and the face of the priest all shaven and shorn is a mixture of Uncle Richard O'Brien and my own dear bearded father.

Thinking of father's observation and sympathy, I remember
his taking my hand for a stroll to the lake. Some small thing
had shaken my nerves and he asked me, very gently, why I was
so easily nervous. 'No-why, father,' I answered, looking him in
the face, for indeed I could not say why I was unlike my calmer
sisters. 'You will grow out of it,' father said, 'but you must not
give in to it. You know you are *quite safe* with Mammy and me
to take care of you. We love you; you are very good and useful
and a dear child to us, thank God.' How understanding he was!
He knew I was full of fears and that I thought too little of myself. Why was I like that? I did not know, but sometimes now I
think it was largely due to the unkindness of a young woman
who came to look after us before we had good little Moll.
Directly Miss O'Connell, as we called her, discovered that our
mother never allowed us to complain or tell tales and that the
thought of speaking of her cruelty did not enter our heads, she
did not spare us. I was her chief victim and she terrorised me to
such an extent that I could learn nothing with her. When she
took us ostensibly to play on Knockfennel, she would secrete
her brush and comb, bringing it out of her pocket when we
had begun our game, and calling me apart, would keep me
brushing and combing her long hair until it was time to go
home. Woe betide me if I pulled, or caught a hair round the
bristles. I was trembling the whole time from fear of this harsh
creature. Fortunately she left us after a year's stay and thanks to
the good character my unsuspecting mother gave of her to
Uncle Richard, she was appointed as mistress to a school at
some distance from Lough Gur so that we never saw her again.

One day Dooley asked me to go with her to cut nettles for
the turkeys—chopped nettles were mixed with their mealy
food—and I went with joy, for when Dooley was nettling she
looked, I thought, like a pirate, with her sharp knife in her

right hand and her left covered with an old woollen sock against the nettle's piercing sting. That sock, I pretended, concealed a sharp hard stone, with which the pirate could smash the skull of any law-abiding seafarer. I carried a rattling tin pail to receive the spoils. As we climbed together over a stone wall, Dooley slipped and fell heavily.

'Oh, darling Dooley! are you hurt? are you broken?' My terror of accidents and sudden death revived.

'I am not, then! 'Tis nothin', mavourneen,' she answered as she struggled up, 'nothin' but another of me ribs broke on me! 'Twill knit together if we take no notice.'

So we went on nettling. Dooley had already broken several ribs and refused to notice them. Luckily this casual treatment succeeded; if she suffered meanwhile she said nothing.

Frequent change of air and scene was supposed to be good for the nerves, therefore I was sent with Bessie and Janie to stay with Uncle Richard at Knocklong for a week's visit. A priest's house seemed unbearably dull after the stir and movement of a farm. Uncle Richard and his curate were happy enough; they were looked after by a middle-aged housekeeper, Martha Clancy, and Morissy who was both gardener and coachman. Perhaps it was because Uncle Richard had no farm that we were so lonely, and for the same reason that we had not enough to eat. All we wanted was plenty of bread and butter and milk; beef and mutton were strange to us as were all fancy dishes. But if the food we lacked had been there we could scarcely have eaten, for the priests delighted in asking us questions at meals, which was enough to take away anyone's appetite; sometimes they laughed heartily at our unsophisticated answers, which hurt our feelings and made us ashamed of being young. After two or three days Bessie borrowed a pen and ink and with much labour wrote her first letter home.

'Dear Mother,' she began, 'we get here ◯ tea and o bread and butter. Your loving Bessie.'

Mother understood and came for us. Our kind uncle looked puzzled but let us go with his blessing. Mother gently chided us for not asking the housekeeper for more bread and butter, forgetting how timid little girls are when away from home.

How wonderful and lively the farm seemed when we were safely at home. Even the bull was rather a dear fellow when tied up in his shed; old gander and old turkey were easily daunted if one brandished a stick at them. As for Lough Gur, it was so perfect in the glow of sunset that one wondered why Queen Victoria did not build a castle for herself and live there.

'Isn't home lovely?' we said to one another as we munched bread and butter ravenously. Father laughed at us, and said to mother, 'Children are happy without knowing it, but they know fast enough when they are unhappy.' Then he turned to us and explained why it is good for children to go away now and then to see something of life in other places and to make friends with people who live in towns and have other interests than farming. Besides all this, even little girls must stand upon their own legs! which made us laugh for whose legs could they stand upon but their own? All the same father was glad to have us back and after dinner he took us *for a treat* to the well-walled paddock beside the lough to have a look at the bull.

'I do believe', said Bessie the next morning, 'that I have got a new pair of eyes through staying with Uncle Richard. Everything looks different and oh! so much lovelier than before.'

After we had helped mother about the house we set out with Dooley to climb Knockfennel, the highest of our hills, and farmed by a cousin of father's. Half-way up is a large cave called the Red Cellar, where, in that sad time called penal days, the poor persecuted people met secretly to hear Mass. I was thinking about them slinking before dawn up the hillside, looking over their shoulders and starting at any sound, even the first note of a lark's song or the distant yap of a dog, then creeping into the cave where the only light was on the stone which served as an altar. There would be the priest, saying *Judica me, Domine* (the forty-second psalm) in a low voice, and after a time the people would leave off trembling and be comforted. I was thinking of the promise of which mother told me: 'where two—or three—are gathered together, there am I in the midst of them,' and the idea of Almighty God being in that bare, cold cave with the frightened Irish people made me shiver, so that Bessie took my hand and said, 'No nerves to-day, Sissy, listen to darling Dooley.' Strange to say, Dooley was also trembling a little, but that was from dread of the *Little People* who were said to live in the hollow hill and who come in and out of Knockfennel through the Red Cavern, their front door. As usual we began asking questions.

'Why didn't St. Patrick banish the *Little People* when he banished toads and snakes?' Bessie asked.

Dooley considered, 'Mebbe they kept quiet in them days; mebbe they were not heathens then but the *Good People* we call them, so there'd have been no need to trouble St. Patrick to throw them out.'

'Or perhaps he did order them to go but when the time came they couldn't be found.'

'Or perhaps they went,' Janie suggested, 'and when St. Patrick's back was turned they came back on fairy rafts.'

'I think', Bessie decided, 'the good Irish *Little People* died of sorrow when Ireland was conquered and those that are here now are wicked Sassenach fairies. . . .'

'They are not, then,' Dooley exclaimed jealously, 'never a one o' *them* belonged to the Sassenach. The *Little People* may be playful about the cows and a throuble at times in the dairy but we wouldn't be without them after all the hundreds o' years they've been livin' beside us in these same hills!' Dooley spoke very loud as people do when they hope to be overheard.

'Darling Dooley,' I whispered, 'if the *Little People* are heathens, shouldn't we pray for them?'

Dooley was shocked. 'Pray for them, is it? Mebbe *they* wouldn't wish it at all! Mebbe . . . but you must ask the mistress . . . if any good would come out of praying for *them*, wouldn't the Holy Father in Rome long since have given us the word?'

On the way home we passed the cottage of Con Curley, an old man whom we dreaded. His amusement was chasing children who came near his house, threatening to sell them to the railway company. 'What'll happen ye then, is it? Ye'll be boiled down to make grease to oil the railway lines!' When the children screamed in terror and ran for their lives, he would stand looking after them, laughing until the tears ran down his face.

There was Curley at his door in his swallow-tailed coat, knee-breeches and tall hat, and to our surprise he said, 'Good evening, ma'am' to Dooley, with the utmost politeness. She answered shortly and we hurried on, but not before he had winked at us children and put out his tongue and jerked his thumb over his shoulder in the direction of the railway.

## 9: CALLERS AT THE DOOR

The monotony of life on the farm was perpetually broken by callers at the front door or the back door. Some came to beg for food, old clothes, old linen for wounds or sores, 'bits' to make clothes for the children and new babies, even for old sheets to make shrouds and a little money to pay for the coffin.

Once or twice a week came Peg Quirke, a useful, obliging old woman who went to Bruff to do errands for my mother and often for my father as well. She was quite illiterate but never made a mistake in her payments or in the money she brought back, having her own highly complicated way of keeping accounts without any knowledge of figures, addition or substraction! I can see her now, the tired old creature, on her return from market, standing before my father.

'Sit you down, Peg. Tell me now, did you get a lift going or coming?'

'Faix then, I did not. 'Twas Shanks's mare had to foot it all the way.'

'What about the turnip seed?'

'Here 'tis, sir, safe out o' me busom, and I wouldn't wonder

if 'tis not sproutin' already wid the heat that's on me from the
long walk.'

'Thank you, Peg. What about the *Freeman*?'

'Glory to goodness! damn the bit o' me ever thought o' the
paper! but hould on a bit, sir. I'll go to Phil Foley after cow-
time an' borrow the loan of the *Reporter* if that'll do ye?'

'Well, Peg, half a loaf is better than no bread, but next time
I'd rather you'd forget the turnip seed.'

One of the maids would sign to Peg that a cup of tea was
ready for her in the kitchen; then they would cluster round her
to hear the news of the town, or in warm weather they would
set a chair for her outside the back door and while she was resting they would sit round playing for her on the Jew's harp, a
tiny metal instrument held in the mouth and twanged with one
finger.

At times Mary-Ellen, a long-nosed spinning woman, came
to spin the fleeces of our sheep and the tufts of wool which
we gathered from the hedges and furze-bushes, wherever the
sheep had pushed by and left little snatches of their wool. The
fleeces had been shaken and beaten and washed in a trough
under the pump, dried in the sun, and combed, but were still
oily from the store of oil which a sheep has in its body to keep
its woolly coat from getting soaked in the rain and to keep itself from getting wet to the skin. With a heap of fleece on a
sheet Mary-Ellen sat at her spinning-wheel for hours together
in utter silence, only nodding or shaking her head, according to
her mood, when we implored her to spin a fine, fine thread for
our frieze, and oh! could she spin a thread which would dye
any colour in the world rather than the hated green of our
school-frocks!

'Why wouldn't ye like the green?' she asked us one day

when the wheel stopped for want of fleece, 'when green is the colour of Ireland, and of the shamrock and the reeds (rushes) in the bogs?'

We were silent. Then Bessie asked, 'Don't they wear green in England?'

'Sorra a thread o' green would ye see over there, nor a shamrock! 'Tis England's cruel red they wear, man, woman and child . . . the red of blood!' Here Mary-Ellen spat into the fire. 'I have an ould a'nt livin' beyond Bruff; she have a way of dyein' the thread with yarbs (herbs) and with the hairy moss from the bark o' trees and with soot and madder. She'll dye some of the thread brown and some grey and some yalla or red; then she'll take it to the weaver and get him to set the weft of the brown and the warp of the grey with a taste of the yalla or the red thrown in here and there. "And", says she to Wally the weaver, "do not care if the thread is a bit uneven with a roughness here and a knot there, for that's the way the quality likes their frize and they thinkin' the world of the smell 'o' turf that it gets with the fire burnin' not two yards from the loom." So quare they are with their fancies for this and for that! Me a'nt was livin' one time with the Lord Lieutenant at Dublin Castle, one of ten or twenty housemaids, and she had the great chanst of inspectin' the clothes thrown off by the visitin' gentlemen after they'd be dressin' for the banquet in their evening suits, black as sin, or mebbe in grand uniforms and cock-hats and fancy swords.'

Perhaps then Dooley would stagger in under a sheetful of fleece and Mary-Ellen would go back to her spinning and her stony silence, while our young heads whirled at the thought of the glory of the castle and the splendour of visiting gentlemen in cocked hats and fancy swords.

Occasionally a pedlar called, on his arm a basket of ribbons, coloured handkerchiefs, cheap jewellery, tapes and cottons.

These the maids turned over, buying odds and ends amid laughter and coquetting. They were often good-looking young men who were born roamers. Matchmakers did not take them into account, knowing that they were already wedded to the road.

Murnane the carpenter was often in the house and about the farm buildings, making and mending, while his donkey dozed in the yard. Murnane was a grey-faced, grey-haired man with a stubbly chin and a bent back. He had a son in America of whom he was very proud because of his success in 'rowling up a fortune'! Young Murnane was one of those who 'keep a heart for the Old Country'; he brought his boy and girl home to be educated in college and convent and beside Lough Gur. He said to mother, 'I'm thinking, ma'am, they will learn the best things in their holidays when they stay with my father beside the lake,' and when mother asked him what, in his mind, are the best things, he answered, 'I'd say contentment with simple things and living kindly among the neighbours . . . like yourself, ma'am,' he added with his charming smile.

Three times in the year came Kennedy, the piper, or, as my mother called him, Kennedy the musician, for he was no mere noise-maker but an artist to the tips of his delicate expressive hands. He was lank and lean, clean-shaven, and wore the cast-off clothes of a priest. He came in at the door with a gentle greeting, 'God save all here,' bowing low to my mother and going over to his place, the piper's corner, beside the hearth, where with a hot ember he lighted his clay pipe and with another bow went out to smoke in the yard, for in those days of courtesy and refinement no one would smoke indoors, whether in cabin or castle, without the invitation of the master of the house and the approval of the mistress.

The coming of Mick Kennedy gave untold joy. At the end of the day's work, the farmboys washed at the pump in the yard, put on their Sunday clothes and their well-polished shoes, while the maids discarded their aprons, replaited their shining hair, tied fresh collars and ribbons round their necks and came happily into the kitchen to meet the shy, self-conscious young men. Then the piper came forth from the chimney corner to the two chairs set ready for him, and sitting carefully down he arranged the bundle containing the pipes on his knee while he tied a leather strap to the second chair on which to rest them, perhaps also to save his threadbare trousers. He then very delicately removed several wrappings, stopping to look up with a smile when an impatient boy or girl tapped heel and toe on the stone floor to hasten him, or when we children in the doorway of the little room wriggled and squeaked with excitement. The last wrapping was a red silk handkerchief from which the bright pipes emerged; they were adjusted and after a few preliminary wails a stately quadrille started the dance, to be followed by reels, jigs, sometimes a hornpipe, and winding up with *Sir Roger de Coverley*. Round dances were never seen at that time.

Kennedy would play any tune called for except one, the *Fox-Chase*, and when in the middle of the evening we children were put up by the maids to ask him for it, he would turn a deaf ear, the reason being that this tune needed re-adjustment of the pipes. Nor would he listen until after my mother had gone to a cupboard for a glass of *J.J.* which she gave him with a smile, bidding him rest awhile. Then the panting dancers seized piggins of milk, standing at the open door to drink as they cooled in the evening air, giggling and joking but ever mindful of the near presence of 'the masther' and 'the misthress', those watchful guardians of their manners and morals.

Fresh wails from the pipes announced the wished-for *Fox-Chase* and with clapping of hands and stamping of feet the dance went on.

Another musician was Mr. Regan, a short, fat, bald little man who was a fine violinist. He played Purcell, Mozart, Schubert, even Bach, and was the 'Opener of the Door' into a new world for us children. Only Bessie demurred.

'I don't *want* to like Purcell because he was one of the English Purcells,' she said.

The little musician whirled round. 'Music is of no nationality,' he shouted. 'The composer is God's son wherever he is born,' which silenced Bessie completely.

Mr. Regan confided in mother and looked upon her as the only one of his friends who had a soul for classical music. He had been deeply offended one day at Castle H. where he 'thought to give his lordship and her ladyship a treat by playing Mozart's *Adagio in D*. You would think, Mrs. O'Brien, that that exquisite air would enthral any mortal man and woman, let alone the cultivated nobility! You can understand the shock it was to me when his lordship, after fidgetting a bit, cried to me, "Oh, Regan, do stop that and give us *Philip McKeogh!*" and the assembled company roared after him, "Yes, yes! *Philip McKeogh!*" and *her ladyship clapped her hands.*'

'That was not well done,' mother said, 'they certainly have no taste.'

'But listen, that was not the worst!' Mr. Regan went on, tears filling his eyes. 'I don't know how it came about, but as I recovered from the blow they had dealt me, I found I *was* playing *Philip McKeogh* . . . and I would sooner have died!'

We dared not laugh, so deep was the musician's sense of outrage, not for himself but for his adored Mozart.

'I tell you, Mrs. O'Brien, that a thousand pounds would not draw me into that castle again.'

He kept his word and from that time he would only play that lovely air for mother.

My mother used to say that life is made up of sleeping, feeding, working—and interruptions. Of these last she had too many, yet great was the patience with which she met them, nor would she ever keep the 'caller at the door' waiting, especially when this was an old father or mother bringing a letter from America to be read. These letters invariably began with the school-taught words: 'Dear Father and Mother, I write these few lines hoping to find you both in good health as this leaves me at present, thanks be to God for His kind mercies to us all.' A letter which did not contain a money-order was called 'an empty one', but useful as these gifts were from the children in America, it was good tidings that the parents looked for and the words which told them that they were loved as of old and not forgotten.

A welcome and beloved visitor was Countess de Salis who used to come on foot across the green hills in her red colleen-bawn cloak, which she wore year after year, perhaps to teach economy and simplicity in her gentle way. For her mother kept the Great Mogul plums which ripened on our wall; for her we picked the earliest mountainy mushrooms; nothing was too good for this friend, whose understanding and sympathy never failed. In truth, the friendship formed with our landlord's family has survived time and change.

Sometimes people came to my mother with 'trouble in the mind', bringing difficulties to be solved. One of these was Bridget Donelly, a decent, devout little old woman. "Tis about the Living Rosary,[1] ma'am. There was no such devotion in me mother's time, God rest her soul! I'd like ye to tell me, if I join it, will I get a higher place in Heaven than me mother have? She wasn't belongin' to any society but the church, and I would

[1] The Confraternity of the Living Rosary, then being started in our parish.

never be content to be higher up in Heaven than me mother.' Old
Biddy went away 'aisy in the mind' to join the confraternity.

A favourite visitor was an old woman called Peggy-the-Caps.
She went her round twice a week carrying on her back a large
hamper of baker's bread from a neighbouring village. I see her
now toiling up the hill holding in her hands the *sugaun* (rope
made of hay) which kept the basket in its place. She, poor soul,
firmly believed that the devil was riding on her shoulders and
stabbing her with hell fire. 'Will I get another bottle of the oil,
ma'am,' she would ask my mother, 'the yalla oil to an'int me
back where *That One* have me burnt.' Peggy-the-Caps would
have scorned to call her pain rheumatism. Her nickname arose
from her secondary occupation, which was making the frilled
caps worn by Irish married women.

Another old creature who came now and then was what
people called a Poor Pity. He wore a long thin brown coat and
a tall hat, round it was a brown veil secured over his chest by
elastic so that no one ever saw his face which was being destroyed by cancer. He was very humble and gentle, weak and
nearly blind, but I dreaded his visits because mother used to put
my hand in his, telling me to lead him safely past the sandpit
which made our road dangerous for those who could not see.
I was frightened by the strangeness of the veiled face.

An extraordinary and merry old man appeared occasionally
in the yard, leaping and whooping to announce his arrival. He
came at dinner time or on summer evenings when men and
maids were free. How they laughed! how we children laughed
as he capered and danced on his bare feet, contorting his pleasant, ugly face in an astonishing way, so that I prayed anxiously
in the midst of my laughter that the moon might not change
while he was making faces! Donnchadh was a welcome visitor;
though he was almost an *omadaun* (imbecile) he gave a vast

amount of pleasure, and was surprised when my father rewarded him with twopence.

"Tis too much, sir, too much entirely!"

Donnchadh had few wants; food was given him in return for his antics, and an old coat or shirt now and again.

'Faix! What more would an ould fella be needing?'

Not boots nor socks, for he had never worn them; not a hat, for hadn't he a tall hat, cast off by half-a-dozen successive wearers, hidden away in a farmer's barn where he often slept, a tall hat for funerals!

'Why wouldn't I go to me friends' buryin's when I have me fine hat an' all?'

A strange sight was Donnchadh in his rags, his feet bare, the tall hat on his rough head, his mobile face fixed in a solemn, mournful stare, walking last in the procession.

The back door of our house was not locked until the farm-boys had gone out after prayers. Once or twice a tall, unkempt woman came in with a baby bundled under her arm. Her black hair hung over her neck and shoulders and partly hid her oval face which would have been handsome but for the hard bitterness of her mouth. No one knew who the tragic creature was, although it was rumoured that she had been sent back from America as a bad character. She came always in dusk or darkness, usually when we were at prayers, giving no greeting, speaking no word as she walked to the fire and poured boiling water into her teapot from kettle or saucepan, never putting down the baby but shifting it from one arm to the other as she went about her preparations. One of the maids would get up from her knees to put a jug of milk within her reach, otherwise she seemed to have all she needed in her basket. The baby made neither movement nor sound, nor did the woman unwrap it to give it food, in fact one wondered if the bundle under her arm was a baby at all. She went as she came, silent and unexplained, into the night.

## 10: MR. PARNELL. GOD'S FAIR INNOCENTS

We never knew who might not come to the farm, but the three we hoped for, perhaps prayed for, never came.

The first was a harper, one who would play on a little old Irish harp like the harp of Brian Boru, that king from whom all the O'Briens are descended.

The second was Charles Stewart Parnell who was our hero. Bessie imagined him striding up to the front door, his beard waving in the wind, if it was long enough to wave, his eyes flashing.

'What would they be flashing about?' Janie asked in her quiet, practical voice.

'Me,' Bessie exclaimed, '*me*!' Then aside to Janie and very fast, 'he would have heard that on Lough Gur lives a young girl who would die for him! Wouldn't he want to see that young girl, silly?' Then she went on in what we called her oratorical voice, 'He is a man! a man worth dying for!'

'Who is worth dying for?' mother asked from the kitchen while Dooley left her dusting to listen.

'Mr. Parnell,' we cried together.

'Och! *him*!' Dooley said with contempt. 'Descended from

67

Sassenachs! Himself a Protestant and his mother from America!
*Him*!'

'Oh!' Bessie shrieked, 'it isn't true, is it, mother? He is a pure
Catholic Irishman? Say he is!' Bessie was hurling herself about
the little room in excitement when a hand came through the
open window and caught her by the arm; the voice of Father
Burke of Limerick boomed round the room.

'*Hibernicis ipsis Hibernior,* that's what the man is, God bless
him—for all his foreign blood which is none of his fault, and
his heresy which please God we'll cure him of.'

Bessie was trembling and pale from the shock she had
had. 'Protestant,' she gasped, 'descended from Sassenach in-
vaders?'

'Come here, me young rebel!' Father Burke ordered when
he had come round by the door into the little room and mother
had gone for *J.J.* 'I've news for ye! What do ye think I've
called in here for?'

'For a dwink,' piped baby-sister from under the table where
she was playing with her dolls.

'What's that?' Father Burke asked, startled.

Annie put up her sweet serious face. 'I said, for a dwink.'

'Babes and sucklings!' he muttered. 'Well, well, that's neither
here nor there! I've looked in, me young rebels, to invite your
father and mother and perhaps—*perhaps* I say—one of you little
girls, to a meeting in Limerick where you'll see and hear—Mr.
Parnell!'

'My God,' said Bessie, blaspheming under her breath, 'my
God! and I'm only the third little girl!' She burst into tears.

'I'll give up my chance, Bess,' Janie said kindly.

My head whirled and my heart thumped. Here was the
chance of a lifetime to see a great man, Ireland's great man! As
the eldest I had the right. I turned away so as not to see Bessie's
face and swimming eyes.

'I give up my chance, Bessie,' I said at last, angrily, and because I knew myself to be a fool I cried too.

'Well, well, I never!' Father Burke cried, somewhat dismayed. 'What have we here! A nest of young politicians and a budding Father Mathew under the table. Mrs. O'Brien! ye've a terrible family, let me tell ye! There's nothing for it but the lot of them must come to Limerick to meet Mr. Parnell! They have me beat entirely.'

Father and mother, Bessie and I, went to the meeting. We saw Mr. Parnell quite closely. He looked tired, his face was pale, his dark eyes glowed in their deep sockets. When our parents were introduced by Father Burke, he shook hands and spoke to them in his English voice and then nodded to us, 'How do, how do,' he said, looking *equally* at Bessie and me and without a smile for either of us. We had secretly agreed to genuflect as we do in chapel, but there was not time before he turned away. When we told mother of our thwarted intention, she said she was glad we hadn't made ourselves noticeable. She would have been ashamed.

Strange as it may be, that meeting with her hero seemed to make Bessie more sensible. She attended to her lessons and we heard less rebel talk. As for me I was glad to have seen Mr. Parnell and that was that.

The third stranger for whom I particularly waited and hoped was a dancing bear. I had a romantic feeling about bears and often made a picture to myself of how the bear and his gypsy leader would appear rather suddenly because the steepness of the road would hide them as they came up. Their heads would show first over the rise of the hill, the sallow-faced gypsy— Pedro, his name would be—with one red feather in his hat and a spotted neckerchief and flashing teeth. Then the round, tousled head of a brown bear wearing the collar of a slave.

I see them. They are standing in the yard; the gypsy is playing on a rough little fiddle, stamping in time with the music; the bear is lurching from one foot to the other, doing his clumsy best to dance. Now mother is bringing him a pail of milk and some bread and carrots, while the maids, giggling shyly, wait on Pedro. He has tied the bear to the pump; very quietly I undo the rope and lead the poor creature to the lawn on the side of the house where mother has a couple of hives. I say, 'There, my dear, help yourself, eat as much as you like.' He turns the skep over and munches the comb, honey-cells, grub-cells, wax and all, and when the angry bees buzz at him, he flicks them away with his hand and rattling nails. I hurry into the house for water to wash his sticky face and hands and to find goose-grease for his road-sore feet. While I am doing his feet I tell him that I know his sorrows and wish he could live with us and be free. He gives my hand a lick and grunts, and then he lies on the grass and has a roll like a horse and after that he goes to sleep while I try to get the honey off his fur. I have only just finished washing his meek face when Pedro shrieks: 'I've lost my bear,' and whistles loudly. The bear gets up and sighs and shuffles to his master.

For some time we had been expecting a visit from two strangers, of whom Dooley had told us, who had lately been wandering about Lough Gur. The people called them by Irish words meaning God's Fair Innocents—an innocent, or a natural, is one who is half-witted, therefore under the protection of heaven.

The day had been wet until late afternoon when the rain ceased and shafts of sunlight divided the backward-rolling clouds. The air was full of sweet scents and below us the dark waters of Lough Gur took on a silver film. We children ran out of the house as father came from the calves' shed and mother from the dairy to see the wild sunsetting, and as the Fair Innocents came through the yard gate, walking in a narrow beam of sun. They were white and terribly thin, a young mother and a boy of about six. Their clothes were threadbare but not ragged, their faces clean, their light, uncovered hair tidy. They came hand in hand through the gate, smiling as though we were old friends but saying nothing.

'God save you,' father said kindly. 'Sit down while we bring you some food.'

'Mary', the woman said introducing herself, 'and Dinny-bawn.'

They sat on a bench outside the back door which was protected by a porch and had a fixed table beside it. Many meals were set on the wayfarers' board in the course of the year, and the maids often sat there to sew or to play on the Jew's harp.

Mother sat down beside Mary. 'You look tired, child. You have come a long way?'

''Twas far, far,' was the vacant answer.

'Perhaps from Kerry—or Clare?'

'Kerry or Clare,' Mary echoed.

'You would like to go home—to mother?'

'No home, no mother,' Mary answered, smiling.

'And Dinny's father? Is he with you?'

'Dinny-bawn,' she corrected and laughed. 'No father.' Mother seemed worried, clearly Mary was half-witted. She went in to consult Dooley while Ellie and Bridgie set bacon and bread and tea on the table.

When mother came back Dinny-bawn was trying to make his mother eat, putting little morsels to her lips and looking anxiously in her face.

'You have eaten no more than a bird, Mary,' mother said.

Mary laid her cheek on her folded hands. 'Dead bird,' she murmured, 'dead bird to-morrow.'

'Come into the kitchen and sit by the fire,' mother said.

'No, hay-shed,' Mary answered, looking about her. Dinny-bawn led her to the little shed where father kept hay and sacks in readiness for homeless wanderers.

By and by Dinny-bawn came out. 'Mary asleep,' he said.

It was a lovely moment, red gloaming over the farm and over the world. The cows were filing out of the byres to go to the pastures for the night; cocks were calling their hens to roost; cooped hens clucking to their chickens and fluffing sheltering wings. Ducks were ambling towards the duck-house, and guinea-fowl running very fast in a bunch to mother's trees where they roosted, while from the lake stalked the great gander with his geese.

Dinny-bawn stood entranced, now and then holding out his arms as though he wanted to embrace the creatures. When it was dark we brought him in and showed him our toys. Mother watched him and decided that he was not 'wanting' so much as undeveloped. He seemed to like looking at father who was dozing in his armchair, his kind face at rest, a smile on his lips.

Ellie called Dinny-bawn to supper in the kitchen; later he knelt with us while we said the Rosary, keeping his eyes on father and copying his movements.

'Bedtime, Dinny-bawn,' mother said, 'good-night.'

'Good-night, ma'am.'

'Good-night, son,' father said with a gentle pat.

Dinny-bawn looked adoringly in father's face. 'Good-night, God,' he answered.

Father Daly found them a cabin where they slept and the neighbours took care of them by day. Their children led Dinny-bawn to school followed by Mary, who was as anxious as a cow whose calf is being carted to market. Dinny-bawn sat among the infants in the lowest class and learnt ABC. When the infants knew XYZ they passed on to the next form, but Dinny-bawn stayed behind and learnt ABC with a new batch of babies. He was always very good; he had a voice like an angel's, but when the children sang hymns, he sang *ah, ah, ah*.

One day Mary was found dead in her cabin. She had been growing thinner and weaker. Doctor Gubbins took an interest in her and tried to trace her parents. Mary, he said, was not imbecile. She had had some dreadful shock. When Father Ryan came with neighbours to bury her, Dinny-bawn fought them with soft fumbling blows, the best his gentleness could do. Anguish was in his blue eyes.

It was Murnane who calmed him. 'Mary says Dinny-bawn must take care of Murnane's ass. Dinny-bawn will ride on the ass to Murnane's house and stay there. *Mary says so*.' Murnane lifted him on to the donkey. Dinny-bawn smiled. 'G'wan now,' he said, kicking lightly with bare heels on the rough sides of the ass.

## 11: FATHER'S FRIENDS

Father's friends usually called when the day's work was ended. There was Jack Mahony, a farmer who at odd times was also a shoemaker. He would come in at dusk with a gun on his arm and a dog at his heels, on his way home from Lough Gur. Sometimes he had snipe or wild duck as an offering to mother, and sometimes he brought his wife to talk to her while he 'discoorsed' father on farming and the price of leather. He and Mrs. Mahony both talked at once, loud and cheerfully, she with an extraordinary sound in her voice like the creak and squeak of new boots which fascinated us greatly. They were never downhearted like other farmers; this was attributed to Mahony having two trades and no children, his circumstances being in consequence considered 'aisy, God send his luck will hold!'

Another visitor, a lively young farmer and near neighbour, had a talent for extemporising clever and amusing verses about events and people. He was—or pretended to be—a red-hot politician; his orations never failed to draw us children from our schoolwork or sewing.

'Now listen to me, ye young gurrls, and I'll tell ye what Ireland wants—she's callin' for a man! A man like meself, burnin' and quiverin' to save her from the tyrant that has his fut on her neck, and she lyin' in the dust that was once a queen, and bawlin' to be saved. 'Twould split your ears to hear her if ye'd but hearken; 'twould bust your heart wid pity for her misery and desolation. Now if I c'd but be king and Misther O'Brien here me prime minister . . .'

'Yes, Mr. O'Herlihy,' piped Bessie, 'if you were king, what would you wear?'

'Wear is it? Wouldn't I wear a collar of gold like King Malachi?'

'A gold collar with a green tie over your Sunday shirt-front?' suggested Janie.

'Silly,' I said to her, being older and knowing more. 'Malachi's collar was big, like the one which Murnane's ass wears to fairs and funerals.'

O'Herlihy set down his glass of *J.J.* and laughed. We all laughed with him.

'That's the way,' he said, 'that's the way ye'll laff when the king and the prime minister here have the last Sassenachs druv out o' the country and they runnin' headlong into the sea, for lack of English paddle-ships to get 'em across fast enough. Ye would laff could ye see them lords and absentee landlords over there puttin' their coats over their heads agin' the noise of the shoutin' of the people and the tootin' of the trumpets, when King O'Herlihy would proclaim the Republic of Ireland from the hill of Tara! But there'd be one ye'd mebbe pity,' Mr. O'Herlihy continued in a low moving voice, 'and that's Queen Victoria, and she dashin' her crown on the floor and cryin' "Och, wirra! me grief! and what worth at all at all is me crown when the brightest jool have gone from it—for ever?"'

'Wouldn't that be splendid?' said Bessie, jumping with

enthusiasm—she was always a patriot. 'And wouldn't *the biter be bit* that time!'

'Please, Mr. O'Herlihy,' asked Janie solemnly, 'what would father be wearing on the hill of Tara that great day?'

'Father', mother said firmly, 'would be attending to his work in his working clothes on his own Carrigeen hill, and you must come and attend to your work.' Over our reluctant heads she murmured to the visitor, 'They are too young for politics!'

'If that's the way it is, I must ask your pardon, ma'am, for lettin' me tongue run away with me. I'm hoping ye'll allow me to sing how Mr. O'Brien went to the horse fair . . .' Here he began to sing an improvisation of father buying one screw after another; taking the dealer's word for their soundness; then bringing them home, and mother's criticisms; after that the master of hounds buying the bunch without inspection, John O'Brien being well-known as the soul of honesty; the sarcastic remarks of the huntsman; the meet, ups and downs, leps and falls, and the ultimate end of the dead screws, shared at a feast by moonlight between hounds and foxes. At the end of each verse we children had to sing

> '*And that is true, we swear 'tis true,*
> *Oh, long live John O'Brien!*'

In which chorus laughing maids in the kitchen and farmboys listening at the door, joined lustily. No one laughed more heartily than father at this satire on his want of horse-judgment, but when we bade him good-night we kissed him warmly in case his feelings had been at all hurt.

A friend who knew all that there is to be known about horse-flesh was Jack Gubbins (no one, not even well-mannered children, called him mister). He cantered over to Lough Gur at any hour, and father jogged on his one well-bred mare, the mother of several sprightly foals, to Bruree, to visit him at the stud-farm. Here, in later years, the famous colt, Galtee More, was born.

Twice a week or oftener came the neighbour, a cousin, who was known to everyone as 'the lord' on account of his likeness to Lord ——. He had a small farm but did not depend entirely on his business, having some private means. 'The lord' was dapper, spick and span, loved and admired by everyone for his kindli-ness and the way he had with him. 'The lady', so called only because her husband was 'the lord', had few admirers. She was a little too fine for plain folk, and seemed to pride herself on being emotional. She used to cry bitterly if a cow or calf died. 'I am so sensitive,' she sobbed, 'my feelings are so fine; but I can't help it; am'n't I one of the Frosts of Clare?'

My father loved 'the lord', with whom he exchanged con-fidences and newspapers, and he was sad—we all were sad—when he fell ill and died from gangrene of the little toe.

Sometimes men from Limerick with whom father did busi-ness came for the day, or some official from the Department of Agriculture to inspect the farm and often to ask father's advice on dairy-farming and other country matters. Now and then Uncle Richard rode over from Knocklong to stay in the old home, to talk over their young days with father and to remem-ber with love and gratitude little Mammy Jug.

We children were usually glad to see the backs of visitors! We liked to have our parents to ourselves. We induced mother to have the aunts, her four or five sisters, 'all in a batch', so as to have done with them, and we begged father to move on people we really disliked. 'Give him two eggs for the road, father,' we urged. This was the polite way in county Limerick of speeding an unwanted guest. At breakfast the host would say heartily, 'Take two eggs, my dear fellow, two eggs for the road.' The hint was always taken.

Grown-up visitors were trying enough but we were indeed put out when father invited two little girls, the youngest children of a business friend in Limerick, called Mr. Finnegan, to stay for a fortnight for fresh air and fresh cream drinking. We were shy at first of these grand city children, who played games we had never heard of, and wore frilled drawers, who played duets on the piano and were learning French and how to make lace. We on our side had a store of country knowledge; we knew about butter-making, candle-making, spinning and weaving even if we could not spin and weave ourselves; we knew how sheep are washed and sheared and the way pigs have rings set in their snouts; how eels are caught and fairies exorcised from dairies. We also knew much more about books and poetry than they did.

· By and by our guests began to like us and to find us interesting. Lough Gur with its ruined castles; Knockadoon and Knockfennel with their caves and ancient forts; the stone-circles, the cromlechs and gowlauns were enchanting places to play in, and in the evening, croquet on the lawn or being read to by mother, ended the long summer days. We could hardly believe that our visitors were unacquainted with *Little Women* and saw to it that before they went away their love for Marmee was as great as our own. 'I'm Jo,' I announced at the beginning, 'Janie is Laurie, and Bessie is Amy, but you can be Meg and Beth, though Beth has to die young.' They decided both to be Meg.

We were glad when the time of their departure drew near because we wanted the rest of the holidays to ourselves, but my gladness was changed to misery when their parents insisted on

my paying a return visit, and in spite of my tears, my father and
mother agreed to my going for a week. They thought it good
for the country mouse to go to the city and in despair I set out
with the Finnegans for Limerick.

'Look at our house! Isn't it big? Hasn't it got great windows?
Don't you like our garden? Aren't the geraniums fine? Don't
you like gravel paths? Here you will have a bed to yourself, a
brass bed! You will be surprised at the size of our church!
There's an organ in it! Have you ever heard an organ? Our
washing goes to a proper laundry! We get real baker's bread
here!' All this with the boasting natural to young children, and
with no intention of disparaging my home. I tried hard to be
well-behaved and polite, but as we had been brought up to be
rigidly truthful, there was nothing for it but silence. I did not
like their fine garden when I compared it with our fields and
green hills; their grand geraniums were as nothing compared
with our sheets of ragweed and willow herb, loosestrife and
furze, our tiny pansies in the short turf, and our bog cotton. I
would rather have our thousand larks than their church organ!
I would rather my clothes should dry in sun and wind than in
a city laundry!

How can I bear, I thought, to stay away from my home for a
whole week?

In the evening we 'small fry' had our bread and milk in the
schoolroom and afterwards joined the elder sisters and their
parents. These sisters were very pretty, especially Teresa, the
eldest, who sang beautifully and had been in Germany to study
music. Several young men came in for the evening. First we
played forfeits and charades, then Teresa sang, both Irish songs
and German, and afterwards they danced. I had never seen
round dances before; they surprised me.

There was a German captain there, who seemed very fond of
Teresa and kissed her hand when he said good-night. 'The fry'

(as our little friends were called) told me afterwards that he and Teresa were going to be married.

It was strange to be in a house where people went to bed without saying the Rosary; I felt more homesick than ever and cried myself to sleep.

The next afternoon the fry went off to their lace class, the big girls went for a walk and I found myself alone, for the maid who had been told to take me out to see the shops was quarrelling with the cook in the kitchen. I thought I would not stay any longer, so without waiting to get my luggage, I crept out of the house and down the street to the place where Fogarty's long car started for Bruff. There by good luck it was, almost ready to leave. I scrambled up; other passengers took their places although the driver was not there. Someone said he was having his hair cut. 'Have a drink for the road, Johnny Daly,' the landlord of the Post Inn shouted when at last he came from the barber's and gathered up the reins to start. Johnny Daly laid down the reins at once, and left horses and passengers once more while he drank his stout. And just then, who should come by but Teresa and her sisters and the German captain!

'Sissy!' they cried, 'where are you going?'

'Home,' I muttered, getting hot and cold in turns for fear the tall German would snatch me from my seat. But they only laughed, not knowing what else to do, and wished me a safe journey. After that they went one way while we went another. Johnny Daly leapt to his seat, shouting, 'G'wan now out o' that,' to the horses which started off at a grand gallop for Bruff.

I got off the car at Grange and ran through the fields as the bird flies, regardless of cows and possible bulls. My fear of horned beasts was overcome by the urge to get home as quickly as possible.

There lay Lough Gur before me, and the farm, deserted and

quiet, showing that milking was still in progress. In the house a neighbour's child was teaching baby-sister to tell the time. How they jumped when from the door I shouted at the top of my voice the war-cry of the Desmonds, which we used because it belonged to Lough Gur. '*Sean-ait-aboo*,' I yelled again, 'hurrah for the old place,' and with my sisters and the neighbour's child, ran hey-go-mad about the lawn.

My loud cheer brought father and mother to the door and seeing how glad I was to be at home they had not the heart to scold me but laughed at me instead. Perhaps they were secretly pleased that their nervous daughter had made up her own mind and successfully brought herself back, even though she had left her luggage behind.

'There was a German officer there,' I told them all later, 'a captain. He is going to marry Teresa, the eldest, the singing one. She will have to live in Germany!'

That was news!

'I will never marry,' I added firmly, 'I will *never* leave home again.'

'I shall marry,' said little Bessie, 'and I don't mind if he is a German or a Chinese so long as he is a good Catholic and a kind man, because I want to see the world. But I would die sooner than marry an Englishman.'

'And I shall marry,' said Janie, our lovely one, 'because I want to be a farmer's wife like mother. Baby can be a nun.'

'So that's that,' father laughed. 'Sissy will stay and look after her old father and mother; Janie will marry Purcell Grogan and live close by at Castle Farm; baby must be a nun, but Bessie . . . don't you be too cock-sure! If I see a smart young Sassenach one of these days, perhaps come over with shooting friends of the Count's, why wouldn't I fix up a marriage for you?'

Here I broke in, encouraged by father's naughty teasing, quoting, '*The English are the finest race on God's earth!*'

Bessie was a spitfire! Her cheeks were red, her little chest heaved. She sprang up and would have fought both me and father had he not taken her by the wrists and kissing her fondly, settled her on his knee, where she wept softly against his shoulder, so deeply did she hate the English.

## 12: TERESA AND THE GERMAN LADY

Three months after this escapade of mine, an invitation came to
Teresa's wedding. Our parents went to it, mother, lovely in a
new dress and her otter-skin cape for the cold drive, and father,
according to Dooley, 'looking as handsome as a sea captain'. It
was a splendid wedding with bishop and priests, flowers and
music, bridesmaids and favours; then off the German captain
went with Teresa to Germany for the honeymoon and to stay
with his mother.

It was not many weeks later that father being in Limerick on
business met Mr. Finnegan and heard of the tragedy which had
overtaken poor dear Teresa. The details which I give here were
told later, when the sorrow was less acute and Teresa could
talk to her sisters about what happened when she was taken by
her husband into his mother's house.

The weather was cold, for it was near Christmas, and the old
lady was sitting in a high-backed chair beside a huge china
stove, doing worsted-work by the light of a tall, unshaded oil
lamp which stood on a table beside her. Teresa saw at once that
they were not expected, and that the shock was terrible for the

old lady when her son told her in words too rapid for Teresa to follow, that he had brought to her the woman he loved. He threw his arms round his mother, but she stood up and pushed him from her. 'My God, my God,' was all she could say as they stood looking at one another, the little, plain, old woman and the tall, handsome man. She signed to Teresa to sit down and sat down again herself, heavily, painfully. Then the son knelt down before her and talked and talked and laid his head on her lap and by and by Teresa saw that he was crying, while his mother talked very low and very fast. She put her hand on his head and he seized it and kissed it, trying to prevent her from getting up so that he could talk again, but she pushed back her chair and stood up and going over to Teresa she took her arm and leaning on her went shakily to the door, while the German captain was still crying with his head buried in the chair.

Teresa did not know what to do, but she thought she had better go with the old mother who was as white as death and hardly able to breathe because of the beating of her heart. She helped her up a short little staircase into a bedroom with another hot china stove, which made the room seem so airless that Teresa feared she would faint. She was still wondering why there had been such a strange scene between mother and son, and she felt sorry that the news of his marriage should have upset her so seriously. So she knelt by the side of the old lady and kissed her hand to show that she wanted to be friends. Then the mother kissed Teresa's cheek and said in very slow, broken English, 'My child, my son has a wife and four children. He has twin boys whom he adores. He and his wife quarrelled and she went to her mother, but that will pass. She is ready to go home with the children and they will be as happy, one hopes, as they were before their stupid misunderstanding. My son talked to me downstairs of divorce, but that can never be. We are

Catholics and so, he tells me, are you. My son has done you a great wrong.'

Teresa sat silently pulling and folding the fingers of her gloves as she tried to take in this dreadful news. She could not believe it; she wanted to laugh as one laughs at the memory of a nightmare. Then the old lady took an album and began slowly to turn its pages. 'Look, my dear,' she said. Faded, inartistic as the photographs were, they told the story of her lover as a child, schoolboy, student, cadet, then as officer, bridegroom and father. The latest photograph was of a group; the old lady slid the picture from the page and gave it to Teresa. It was of the young father and mother, smiling at one another, with four children at their feet. There was writing underneath: 'For the beloved grandmother from her son Karl, her daughter Augusta and the children, Lili, Rudi, Wilhelm and Mariechen.'

The next thing that happened was a knock on the locked door. The old lady turned the key and let in an elderly maid who carried a tray with coffee, bread, butter and cold sausage, which she set down, saying in German, 'Eat, please. I beg you to eat.'

'A trouble, a great trouble, has befallen us, Anna.'
'May God help us to bear it,' the maid answered.
'We will speak of it—another time. Will you make up a bed in here for this good child who is very tired. Our trouble is also hers. In the early morning I shall start by train to take her home to Ireland—a long way off, Anna. It may be a week before I come back.'
'And Christmas here,' the maid whispered, 'and in all this snow! May God take care of you.'

She bent and kissed the old lady's hand and went away to
fetch sheets and blankets to lay on the sofa.

'We must eat,' said the old lady, pouring the coffee with a
trembling hand so that it flowed upon the tray. Suddenly she
began to cry. 'I can't go on,' she said.

Teresa sat very still. Nothing was real to her. Later on she ate
and drank, she undressed and brushed her hair and said her
prayers. Then she looked at the narrow sofa with its single
pillow. Life suddenly became real.

The maid tucked the old lady away between two feather beds
and immediately she was asleep. Then the good creature helped
the shuddering Teresa into her little bed and sat beside her, patting her gently, as one pats an infant, till she too slept. So deeply
she slept that she did not hear the knocking on the door, the
angry rattling of the handle, nor see the maid draw bolts at the
top and bottom to keep out the desperate lover.

The next day, while it was still dark, the three women crept
down the stairs and out into the silent street where the snow
cried shrilly under their feet. The maid walked in front carrying
a lantern with a candle in it, leading the way to the station. Here
it was icy cold, the darkness pricked with a few oil lamps on the
platform. The street watchman, muffled in cape and scarf, met
them at the ticket office with their luggage on a small truck,
Teresa's wedding trunks and the old lady's ancient box covered
with the skin of a black and white cow, ornamented and ini-
tialed with square-headed brass nails. The train came clanking
in led by a red-eyed engine, its high funnels smoking and steam-
ing; cold foot-warmers were pulled out with a clatter and replaced by hot ones, passengers were pushed up into freezing
compartments; a bell rang and a whistle screamed; with jolts
and loud puffing the train gathered way on the icy rails.

Three days later Teresa and the old lady came to Limerick. The cold of Germany had given place to Ireland's winter softness. No one met them at the station for there had been no time to write the dreadful news. The jarveys lolling on their cars, stared at the strange old figure in a velvet bonnet, a fur tippet over a 'mantle', and black cloth boots. They stared still more at Teresa.

'That's never Miss Finnegan,' they said, 'though she do have a look of her. Mebbe 'tis one of her a'nts.'

When they came into the house, Teresa forgot her own grief in the greater sorrow of her lover's mother, the humble figure bowed under a load of shame, who, when she tried to speak could find no words.

'I tell you, John,' Mr. Finnegan said to father, 'that old German is a great lady. She stood there, trying, I am sure, to ask our forgiveness for her son's villainy. She had to give it up. Didn't her tears speak for her? Her head was sunk so that her tears dripped on the carpet. And she turned to go, to start right away home and she'd been travelling three days. My wife wouldn't hear of it. She just clapped the old soul into bed, cossetting her like a sister. And there was Teresa, my poor girl, unpacking a comical old cowskin trunk to find the old lady's night-cap.'

There was a great wagging of tongues in Limerick. Everyone sympathised with Teresa and her family. The Bishop decided that she should be called by her married name. One thing puzzled us children, The fry, some months later, told us privately that the other two big sisters were given penances by their confessor because they hated and would not forgive the German captain, whereas Teresa was given a penance because she could not leave off loving him.

## 13: MARY DEASY. MY CONFIRMATION

Our mother seldom had time to go for a leisurely walk: she was too busy, or too tired after strenuous work, or she had to go 'just there and back' when she visited sick people, so that when one day she asked me if I should like to go for a walk with her I was astonished and delighted.

'Is anyone ill?' I asked her, 'is Mary Deasy worse?'

'I haven't heard,' said my mother, 'but we will take her some cough mixture as we go by. I thought you and I might go down to the lake.'

This was so unusual that I felt half afraid I might have done something for which I deserved a lecture, but mother's face re-assured me.

The Deasy children were playing in the dust of the path outside the cabin; all except Timmy, the eldest of the six, who was minding his mother in the bedroom where they all slept at night. The cabin had only two rooms, a kitchen and a bedroom, small and stuffy, with panes of thick glass built into the wall to let in a little light. A hen dashed out, cackling, as we entered, leaving an egg behind her on the hearth.

'Must I go in?' I whispered, hanging back.

Mother nodded and we went into the inner room where Mary Deasy was propped up in bed by a bundle of sacks surmounted by a dingy pillow. She was flushed and exhausted by a bout of coughing, but smiled gallantly. Mother gave her a dose of the carrigeen mixture and talked quietly while the sick woman recovered her breath.

'I d'know will I get it done in time,' she said, patting the white linen which she had been sewing, 'I've another yard and more to seam up before it'll be done. I d'know can I hold out so long?'

'If you will lend me your thimble, I will sew some of it,' mother said.

Mary was unwilling. "Tis like your kindness, ma'am,' she said, 'but I'm wishful to set the last stitch in it meself if so be I can. I'm thinkin' 'tis havin' the sewin' that keeps me here for another day—or mebbe two—with himself and the childer, God help them!' She smiled again. 'Ye'll give an eye to them, I know, ma'am, till himself gets married to me cousin, Nancy Sheehan. If ye could take Timmy on the farm I'd know he'd get plenty to eat.'

My mother signed to me to go out; my knees were knocking together and I felt faint. Timmy, in the kitchen, stared at me.

'Could ye beat up the egg while I heat a drop o'milk?' he asked me, and I responded as best I could.

From the inner room I heard my mother's voice, gentle, reassuring, and the low, continuous coughing of the sick woman.

'Me mammy's been anointed,' Timmy told me confidentially. 'Father Ryan was here last night. He told me father she wouldn't last the week out. 'Tis a grand place where she's goin'; 'tis the other side of the world annyway, an' she'll thravel there in a box. . . . Mammy said not to mind about that and about her looking quare, because she'll be enjoyin' herself when she gets there—'twill be better than a fair! But . . . it's lonesome I'll be for her . . . and I d'know will I be able to mind the childer and them so bold.'

Mother was saying, 'Good-bye, my dear; God be on the road with you.'[1]

Mary answered very cheerfully, 'And with you, ma'am! Me blessin' on you for scatterin' me fears. *Timmy! Timmy!* Let you have a look for me thimble under the bed. I'll get on wid me sewin' before 'tis dark.'

It was her shroud that she was making.

For a time we walked on without speaking. I was still trembling.

'What is it, child dear?' mother asked me.

'It's everything . . . poor little Timmy . . . he doesn't know how he will manage the children . . . and Mary sewing like that and being so smiling. . . .'

'Mary knows she is going to die . . . death isn't terrifying when it comes near—it frightens us much more when it is far off. And of course it is frightening and terrible for those who are not ready and prepared. Our religion teaches us that, it teaches us how to live and how to die.'

'Did you know when you were a little girl like me?'

'Mammy—my mammy—helped me. When she was a very small girl our holy religion was persecuted and forbidden. The priests were hunted. They took their lives in their hands every time they said Mass in a barn or a lonely house or in the caves of the mountains—for half a dozen people at a time. They who were heroes and saints were hunted as criminals. You can imagine that there was little chance for them to teach religion to the children. So they gave certain words to fathers and mothers for them all to live by. When I was a child things were very different, thank God, but still my mammy taught me what she

[1] An old Irish farewell.

had been taught, what her mother learnt from a priest who was *in keeping* in her father's loft.'

'Do tell me what the poor priest taught her. Did he have to whisper all the time?'

'I expect he had to talk very low. He said, "Be just, love mercy. . . ." '

'Why, that's like father!' I cried, remembering how just he was with Meggy-the-Eels, and how merciful to old Paddy when he might have punished him for keeping back the fat eel. 'Please go on, mother.'

'He said, "Keep the faith. Hold fast to our holy religion. Love God with your whole heart. Love your neighbour as yourself." You see when hardly anyone could read, the priests had to teach them in short easy sentences. They couldn't say: "Learn the Sermon on the Mount by heart," when no one had a Bible and few could read. So they said: "Visit the sick, feed the hungry. . . ." '

'Oh, mother! Is that why you are so kind?'

It was a new idea. I had taken it for granted that mother was kind because she was herself. Now it seemed that there was Something, Someone, for whom she was good. In that moment I had a glimmering of what is meant by idealism, a new light was shed on the difficult word religion.

Mother considered. 'I began by obeying those words against my will. It took me a long time to get used to dirt and bad air— and insects—in the cabins, and the begging and persistence of the people at the door, and being bothered for things—medicine and clothes—when I was busy. I had to say to myself that if we do kindnesses to the poor, the hungry, the naked, to those who are, in a way, imprisoned by poverty in dirty rags and dirty rooms, we do kindnesses really to our Blessed Lord. That helped me, and helps me still. We see Him in them.'

'Oh, mother! not in the man in the brown veil. . . ?'

'Yes, child dear.'

'*Mother!* surely not in Donnchadh—not in an omadaun?'

'In everyone . . . in the very least.'

'Oh, mother, mother,' I cried. 'I never can feel like thàt! I never shall be able to love beggars . . . I know I shall have death rattles like Dick Dooley. . . .' I burst into tears.

We had come to the lake which lay calm and smiling in the sunshine. Mother drew me down to sit beside her on a rock. 'Hush, darling, hush. There is nothing to be afraid of. You are learning all the time to have courage. It will be easier after you have been confirmed at Easter.'

'Confirmed!' I began to cry again. It is dreadful to be a confirmed person at ten years old—eleven, soon after Easter. A child leaves off being a child after confirmation. She turns into a *responsible person*—so I had heard. She becomes a grown-up person and to be grown-up is dreadful. It is being a lost child.

Mother was oh! so kind when I poured out my fears. She comforted me. I should like to write down here the words she said—still bright in the treasury of my memory—but they were spoken only for me.

As I lay awake that night I resolved to live for God. I determined to copy my father and mother in all things. Like them I would do works of mercy. I would visit Mary Deasy by myself-early the next day.

There was, however, no call for me to do this for Mary died in her sleep early in the night. Dooley was with her. While the father and the children slept all round her, Dooley finished sewing the shroud.

I was prepared for my confirmation in a class with my schoolfellows, examined and passed by the priest. The intervening days were heavy with anxiety and foreboding lest I should fail to answer rightly and promptly the questions that would be put to me by the Bishop. I wished with all my heart that he would take the priest's word for my fitness instead of disturbing me with questions at a time full of mystery and expectation.

The Archbishop of Cashel came himself to St. Patrick's Well, to our humble chapel. We stood and knelt before him in our white dresses and veils, looking, as Dooley said, like a flock of little angels. The dreaded moment passed and I received the sacrament which gives strength and wisdom to the least of the little ones.

My mother helped me to take off my white dress and veil; she seemed to be waking me from a beautiful dream and leading me back to the everyday world. 'Here, my dear,' she said, 'are my presents for your confirmation.' The presents were a small gold cross on a chain for my neck and a Thomas Kempis. 'In times of trouble and sorrow,' she continued, 'read the chapter that opens to you. You will surely find the help and comfort you need.'

My sisters stared at me when we sat down to dinner. 'You look just the same,' Janie said, 'do you feel different?'

After that day I was put in charge of my three sisters. I had to see that they were neat and tidy, that they brushed their nails and their teeth and did not shirk their tubs. Their hair was my special duty. I brushed and combed the brown, the gold and the baby-flaxen heads until they shone—in spite of protest, wriggles and tears. The tears were my own, shed over their waywardness and over my difficult duty.[1]

[1]Bessie, sixty-five years later, writes: 'How we all looked up to you, but too great a responsibility was laid on you to manage the younger three of us and keep us in order. Naturally we resented it and gave you all the trouble we could.'

## 14: THE CONVENT SCHOOL

The little town of Bruff is only two miles from Lough Gur, yet it seemed a far place when the time came for me to go to school at the Convent of The Faithful Companions of Jesus. I felt as if I had died from my dear home and had entered the Kingdom of Souls, so unearthly were the ways of life in this strange place.

Everything was different: the vast size of the rooms, the endless stairs, the long, uncurtained windows from which no one might look out, the cold bright light reflected from painted walls, the black clothes of nuns and pupils.

The first thing I noticed when the big front door shut behind mother and me was a sweet scent of beeswax and the bright shining of woodwork, produced, as I learnt later, by the fervent work of lay-sisters who rubbed and polished with might and main because they were the servants of no earthly master, but of God. The next thing that struck and bewildered me was the great number of people in the house: nuns, lay-sisters, the ninety pupils, besides many parents who had come with them, some bringing new little girls, tremulous like myself and trying not to cry when the bell rang which warned visitors to take their leave. It warned my mother to go with the rest.

Oh, my grief! The pain comes back when I remember the great door closing between my darling and me and the flood of anxiety which overwhelmed me. I could not tell what danger might await her on the way home. The horse might fall, mist might hide the road and the car fall into the lake or the sand-pit; Fenians might shoot her from behind a hedge, mistaking her in the dark for an agent or a landlord; or she might die of sorrow to be leaving me alone at school. Her eyes were brimming with tears when she said goodbye. She might so easily die, pale and delicate as she was—and so good.

The bell rang again, this time it was for supper. Crowds of children surged round me. I was swept in turn into the refectory, the chapel, up the endless stairs, into the vast dormitory with its rows of curtained beds.

I heard a nun's voice say, 'Mary O'Brien, this is your bed.'

Mary O'Brien seemed a stranger to me, a puppet for whom Sissy O'Brien must pull the strings, whom Sissy O'Brien undressed and enveloped in a long, loose nightgown, buttoned at throat and wrists and down the front, and finally put into a bed as cold and lonely as a grave.

A nun, reciting the Rosary, marched up and down, keeping a vigilant eye upon the dormitory until the last child was in bed. Then, for the benefit of new-comers she announced, 'No talking or whispering! Silence must be unbroken! The curtains between the beds must be kept drawn.'

Crying is not talking or whispering therefore not disobedience nor a sin to be confessed, but crying must be smothered by bedclothes so that no one is disturbed. The girl in the next bed heard my stifled sobbing; she pulled back the curtain between our beds and felt for my hand and held it until I fell asleep.

When I hear or read the story of our Lord walking one day through a cornfield with His disciples, who picked the ears of corn to eat the grains and so broke the law of the Sabbath, I think of sweet Lena O'Farrell who broke the law of the convent to comfort an unhappy child.

When we were roused in the morning I was dreaming about Dooley, which reminded me of her agitated farewell at the gate as we drove through: the way she gobbled my hand, which was her idea of kissing and her exhortation to mother, 'Ye'll be sure, ma'am, to tell the nuns the way it is with her, the tricks her nerves do be playin' her and the good intentions of the doty[1] child! Ye'll tell them how we have her brought up—innocent as a flower.'

The nun who called us at six o'clock gave a tug at my bed-covering saying, 'Praise be to Jesus,' and hurried on from bed to bed waking one child after another with the set words.

'Night will come again, please God,' I said to myself. I dreaded the plunge into the new life, and into the bleak dormitory to wash at the long line of basins set under taps of cold water. I watched girls slipping their nightgowns to their waists and tying them there by the sleeves while they sluiced their faces, necks and arms and hurriedly dried them. I did the same and was proceeding to stand on one leg to wash the other when a bigger girl stopped me and hurriedly covered my bare knee and foot. 'You mustn't do that,' she whispered, 'it's forbidden; you'll have a foot-bath twice a week.' With that perfunctory performance I had to be content although my body rebelled, used as it was to be washed all over every day. That's what Dooley would call a *lick and a promise*, I thought as I went back to my cubicle.

'Two minutes for hair brushing,' my neighbour said under

[1]Darling.

her breath, 'and put on your *peignoir*.' She pointed to a funny little print cape which I buttoned under my chin, and then proceeded to do my hair as best I could with the help of a tiny handglass which reflected one eye or a nose or an inch of hair. As there was no way of making a straight parting I combed my hair back, and secured it with a round comb. I looked and felt in more ways than one like Alice in Wonderland.

The business of getting up went at full speed so that we should have time to make our beds.   Nannie O'Brien, a kind little cousin from Limerick, was sent to help me, and to show me, by signs, exactly how my bedclothes must be arranged. When we left the dormitory with the rest and were clattering downstairs, Nannie whispered, 'That's the French way of making a bed; all the rules are French because the foundress of F.C.J. was a Frenchwoman.[1] We even have to go to bed at eight like babies.'

'Silence,' said the nun, 'tread lightly. Gentlewomen make no sound when they walk.'

The clatter ceased instantly; noiselessly we adjusted small black veils edged with blue, and short black cashmere capes, and filed into chapel, as quietly as cats, attending to our steps instead of lifting up our hearts.

That's a sin, I thought, when I recalled my mind from my feet, but it is the nun's fault and will be on her soul.

After chapel came breakfast in a great bare refectory. A nun sat at the head of each of the four tables, silent and watchful, her hands hidden in her sleeves; she did not share our meal. A senior pupil read aloud from some pious book while we consumed bread and butter and tea already mixed with sugar and milk, poured from a huge tin tea-pot by a lay-sister. I was so deeply occupied in looking about me that I forgot to eat until

[1]Marie Madeleine Victoire de Bengy, born 1781, married Monsieur de Bonnault, son of Vicomte de Bonnault-Houet.

my neighbour nudged me and whispered, 'You'll faint if you don't eat and you won't be able to work.'

Work! I intended to work hard, for father was paying a high *pension* for me; besides I liked lessons and was ambitious, so that when the nine o'clock bell rang and classes were formed, I began to feel less frightened and strange. I was put into a class with children of my own age and found the work too easy; later, Mother Aloysius, the mistress of studies, moved me into a higher class. We worked until eleven and then had individual lessons until mid-day, when we stood to say the Angelus before filing into the refectory for dinner.

Everyone was hungry; the silence, which seemed crushing at other times, was endurable while we were occupied with hot roast meat and vegetables. A clapping of hands greeted the lay-sisters who carried in the girls' favourite pudding, known as the stocking, a light roly-poly. Under cover of the clapping the girl sitting next to me muttered, 'It's called the stocking because it looks like a fat leg. Next favourites are spotted dog, dog-in-a-blanket, jam-tart and . . .'

The nun's eye turned in our direction—and rolled on. I glanced at my neighbour who looked as good as a saint in the religious pictures which we kept in our prayer-books. No one would have thought that she had just sinned. I had not yet broken silence, but it was a hard rule to keep.

After dinner we had recreation, indoors or in the garden according to weather. At last we were allowed to talk and laugh and make a noise until the two o'clock bell recalled us to the classroom for two hours of plain and fancy needlework, and *bonne-tenue*, this included deportment and etiquette.

Tea at four was a fraud, for it consisted of a glass of cold water with bread and scrape.

By this time I felt worn out, but the day had not yet ended. An hour and a half of preparation for the next day's lessons fol-

lowed and then chapel—in our little veils and capes—to make
the Way of the Cross and say the Rosary. Lastly came supper—
and silence—in the refectory, more bread and butter with tea or
milk, followed by a rómp in the playroom where we were encouraged to hop, skip, jump and run so that we might get
warm before going to bed in our cold dormitories.

There were many moments of misery for me in my first six
months at school. The sudden change from freedom to capti-
vity; long hours indoors, stifling in their monotony after the
outdoor life in the sweet fresh air of Lough Gur and the variety
of happenings on the farm; painful silence at meals after our
lively talk and happy laughter; perpetual anxiety lest one should
break rules or, having broken them, that one might forget to
confess the sin. Some of the rules seemed to me meaningless or
arbitrary and after the reasonable rule of my parents and my
care-free existence, they weighed on me like fetters! No hardship, however, mattered in comparison with the lasting un-
happiness of being separated from mother. For this there was no
solace, yet it turned my mind to religion and I prayed as never
before, for her and for all whom I loved.

After poor little St. Patrick's Well, stark and bare in its poverty, the chapel in the convent seemed a beautiful, unearthly
place. On the high altar were flowers in fine vases and candles
which blazed in splendour before my astonished eyes. Flowers,
light, incense, soft-stealing music, sweet singing, combined to
carry me away; again I seemed to be in the Kingdom of Souls,
remote from the life of every day and I had to pinch my arm to
keep myself from drifting into some unknown world.

It was not easy to get to know my school-fellows, and at
first I used the silence of meal-time to examine faces. It was as

hard to know them apart as to tell one goose from the next in
our flock at home, or to distinguish between one rook and another as they followed Con and the plough on the furrows,
seeking grubs. We ourselves were not unlike a flock of young
rooks in our black uniform and our sleek heads. There was
nothing bright about us, but our eyes and cheeks, and nothing
warm but our friendliness. We should have been lively and
joyous, but for incessant repression and the haunting fear of
breaking rules, especially of breaking silence.

'God loves silence,' we were told, and 'He is nearest to God
who knows how to be silent.'

Later, I decided that our pain and grief—like King David's
when he kept silent even from good words—were balanced by
the advantage silence gave the nuns. If we had all talked at
once, they, poor things, would have been too moidhered by
the noise to do their work.

The nuns were an interest and a mystery, I longed to be
friends with them, to hear why they were nuns and how they
contrived to be good all the time; how they brought themselves to leave home and family and give up their freedom to be
mewed in a convent with a lot of other nuns. Oh, poor nuns!
never to be able to run out to see the sun rise, or a comet in the
night, or the full moon shining on a lake; never to go out alone
to hear skylarks singing, to see plover falling to their nests in
the soft plough-land! I pitied them for having to be obedient to
the clock, praying, watching, teaching by the clock, on and on,
all their lives; for being obliged to wear thick heavy clothes all
the year round; to have no hair, no necks, no looking-glasses,
no fires, no fun—ever.

I learnt before long that my pity was misplaced. Our
nuns, the Faithful Companions of Jesus, were happy; they had
the habit of happiness. They had sweet, smooth faces: no

temper or worry wrinkles were there, nor tear-lines under their eyes.

'Nuns are happy', I was told by a big girl, 'because they have no wills. They try to make us happy by breaking our wills.'

I was born with a small will; one which could easily be broken. If that should happen, people would say, 'She has a vocation! The dear child has a vocation!' Before I had time to resist I should find myself a nun.

This was a new fear for me. I prayed fervently that God would strengthen my will; that He would arrange for me to go home to Lough Gur; that He would protect me from a vocation and yet let me go to heaven when I die.

In the course of three years at school I learnt to know the nuns fairly well and to respect them for their great goodness. One or two of them I loved.

Reverend Mother, Madame Caldwell, was a Yorkshire woman, tall, slender and stately. We loved and feared her. If we all froze when at 4.30 every afternoon, she came into the class-room, walking down its great length and observing us as we worked in utter silence, so did we thaw when on feast days she came among us, setting us at our ease, chatting and making us laugh. At those times we talked freely to her, although I never summoned enough courage to ask her if she had met the Brontës or ever been to Haworth.

We were allowed to ask to see Reverend Mother at any time, and often a child, lonely, homesick, or in difficulties in her religious or school life, would go to Reverend Mother or to her assistant, beloved Mother Margaret Pigott, for what was called a croak. She would come away comforted and strengthened.

Mother Aloysius, who in later years became Reverend Mother, was my mistress of class. She was over six feet in height, and as straight as a poplar tree. She was so energetic that everyone else seemed to be idle beside her; when she looked at us, we straightened our spines and worked hard; she was a strict teacher, especially at music lessons, and we were afraid of her displeasure. But in chapel, where she was the organist, Mother Aloysius was different. She and her music seemed to me to be one, and often I thought that the notes were words which led one to be good. It was to this Mother that I went with my childish scruples and fears. If I had broken silence after making my confession, I hastened to ask her whether I could still receive the Holy Communion. She would re-assure me, respecting my tender conscience, understanding my dread of committing sin.

We were forbidden to have 'pet nuns', but I secretly loved and worshipped Mother Berchmans, so called after Blessed John Berchmans, a holy Jesuit. She was young and pretty and reserved. For her sake we took a pride in our sewing and in making elaborate samplers, trying to ply our needles with grace while we watched her thin white fingers moving in lovely curves as she embroidered vestments or hemmed fine linen for the altar. For her sake we strove to walk and move quietly. I recalled the orders of Lavery, our little dancing-master. I held up my head, let my hands hang naturally and felt myself a model of *bonne tenue*. We imitated Mother Berchman's low voice when, obeying the direction of the Foundress, she gave orders to imaginary butlers and footmen for our instruction, and taught us how to reply if addressed by royalty or the Lord Lieutenant. A giggle, even a twinkle of the eyes between two girls over these exercises, would cause Mother Berchmans pain; loyalty to the Law of the Foundress must be upheld at all costs. For us, the Foundress was the tyrant who made us wear scarlet *capelines* when we went for walks and ridiculous turned-up sailor hats in summer, nightgowns large enough for elephants, and in winter, felt boots lined with red flannel. It was she. who wouldn't let us have hot water to wash in and who sent us to bed at eight, who invented silence, and made sins out of the most innocent actions, such as looking out of the window. We prayed for her soul in chapel every day.

Mother Berchmans was still more pained when some parents who had heard of the butler-footman-and-royalty lessons, called on Reverend Mother to tell her of their disapproval! That sort of teaching, suitable for girls in one position of life, was, they remonstrated, unnecessary and ridiculous for those in another position. They were told that no discrimination could be made between county, country and town pupils. Children in the care of the Faithful Companions of Jesus were educated as gentlewoman by gentlewomen. It was the law of the Foundress again. She was the target behind which Reverend Mother sheltered while the parents grumbled. As it was of no use talking to a target, they went away.

I liked lessons in *les convenances*, because I loved Mother Berchmans, but I knew that living with mother was to learn more of the ways of a gentlewoman than I could learn in a lifetime of convent etiquette.

I have spoken of Mother Margaret Pigott, who taught mathematics and whom we dearly loved and trusted. She and her sister, Mother Julie, came from Dublin. Mother Theresa, who trained the choir, was English and beautiful; little Mère Philomène came from France and taught us her language. There was Mother Magdalen, the infirmarian, whom I scarcely knew, as I was never ill, and Mothers Josephine, Euphrasia and Victoire, teachers of classes, who took us for walks, and Mother Rosa, a much-loved Austrian nun. There was great competition on these occasions for the honour of taking the nun's arm, each one having two supporters, but it was the custom to avoid

coming face to face with nuns if they were in the garden in our
recreation hour. This arose, perhaps, from a wish to assert our
independence now and again. Sometimes we watched them
from the playroom window—although the Law of the Foundress forbade us to look out—and thought how like black
ladybirds they looked, moving slowly on invisible feet up and
down, to and fro, until a bell rang shrilly; at the first tinkle they
turned like one nun, to go in. Now, I thought, surely like ladybirds, they will let out unsuspected wings and fly to the door in
a black buzz.

It was against the rules for pupils to go to the community
sitting room, but we were told that the nuns enjoyed their recreation gathered round Reverend Mother, who liked them to
forget their work and their cares in the time that was their own:
The nuns did not speak to one another, but made their remarks
to Reverend Mother, who distributed them to the company.
'Mother Berchmans says . . . What is your opinion, Mother
Victoire . . .? I wonder if Mother Aloysius agrees with that . . .?
And Mère Philomène?' In this way every nun was drawn into
the conversation. Reverend Mother had a great sense of
humour and made the nuns laugh until they crowed.

Among the lay-sisters was one who seemed nearer to heaven
than anyone in the convent. Sister Josephine Ryan was small
with bright dark eyes and rosy cheeks. She went about her
work with joyous fervour and a radiant face, making frequent
ejaculations of love and thankfulness to God. She was our
*Little Flower*, not clever nor educated nor wise, she was only
good. The nuns were good, and so, the Dean said, were all
the children, but the goodness of the nuns was mixed with
other qualities: they were clever, learned or musical, linguists
or artists, or they had a background of France, England, or

of some grand family. Sister Josephine had love, and that was all.

Sometimes the monotony of life was broken by visitors for me. A nun would come into the class-room: 'Mary O'Brien is to go to the parlour.' Who would the visitor be? Uncle Richard, who came once and gave me a gold piece; or cousin Mac, whose visits I dreaded because of his way of ridiculing me; or Teresa and the fry from Limerick with a box of sweets; or Janie, our lovely one, in a brown holland frock and mushroom straw hat, bringing me a cake. Once in two months mother came to see me. When I came into the parlour she would be sitting on the sofa, several parcels heaped on the floor beside her for she brought all kinds of good things for her hungry child, besides an offering of cream cheeses or honey in the comb and flowers for Reverend Mother. I looked anxiously at her pale, tired face. Was she well? Would she go on living for a long while? She smiled at me. She was well. She would take great care of herself until the holidays when I should come home to look after her.

The time went all too fast. I wanted news of everyone, from father to Dinny-bawn, from Laurie, my dog, to the youngest kitten. I wanted to hear what was going on that very morning.

'Well, father was busy with Tom Hickey and Murnane, looking over the carts and harness and implements. Con (the ploughman) was twisting sugauns (ropes made of hay) while he kept an eye on the young lambs in the rickyard. Ellie had the first hatching of chickens in a coop by the back door with the speckledy hen. The grey goose was sitting. Old Biddy called, just as mother was starting, with a letter to be read to her from Me-John in America. He is married and has two children. He has a good place and is making money. He sent his mother a pound.

'Dinny-bawn is well; he is still devoted to father and flits about the farm after him. He is always happy and good and he is proud because at last he can spell c-a-t cat with the infants. The other day he slipped into the confirmation class, but of course he could not understand the teaching. Father O'Dwyer told mother about it. "You are too young to be confirmed, Dinny-bawn," he said. The little fellow smiled at him. "Not too young, Father," he answered, "I love God!" '

Does Father O'Dwyer know that Dinny-bawn calls fa . . .'

'He calls father *sir*, now, because Murnane told him he would have a beating if he called him—anything else, but when he says *sir*, he looks at father and laughs gently, as if they shared a secret joke. "Mary's child," he calls himself to Father O'Dwyer, very earnestly. The neighbours think he is a saint as well as a Fair Innocent. Dinny loves everyone, even old Con Curly, who gives him cakes and lets him feed his hens, but he loves no one so well as father. The only person he is afraid of is Billy-the-Clerk who turned him back on Christmas day when the little fellow was going up to the altar with the rest.'

## 15: EASTER HOLIDAYS

Father came for me himself, the darling man! One would have
thought from his good spirits that it was he who was starting
off for an Easter holiday; he seemed delighted to be taking me
home and no one could measure my joy when I hopped on to
the car with my little leather bag and waved good-bye to the
lay-sister at the door. It was six months since I had had a drive,
not since the same car brought me to school after the summer
holidays. How I loved the spring and the bounce of it, the
homely smell of horse and the whistle of the whip, which
never even flicked old Beauty's clipped sides or her rough un-
clipped legs. At the gate stood darling Dooley with a bunch of
primroses and willow catkins for her 'doty child', and there on
the edge of the orchard was old Malachy teaching his new
young dog to chase trespassers, with Timmy Deasy, the crow-
scarer, for quarry. I felt shy of everyone after my long absence,
even of old Paddy who was waiting about to take Beauty from
'under the car' and of the smiling maids who clustered at the
door clapping their hands.

My shyness vanished when mother appeared and my sisters
crowded round, Janie, Annie, and Bessie who waited for

silence to read solemnly from a primer of the Irish language *Caed míle fáilte roimh m'ingin dílis*, a hundred thousand welcomes to my dear sister.[1]

We chattered like a nest of young sparrows, even Annie, our little one, putting in her remarks and laughing when we laughed. How I talked, and what a nuisance I must have been to my parents with my constant allusions to school life! Reverend Mother says this, Mother Aloysius thinks that! Fortunately after a day or two the convent faded from my mind and I was absorbed in my home. I was often to be found gazing at the great hearth in the kitchen—I had not seen a fire for six months—or in the dairy begging for milk and bringing a slice of bread to be spread with a quarter-inch layer of butter. It was good after the too sweet tea, the bread and scrape that we had at school.

On Easter eve we got ready our pretty new dresses of brown lustre and our gypsy bonnets trimmed with brown ribbon to match, and laid them on the bed in the spare room beside our new gloves from Bourke of Limerick, our prayer-books, beads and handkerchiefs, so as to be ready when father would call us to go to Mass early on Easter Sunday morning.

The hedges on the way to St. Patrick's Well were full of primroses; lamb's tails dangled from the hazel boughs, sending tiny puffs of pollen into the sunshine; from the sky fell the song of larks. The clip-clop of Beauty's hoofs, the whistle of the whip, the ding-dong of the chapel bell were the only other sounds.

The chapel was packed to overflowing: old Malachy was

[1] Irish was hardly ever spoken in these days. Our parents sometimes talked to one another and mother said Irish is the most expressive language to pray in.

there, the Murnanes, the Heffernans, poor Biddy who was praying aloud for Me-John-in-Ameriky, Tom Hickey, Con the ploughman, Con Curley and many more, all of them come to make their Easter communion. At the door of the chapel Joannie stood and near her, half in and half out, was Dinny-bawn, longing to come in but afraid of Billy-the-Clerk. He was thinner and whiter than ever and with the sun shining on his fair hair he looked like a spirit rather than a boy. Joannie saw him and drew him in just as Billy-the-Clerk shut the door, leaving the sweet fresh air outside.

Perhaps it was because of the scent of jonquils on the altar, or because I had come fasting to Mass, or because the service lasted so long and the air was exhausted that I fell into a state between being asleep and being awake. I seemed suddenly to be on a narrow strand beside a lake. There were cliffs and low hills on the opposite shore and at the head of the lake rose a great snow-capped mountain. The place was quite unlike Ireland; someone said the mountain was called Hermon. I knew this was true because I had seen a picture of Hermon with the lake and strand in Uncle Richard's dining-room at Knocklong. There were people sitting comfortably on the sand and grass, listening to a man who was talking to them, telling them stories as he sat in a boat drawn up on the beach. I was sitting too, but suddenly I knew whom He was, and I stood up, just as we do at school when Reverend Mother comes into chapel or class-room. Only one other person was standing and that was Dinny-bawn. He was crying as he told his trouble—there on the shore of Galilee. Billy-the-Clerk, he said, had turned him back because he was *distant in his mind.*

'Don't trouble about your mind, Dinny-bawn,' said the gentle voice.

'And 'cause I hadn't the sense to confess me sins.'

'Never mind about that either,' the gentle voice went on. 'Father Ryan will not turn you back, Dinny-bawn.'

The picture faded away. I could only hear the lapping of small waves and feel the wind blowing coolly from snowy Hermon. When I opened my eyes mother was holding me and fanning me with a book while Joannie was holding a glass of water to my lips. They thought I had fainted.

'Have I made my communion?' I asked mother.
'Come now,' she said.
We knelt side by side, the last to communicate except for one who was before us. Father Ryan was bending over the fair head of Mary's child.

'A happy Easter,' we said as we came in at the door on our return from chapel. 'And to you,' replied the maids, echoed by the farmboys as they shuffled up from their forms and looked bashfully at the gay pile of eggshells on the table. On Easter Sunday the servants ate as many eggs as they wished—six per man being a moderate average, and the shells must be coloured for luck.

In the little room father was looking doubtfully at a crimson goose egg, which Bessie declared was laid by a fiery dragon.

Our eggs red, white and blue, were in a nest of moss, with a yellow one for Bessie who would have scorned to eat an Irish egg masquerading in British colours. Mother did not encourage Bessie in her patriotism, but the maids highly approved. "'Tis Miss Bessie that have the heart for the ould country', they said, and loved her for it.

After breakfast we children carried a large flat milk-pan into the sunshine on the kitchen floor, filled it with water and gently shaking it made the sun dance on the ceiling. We little knew that in keeping this Easter custom of Lough Gur, we were honouring the sun exactly as pagan sun-worshippers did a thousand years ago.

## 16: THE STORY OF MISS BAILY

On the lawn were two arbours, one of beech so thick that its green walls and roof sheltered those who sat there from wind and showers; the other of hawthorn and ivy with built-up seats finished with slabs of marble from a tumbledown house on Lough Gur. Mother came now and then with Dooley to rub and polish the marble for Miss Baily's sake. Miss Baily was an old friend of mother's long ago.

One lovely April afternoon towards the end of the holidays I was sitting by myself in the hawthorn arbour on the marble seat and on the duck-feather cushion which Dooley had made 'against the chill of Miss Baily's old mantelpiece'. I had brought *Pilgrim's Progress* with me, an old illustrated volume which had Miss Baily's name in it and written underneath, 'Given to Anne O'Brien by her friend A. B. 1845.' *Pilgrim's Progress* was a book I felt bound to read, for my sisters had read it with mother while I was at school; I could not let them know more English literature than I did. I was thinking about Miss Baily and wondering if she had reached the Celestial City or if she was detained in the Enchanted Grounds, and whether anyone remembered to pray for her soul, when mother came to sit with me and read. I asked her about these things and she told me that she remembered Miss Baily every night at prayers when we pray for the souls of the departed. 'All the same,' mother said, 'your having this idea may mean that Miss Baily is needing prayers; it may be a message allowed to come to you.'

So we prayed for the soul of Miss Baily in the arbour, and afterwards I asked mother to 'remember' about her.

'These marble seats', mother began, 'were part of a fine mantelpiece in her drawing-room. When I came to Drumlaigh as a bride, she was my greatest friend, even though she was very old. She was born, I think, in 1769, the same year as the great Napoleon, and the Duke of Wellington whom she called Arthur Wesley. They had, I believe, played together as children in the county Meath. If I shut my eyes,' mother went on, 'I seem to go back into the past. Everything is real. I go into the drawing-room; there is a carpet, rather worn in places, with a large flowery pattern; the faded curtains are of embroidery on velvet. The high-backed chairs have seats and backs of silk cross-stitch. A fire burns cheerfully and there is a sweet scent of lavender and dried roses. A harpsichord, an inlaid bureau, a corner cupboard for china, and a bookcase full of old books, make the room very interesting and delightful. There is a small table in a window with flowers in a great glass loving-cup which had strange words engraved on the rim: *The glorious, pious and immortal memory.* There is another curious glass in the drawing-room which Miss Baily calls the stirrup-cup. It is large enough to hold a bottleful of wine. In a corner stands a harp on which Miss Baily plays Irish melodies, and beautiful accompaniments when she sings in her thin old voice. Her hands on the strings are white and transparent with outstanding violet veins; she wears many thin old-fashioned rings which now and then slip down her fingers and jar upon the strings. Sometimes she reads aloud, but more often we talk as we sew or knit innumerable garments for the poor.'

'Dooley told me there was another Miss Baily, who was burnt to death in the pantry!'

'Yes, the poor thing! That was Miss Susan. Sometimes she came to sew with us and then the two old ladies told me stories of the past. They seemed to know the genealogy and family history of half Ireland, and they liked to tell the legends and stories of Lough Gur. They firmly believed that 'Desmond the Earl' appeared now and then.

'You don't believe in ghosts, mother?'

Mother hesitated. 'I don't believe they are the spirits of the dead,' she said, 'I don't know what they are, but they can't be entirely imaginary.'

'I do so want to hear about Miss Baily's ghosts.'

'She had three stories; the first was not about Lord Desmond, but a ghost of later days, perhaps an old Baily.

'The motherless children, Anne, Susan, Kitty and one or two more lived with their father and a governess in the house which you only know as a ruin. It had a number of small low rooms and was built up against the old square tower of the Desmonds' castle. A narrow archway led into a great gloomy room in the old castle, lit by small windows in the thickness of the wall. It was called the Earl's Hall. In my time it was used for storing wood and turf, but in those days it had some benches and a heavy oak table at which the governess liked to sit to read or work. One day when she was there alone, a gentleman with a grave face and wearing old-fashioned clothes, suddenly stood beside her and by signs called her attention to a rod which he had in his hand and which he measured against a mark on the table so that she should know its length. Then he measured with this rod a certain distance from two of the walls. At this spot a hole of a certain depth must be dug; at the bottom, treasure would be found. Then he disappeared and the governess hastened to tell Mr. Baily, who only laughed at her; but after the ghost had appeared a second and third time, repeating the measurements with an angry air, he consented to have a hole dug in the floor. The governess and children were present. At the given depth, a flagstone was uncovered, beneath it was a cavity and on the earth floor were deep marks where a heavy vessel had rested. The crock itself had vanished and what treasure there may once have been.

'Miss Baily and Miss Susan saw no ghosts, but they heard the summons of Ainë the banshee, before the death of their sister Kitty. This was no blood-curdling scream or trampling of horses' hoofs, but sweet sad music as of a choir singing with stringed instruments. It came from the air, east, west, south, from the old castle, from far off, now near-by. Both sisters heard it at the same time and at first ran distractedly about to find the singing band. When they realised that it was *ceolsidhe* they heard they went back to Kitty's bedside and watched her as she died. Then the fairy music ceased.

'There was a very old woman called Moll Ryall, who told Miss Baily, then a child, stories of bygone days. Old Moll remembered her father and the neighbours round Lough Gur cheering when the news came of the death of King William of Orange. She had worked all her life for the Baily family, In the grandparent Baily's days, a number of poor, young girls worked in the kitchen, laundry or poultry-yard, earning nothing but their keep, with a present, perhaps, of a petticoat or a shawl now and again. One early morning in summer young Moll was washing clothes on the edge of the lake, standing in the water with her petticoat pinned round her hips and smacking the linen on a flat rock with a beetle (a flat beetle-shaped bat) when a gentleman in a purple cap and a fine silk cloak came down the path from the old castle. Very grand and out of the common, Moll thought him, and when he took a ring from his finger, and laid it on the ground, inviting her by signs to take it, she might have spoken to him had she not noticed as she let her petticoat down, that the water rippling over her feet was red as blood. 'Och! my God and Jesus Christ,' she cried crossing herself, and at the holy name and sign the gentleman vanished. But for the red water Moll would have spoken, she would have picked up the ring and so have been bewitched. The gentleman, Miss Baily said, was certainly Lord Desmond.'

'Why did he want her to speak?'

'The object of ghosts is to get a mortal to speak to them. The mortal, if he speaks, is bewitched and this shortens the ghost's time of punishment.'

'Why is Lord Desmond being punished?'

'Because he was a magician. He made wicked spells and frightened people.'

'So now he has to be punished till the silver shoes of his horse are worn away?'

'That is the legend. There was a blacksmith named O'Neill in Miss Baily's time, who owned the forge at the top of the hill on the road to Cahirconlish. He was alone in the forge one moonlight night when a strangely dressed fine gentleman rode up on a white horse followed by a number of horsemen. He signed to O'Neill to look at his horse's hoof, so the blacksmith lifted a fore-leg and saw that the shoe was of silver and worn very thin. O'Neill was frightened; he dropped the hoof and made the sign of the cross. 'God be between me and harm,' he prayed. At that the rider lashed furiously at him with his whip, which seemed to cut with an icy blast but left no mark. The next moment he and his followers galloped away, the horses leaped into the air and the whole company disappeared in a flash of light like a shooting star.'

'I am glad the silver shoes were nearly worn out,' I said, 'perhaps by now Lord Desmond's punishment is over and there's no fear of our meeting him?'

'You won't meet him, have no fear,' mother answered. 'I don't believe he has haunted the lake at all. . . . Remember I'm telling you Miss Baily's stories.'

I had often heard of Miss Baily from Dooley, whose aunt had been the old lady's maid; her stories were of the vanished grandeur of 'the family' and anecdotes such as old servants collect and remember. 'Miss Baily was', she said, 'queer and cross, full of dreams and for ever listening. . . .'

'What was she listening for?' I asked her.

"'Tis the way people have and them old and sitting alone. She'd think she heard Miss Susan's voice— and she for years in her grave, God save her—or, "Was that Miss Kitty laughing?" she'd ask me a'nt when she'd be bringing her tea. "Kitty is so merry these days. . . ."'

Mother had noticed the way Miss Baily listened. 'She was very lonely after Miss Susan died and when she remembered that she was the last of the Bailys who had lived on Lough Gur for a hundred years, perhaps two hundred—she could not remember—and at her death the family would die out. She counted on her fingers the Bailys she had known, but her memory began to fail and her mind to grow perplexed. All the day long she sat beside the fire and often she seemed to be listening, perhaps for the fairy music, for she would turn her head and look from the harpsichord to the harp as if to say, "Did you speak? What was it you said?" When the wind roared over Lough Gur and cried in the chimney, she grew uneasy and spoke of hearing flutes and drums.

'Miss Baily lived latterly in two rooms, which Murnane and Dick Dooley—young men in those days—kept watertight and sound. The house, which was not in good condition when I first went there, was going from bad to worse; its many little rooms were damp, empty and forlorn.

'After Miss Baily's death her heir took away all her belongings that were of value and sold the rest. No one came near the house which was left to moulder and rust. The roof leaked badly; window frames, already rotten, were blown in; ceilings fell down; sparrows roosted on the gilt curtain poles and nested in the deep cornices; bats hung in festoons hooked to laths from which the plaster had fallen. On floors and shelves, in cupboards and cellars, fungus grew and spread until it was like a dreadful nightmare to go into the house.

'Then tinkers came and camped in the tangled garden; they stabled their donkeys and little carts in what had been Miss Baily's drawing-room. They called it the coach house! It was sad, child dear!'

'Yes, mother, it was very sad for you, but if it wasn't for that, did it matter?'

'What do you mean?'

'I mean it didn't matter to Miss Baily for she was dead, and it didn't matter to the owner for he can't have cared for the place, and it didn't matter to the house because houses can't feel or know....'

'I wonder!' mother said.

'And it's a nice home for bats,' I said to cheer her up.

Then we settled down to read; it was lovely having mother to myself and being able to go on and on without questions from younger people like Janie and Bessie. Afterwards mother told me about Bunyan, the child of tinkers, who was bad before he was good. If he hadn't been shut up in Bedford Gaol, where time hung on his hands, we should never have had this lovely and exciting story. Good came out of his being kept away from home. I hoped that good would come out of my being away at school, but I doubted it. I was on the point of falling like Christian into the Slough of Despond, in which I should have had to wallow alone as mother had gone in, when I heard father calling me.

## 17: DIGGING WITH ANTIQUARIES

'Oh, there you are Sis? Come in. Here's a visitor for you.'

The visitor was Peter, the young antiquary who knew about the ways of the *Little People*. Behind him, talking to mother was the fat Sassenach, the chief antiquary. They both stood up to shake hands and I felt very glad that I had on my new brown lustre frock.

'We have come', Peter said in his grown-up voice, 'to ask Mr. O'Brien to get leave for us to dig in the bogs round about Lough Gur.'

'What do you think you will find in the bogs?' I asked him.

'Butter,' he answered, and then I knew he was teasing, for who ever heard of butter from a bog?

'Butter and bones, perhaps a four-horned sheep or a long-nosed pig, and—fireplaces, perhaps bodies, perhaps treasure.'

'A crock of gold?' I suggested.

'That's it. Will you come and direct us?'

'How could I?'

' "Dig there," you will say to Mr. Tilecote, and at once he will unearth a few diadems and torques. "Dig here," you will order me and instantly I shall exhume the leather body of your remote ancestor, nicely tanned by peat water.'

'All my ancestors were buried in graves,' I told him, 'they are all respectable skeletons in holy ground.'

'That's all you know about it,' Peter mocked. 'Please, Mr. O'Brien, may your daughter go with us to-morrow to the bog as a luck bringer?'

Father looked at mother and she looked—rather coldly—at Peter. 'Yes, if her sisters go too.'

'They're too young,' I said hurriedly—I didn't want our lovely one and our clever one to be friends with Peter—'and they know nothing about—about—'

'Archaeology,' Peter suggested. 'Whereas Miss O'Brien knows quite a lot and will be of the utmost help to us.'

'I am afraid Sissy can't go alone,' mother said decidedly.

'Oh mother! I would so love to see butter oozing out of the bog!'

'And so should I! Any dairy-farmer would!' father said, laughing. 'Sissy and I will go together. To-morrow is a holy day so we are free.'

'A good day for getting diggers,' the Sassenach said. 'There will be plenty of idle fellows glad of a light job.' Being a Protestant Sassenach that is what he would think and say, with never a backward glance at St. Mark on his holy day.

It was a good day, though mother would not let me wear my new brown lustre frock. 'Not suitable,' she said, and that was the first time I realised that one must dress to suit the occasion and not to suit one's face. So I wore a homespun jacket and skirt which mother had had made as a surprise for me; it was sparrow-colour, mixed brown and grey, in a weave invented by Mary-Ellen's aunt, the one who lived with the Lord Lieutenant. I put on my thick lace-up boots, and wore no hat because mother wanted me to get sunburnt. My cheeks were pale from the shut-in-ness of convent life.

By the time we arrived at the bog-side a hole had already been dug; Peter had almost disappeared in it and was fumbling about the sides for fragments of black oak. Further on three men were making other holes and as soon as father joined us after leaving Beauty at a farm he began to dig, throwing up the turf with long, strong strokes which made the antiquaries stare. They even tried to imitate him, but the Sassenach very soon had a blister and had to sit down on a dyke to pant.

'I've got a good hard lump on my hand,' Peter boasted, adding 'from spade work', and I expect he said that lest I should think he had killed a robin.[1]

'Everyone is working but me,' I said disconsolately, 'what can I do?'

'You can tell us where to dig,' Peter said, hoisting himself out of the hole, and I was glad he did that because it was not at all nice to talk to a face which seemed to be growing out of the ground like a mushroom.

'Do you remember the day we met and talked about—the *Little People?*' Peter continued.

'I do remember, but I don't believe in fairies now.'

'Oh, Miss O'Brien! you disappoint me! However, that day, when I was telling you about the poor mortal inside the hill blinking in the strange green light while *they* buzzed all round him—you *were* that man!'

'Oh Peter! I was not.'

'You were. You felt them tickling! You tasted the swallow-meat and it nearly made you sick!'

'You are quite wrong! I never thought I was he or he was me. . . .'

---

[1]The robin is sacred. If he is killed a lump grows on the palm of the murderer's hand which prevents him from working.

'Or me was him and them was us.'

'You worry my brains . . . but I did think he might be father or brother.'

'It's all the same. You were as white as you are now and your eyes were fixed and squinting.'

'They were not!'

'. . . which shows that you were in a trance. I wish you would make your mind a blank—think of nothing at all and just walk about until you come on things lost by long-ago people. You will say, "Peter, I've found it! Dig here." I'll take care you do not fall into a hole.'

'I shall go home,' I cried, 'I will not make my mind a blank . . . no one shall make me squint.' I was about to walk away when Peter said I needn't do it if I would rather not, but it was a pity. He looked so disappointed that I stayed with him on the dyke and managed to overlook what he had said.

'Why must you dig?' I asked him, 'isn't it as useless as a child's digging on a strand?'

'It's my holiday task. In term time I'm at Trinity College learning to be a schoolmaster or a parson.'

'Is that a priest?'

'A clergyman—Church of Ireland—Protestant.'

'Oh dear, Peter! You mustn't be that! Be *anything* else. Don't you know that all Protestants are damned and Protestant clergymen are double-damned? A girl at the convent told me, a big girl.'

'Oh thank you! Thank you for warning me! I'd simply hate to be double-damned! What would you advise me to be when I'm grown-up? I'm only twenty-two. Shall I be a farmer?'

'You might—if you aren't afraid of bulls.'

'I'm scared of them. Cows too. Think again.'

'I suppose you couldn't be a poet? I don't mean the kind who write the sort of poetry that nuns like and teach us at school . . .'

'Such as?'

> *'Oh call my brother back to me,*
> *I cannot play alone.*

or

> *The dew was falling fast, the stars began to blink,*
> *I heard a voice; it said: drink, pretty creature drink!'*

Peter laughed. 'A good many people hear that voice! But go on, please; I could listen to you all day! What kind of poetry must I write to please you?'

'I'm afraid you couldn't write like Milton—no one ever will again—but there are others you could take after. Mother makes us learn a lot of poetry in case—when we are old—we aren't able to use our eyes for reading. One day at school we each had to say our favourite poem. You'd be surprised how many girls chose Longfellow.'

'I know, *Excelsior*.'

'Not that, because of

> *O stay, the maiden said, and rest*
> *Thy weary head upon my breast.*

The nuns don't like that maiden, but I think she was a kind person. The girls mostly said,

> *Tell me not in mournful numbers*
> *Life is but an empty dream.*

'One of them wanted to say *Hiawatha* all through, but she wasn't allowed.'

'Wasn't that a shame when the poor girl had taken the trouble to learn it? What did you recite? Can you say it now?'

'I said some Milton:

> *Sweet is the breath of morn, her rising sweet*
> *With charm of earliest birds; pleasant the sun*
> *When first on this delightful land he spreads*
> *His orient beams on herb, tree, fruit and flowers,*

> *Glist'ning with dew; fragrant the fertile earth*
> *After soft showers; and sweet the coming on*
> *Of grateful evening mild; then silent night*
> *With this her solemn bird and this fair moon,*
> *And these the gems of heaven, her starry train.*
> *But neither breath of morn when she ascends*
> *With charm of earliest birds, nor rising sun*
> *On this delightful land, nor herb, fruit, flower,*
> *Glist'ning with dew, nor fragrance after showers.*
> *Nor grateful evening mild, nor silent night*
> *With this her solemn bird, nor walk by moon*
> *Or glittering starlight, without thee is sweet.'*

'No one could find fault with that?'

'They did! One of the nuns said it was idolatrous, worship of nature, another said it was worse than that, it was a love-poem. Love is wicked.'

'Is it?' Peter exclaimed, arching his eyebrows with surprise. 'I never heard that love is wicked! I am ignorant! I shall never make a schoolmaster, but I can say the *Ancient Mariner*.'

'So can I! Let's say it turn and turn about.'

We repeated it, prompting one another until we came to the *painted ship*, when we were startled by a loud cry.

'Hullo,' Peter cried, jumping up from the dyke where we had been sitting, 'come on, run! They've found something!'

Mr. Tilecote was yelling like a hound that has found a fox. Father ran like a hare.

'What is it? What is it?' we all asked.

Whatever it was was being gently cleared, the turf—which Mr. Tilecote would call peat—was being crumbled away in handfuls until there appeared a big wooden disc with a hole in the centre through which was the head of a thick piece of oak.

'It's a wheel, father told the excited antiquaries. 'Go easy now,' he said to the labourers, 'and you'll get the cart and maybe the horse that drew it . . .'

'. . . who can say how long ago?' said the Sassenach reverently.

We were all quivering with excitement, like terriers waiting for rats at threshing time, when at last the little cart was freed from the bog that had held it. It lay on its side, perfectly pre-served to the last oak bolt and pin, unbroken, but for the ends of the shafts which were cut in one piece with the body of the cart. Very carefully they righted it to stand upon its wheels.

'There was a cause'ay across the bog just here,' said Paddy Regan, a little old man who seemed to be the keenest of the labourers. 'We've been diggin' and burnin' the ould piles. for years.'

'Can't you see it all.' Peter cried, grabbing my arm and shak-ing me gently. 'The cart was going along the causeway when a mist rose up from the bog and hid the track. One wheel went over the side; the horse struggled to hold the cart and broke the shafts and traces; horse and man were safe, but over went the cart, sinking down and down in what was then a swamp, and everything that the man was taking to market was lost.'

'Shut up, Peter,' growled the chief antiquary who wanted to talk himself and quite right too as he was the oldest.

'That stuff which we heard about, found by peat-cutters near here ,where is it?'

'Father Ryan have it, sir,' the second labourer answered. 'He's a great one for the ould times! He have the bones of a big deer[1] that was destroyed in Noah's flood. and the two halves of a quern and other quare ould contraptions. His reverence would be proud to show your honour the little barr'l we brought him from the bog we're standin' in.'

'If 'tis a barr'l your honour is wishful to see,' said the third

[1] Said to be moose.

labourer, 'sure I threw one out of yonder hole the very spit of the first one, at the minute your honour shouted me to see the little ould cart. 'Tis lying there now.'

'Where! Which hole? Show me! Quick man!' Mr. Tilecote shouted, seizing the man with such violence that he almost hit back. Locked together they ran to the farthest hole, while from the road there came a long-legged priest, leaping over the heather, determined to arrive first at the goal. Peter outran him and stood across the hole looking as proud as the Colossus of Rhodes in mother's *Ancient History.*

'Now then, sir,' said the priest, who was our own Father Ryan, 'who are you, and by whose leave are you digging in this place?' He was very red and blustery until his eyes fell on father and me.

'Oh, 'tis you, Mr. O'Brien, and Sissy!' he said mildly, for having been Uncle Richard's curate at Knocklong he was always respectful to father.

The antiquaries were introduced and when Father Ryan heard the name Tilecote, he bowed as low as he does in chapel, because though Mr. Tilecote was a Sassenach, it seemed he was a well-known archaeologist and the author of a book which Father Ryan actually had in his bookshelf.

'Will I give ye the little barr'l, Father?' whispered Paddy Regan who was jealous of a stranger handling our old Irish curiosities.

'Give it to the gentleman, and be proud to have that honour,' Father Ryan commanded.

'Mr. O'Brien must open it,' interrupted Peter, who had no fear of his chief. 'It's sure to be the butter he wanted.'

'Butter made by a pagan woman, perhaps *more* than a thousand years ago,' Mr. Tilecote added, more reverently than ever.

Father and Father Ryan looked at one another, but said nothing. They knew that even in their grandfather's time, butter, flavoured with wild garlic and unsalted,[1] used to be put in a bog-hole and left to ripen.

About midday the labourers went away to their cabins to have their dinners, delighted to take with them the antiquaries' huge beef sandwiches. Father had invited Mr. Tilecote and Peter and Father Ryan to lunch with us. He had left the hamper in the shelter of a turf-rick where we could eat in the warm April sunshine. On the way he asked Mr. Tilecote if the cart we had dug out could really be a thousand years old, as he remembered carts made in the same way, only larger, when he was a boy. 'It might not be so old,' Mr. Tilecote said, 'as it was only two or three feet below the surface. Some bogs are older than others.' Both he and Father Ryan had seen a bog which had been made by the destruction of ancient forests, and under tree trunks, fifty feet below the present surface, furrows could be seen in the ground where it had been ploughed, which showed that the bog was formed after the invention of the plough.

I could not see how the ground had been ploughed in a forest where the trees stood thick together, all tangled with undergrowth, unless the furrows were there before the forest grew, but I was afraid to ask, for Father Ryan was saying how strange to think that the furrows should remain when the ploughman had long since turned into dust, and '*what mysteries do lie beyond (that) dust*', which was a line he learnt from mother one day when he happened to come in and found her teaching us, line by line, as we sewed,

> '*I see them walking in an air of glory,*
> *Whose light doth trample on my days.*'

Peter and I unpacked the bounteous luncheon which mother had prepared of home-made bread, butter, cream cheese,

[1] Salt cost too much for the poor to buy it except in small quantities.

home-cured ham, hard-boiled turkey's eggs, and young water-cress from the eel-stream. When I was waiting on the older people, Peter prepared a tiny three cornered sandwich, tightly pinched together, which he gave me in a dandelion leaf, whispering, '*Swallow-meat.*' The mere thought nearly spoilt the picnic for me, but I was determined that he should not think he had the power to make me sick, so I gulped it down looking defiantly at him.

'Good, obedient child,' he said to torment me, 'it wasn't swallow-meat after all, I made it of cream cheese and primroses.'

I took no further notice of Peter because father was remembering about old times and telling Mr. Tilecote about country carts.

'We had one when I was a boy,' he said, 'with solid wheels cut from the trunk of a large tree and shod with iron. It had a strong floor and upright bars all round. The last time it was used was to carry my grandfather to the grave. My father nailed boards across, above and beyond the bars, to make a platform; a feather-bed was laid on the boards and on this the coffin rested, well roped on. I and my little brother, being too young to ride, sat alongside, holding to the ropes as the cart lurched along. The old country roads went up hill and down dale in those days; in places the rock rose half a foot above the surface, there were holes a foot deep and ruts deep enough to hide a man. Good roads were made later,[1] when people left off riding on horseback and took to coaches and cars. To-day, from the new roads which wind about among the hills, you look up and see the old road cutting across the top, and where you now cross a river by a bridge, you may see traces of an ancient ford. There are still old people who would rather take the old rough

[1]Roads with foundations were made by Telford and Macadam early in the nineteenth century.

tracks their fathers used than go by the dusty or muddy high-roads which have neither memories nor romance for them. Here and there the new roads follow the course of the old ones, but not for long. When I was a boy there was one of the old roads near enough to my home for us to hear at night the shouts of drunken men, wastrels travelling from town to town. We children used to tremble as we lay in bed, knowing that these dreaded rascals were so near.

' "Oh mammy, mammy," we cried to our mother, "put out the light, quick!" She would pinch the wicks of the home-made rushlights to put out the flame and rake wood-ashes over the fire

' "Hush, hush now, my darlings! Not a glimmer is there in this house! The doors are locked and bolted, the shutters are barred! Let you sleep in peace."

'We seldom slept until we knew she was in bed with the two youngest of us nestled against her.'

'Was there any danger?' Mr. Tilecote asked.

'There was danger when there was no man in the house. We had one or two frights when a man banged and kicked on the door in his efforts to get in. Then mammy crept to our beds in the darkness whispering that the locks and bolts would hold; we need have no fear, for *God is nearer than the door*.[1] We used to go to bed when darkness fell, for so long as there was a light, people might demand shelter for the night and food. The law of hospitality was hard to evade. As a rule, however, beggars went by daylight to farms for food, and at nightfall to a cottage for a lodging.'

'The poor never refuse shelter to a wanderer—that is one of their best points,' Father Ryan said. ' "Come in and kindly welcome," they say, even when their home is a one-room cabin and the floor already thick with sleeping children.'

[1] An old Irish saying for times of anxiety.

'That is so,' father said, 'I have known of poor people, five and six in the family, sleeping in a one-roomed cabin so small that none could lie flat on his back for want of room, but each one must lie on his side. And in another hovel where the floor space was already occupied, a beggar asking for shelter was given "the length and breadth of herself" under the table. There was no other place.'

'Those were the bad days,' Father Ryan said, 'I have heard stories from my parents and grandparents that would not bear telling. Mr. O'Brien saw for himself how the poor starved.'

'I don't care to speak of miseries,' father went on, 'but I can never forget the efforts my mother made to keep life in the families who lived on the farm and worked for her, and yet not rob her children of food. Farmers like ourselves had cows and hens and a little corn and oats, so there was no fear of starvation for us, but we should have been ashamed to eat more than was strictly necessary when children all round us were famished. Often a labourer was so weak that the spade would fall from his hand and when he stooped to pick it up, as likely as not he would fall beside it. The worst time of the year was when the potatoes were finished and the new crop not ready for digging. Those were called the meal-months, when there was nothing to eat but stir-about made from siftings of flour more than half bran. And then, at times, after the months of dreadful hunger, disease came in the potatoes, or the crop failed entirely. . . .'

Father's voice grew husky and went out for a time.

'There was a potato famine in the winter of 1821-2, when I was a little fellow. The roads then were cumbered with people making for Bruff and Limerick to beg for charity, old folk, desperate men without work, mothers with long trails of half-naked children. . . .

'I daresay you have seen a ewe lying dead in a field and her day-old lamb butting and tugging at her? So I have seen little children patting and pulling at their mother to wake her, and she lying by the road-side, dead.'

The Sassenach had been fidgetting while father spoke about those terrible days of which I had never been told; Father Ryan and Peter had turned their faces away; I was crying.

'Surely they had parish relief?' Mr. Tilecote asked.

Father Ryan answered. 'There was no poor law for Ireland.'

'Yet Mr. O'Brien tells us there were drunken men! How could they afford to drink?'

'Not in famine years. I was quite a little fellow when the first of the I.C. (Irish Constabulary) came to Limerick. They made the country safer. We were safer too, because my mother decided to take in a Poor Scholar. He had a room in the yard, and a gun to frighten vagabonds, but he never had to use it. Later, she had two permanent farmboys as well. But to go back to drunkenness. I have often asked myself how, even now, a man earning ninepence or a shilling a day who has a wife and a family to keep and rent to pay, can afford to get drunk? I can only think that for an under-nourished man a mouthful of whisky is too much.'

'I'm thinking', Father Ryan said, 'that Regan and his friends have struck something in the hole that we got the cart from. Look at their three heads put together. We had better be moving.'

He strode off on his long legs and Mr. Tilecote, sober-faced, prepared to follow. But first he took father by the arm and thanked him. 'You have lived through great tribulation and are not embittered. You have my honour and respect, sir.'

They went off together, leaving Peter and me to follow.

The men had found a brogue, a very little one to fit a child. Further digging revealed some bits of leather which might have been harness and that was all. When we left them they were still

digging here and there. Father Ryan came with us; he had to
·get ready for the antiquaries' inspection of his collection.

The next day Mr. Tilecote and Peter went away to dig in
county Meath and we heard no more of them until the following Christmas, when Peter sent me a box of chocolate and
*Grimm's Fairy Tales* (which I thought rather young for me) and
Father Ryan had a letter from Mr. Tilecote enclosing £50 for
the poor of Lough Gur. Even Bessie had to admit that it had
pleased God to make one Protestant Sassenach with a good
heart. We prayed for him for several weeks. I prayed secretly
for Peter for a long time.

## 18: THE CONVENT SCHOOL AGAIN

The holidays came to an end, the agony of leaving mother had to be endured once more, yet when I was again at the convent I was not unhappy. Lessons were interesting and I worked hard, earning the approval of Reverend Mother and my teachers. Mother Aloysius was pleased with me.

Another interest at the beginning of term was hearing from my friends of their doings during the holiday, their parties, picnics, visits, journeys—perhaps as far as to Dublin or even to England. The happenings of my holidays seemed dull to them! 'You read a great deal! Why on earth did you read *in the holidays?* You were digging in a bog with some antiquaries? Oh, how stupid! But then you live on a farm and nothing ever happens on a farm!' They pitied me. I let them pity me and said nothing. They would never understand how rich and full our days were on Lough Gur.

One of my friends, Ellie Byrne, confided in me. 'Listen, Sissy, dreadful things happen when you live in a town and go to parties, half grown-up parties! Things that don't seem dreadful at the time are awful when you are going to confession. Then they swell like air-balloons that are being blown up. I went to confession before I came back to school. I thought I'd better. Father Bourke was tired, he must have been, because he was impatient and that frightened me. I could only stammer, 'Father. . . Father . . . oh, Father . . . I can't . . .' He said very crossly, "Leave off your Father—Father and tell me your sins." So then I began to cry and at last I managed to confess, "I . . . I kissed . . . a Protestant gentleman," and even that, Sissy, wasn't true, because it was the Protestant gentleman who kissed me. I thought Father Bourke would have been shocked, but he gave me absolution and said he would rather hear the confessions of a whole regiment of soldiers than of a person like me.' I thought Ellie was wise to make such an uncomfortable confession before she came back to school; our confessor might have taken a more serious view.

The nuns discouraged friendship between girls so that I did not get to know anyone very well except the two who sat beside me at meals. They were in the same dormitory and we walked together when we made a *promenade* on the high-road. Sometimes we walked in a class of twelve or fourteen girls with two nuns to shepherd us; occasionally the whole ninety of us set off with several guardian nuns. Walks were popular, partly because we were admired by passers-by for our discipline and good looks, partly because we hoped to meet people we knew. Occasionally Dean Cregan came by on his car, taking off his hat to us several times while a ripple of bows ran along our ranks. We never forgot *bonne tenue* and the proper bend of the neck for a dean. This was deeper than for a plain priest, but not so marked as for a bishop, which has to be a bend of back as well on account of kissing his ring. This, however, was only called for at the distribution of prizes at the end of the summer term, a great day, when Reverend Mother and the community entertained priests and parents, old pupils and friends to *déjeuner* in the refectory.

My favourite walk was the road to Lough Gur. Supposing, I thought one day as we neared the first milestone, *supposing* the nuns were to be absent-minded and let us walk on until we came to the lake, to our gate, to the orchard, to mother's trees! Oh, the racket of old Turkey giving warning of intruders, the sympathetic yelling of young pigs, the barking of Tear'em and Ate'em at the sound of our young feet on the road, the running of farmboys to see the 'quare company', the astonishment of the maids and my sisters—father, quietly amused, and mother...

'What are you giggling about, Mary O'Brien?' my companion asked.

'Only my thoughts,' I had to answer, for no one, but myself could see the nuns as they come out of their reverie, their fluster and bewilderment mixed with politeness and the desire to be as calm as mother, who is smiling as she watches her ninety unexpected visitors drinking milk and cream from cups, mugs, glasses, piggins, jampots and even from Mammy Jug's jugs.

'I wish you would leave off giggling, Mary O'Brien.'

How could I help laughing at the picture in my mind, and at father when he whispered to me, 'They look jaded, the poor nuns! They would be better for a glass of J.J.!' Who could help laughing at such an unreligious idea?

Alas! At the milestone the vigilant nun in front cried, 'Stop! Turn back!'

We turned on our feet and were facing Bruff. The last girls were then first and the first last. 'Avancez!' cried Mère Philomène.

Back we went into capitivity.

Walks, work, recreation, meals, sleep—so the days passed, leaving a memory of monotony broken by one or two small excitements, and one shock which stunned the whole school. This was the expulsion of one of the girls.

It began with a dreadful whispering. 'One of us has done something wicked.'

'Who is it?'

'What has she done?'

No one knew. Over us all fell a cloud of shame and disgrace and fear. We looked suspiciously at one another and then frenziedly into our own hearts. Is it I? Have I *unawares* done something wrong? It was a time of trembling, and rocking on shaking legs, of jumping violently when spoken to. *One of us knew.*

'Lucy O'Connell is to go to Reverend Mother.' The nun who brought the summons burst into tears. Lucy O'Connell walked slowly across the room, her head in the air and a smile on her lips. The sobbing nun went out behind her, shutting the door. No one spoke; we were all stupified. *Lucy O'Connell!* one of the oldest girls seventeen, pretty and lively. What had she done? She was an orphan, without brother or sister and lived with an uncle and aunt. Poor Lucy! Some of us were crying, and when Mère Philomène came in and said, 'Bedtime, *mes enfants*,' we were glad to creep upstairs, each with her burden of trouble.

Lucy's bed in St. Joseph's (dormitory) was empty. No one saw her until the next day when we were assembled in the classroom. The blinds all over the house were pulled down, the chapel bell tolled as for a death. No one spoke or moved. Then Lucy came through the long room on her uncle's arm and out into the hall, into the road where a covered car was waiting. The front door clanged. The tolling of the bell ceased.

Mother Aloysius came into the darkened room.

'Let the fate of Lucy O'Connell be a warning to you all,' she said, and went away.

Sister Josephine came in and pulled up the blinds. We felt happier for seeing her.

From that day I lived in constant fear of committing the same offence without knowing it. No one was ever told what Lucy had done and we dared not ask.[1] Reverend Mother and the nuns knew nothing of the suffering endured by nervous children like myself after Lucy was expelled.

Dean Cregan, who came once a week to give us religious instruction, unconsciously reassured the anxious ones among us. 'I can say of all of you here now and looking back over the past, that not one of you has committed a mortal sin.' Not even Lucy, I thought with a sudden uplifting of my heart.

The Dean taught us how to live, how to overcome difficulties and to profit by the happiness which he trusted life would bring us. His teaching was more inspiring than that of the nuns which led the diffident among us to mistrust ourselves and to fear the world outside the convent walls. The future of the soul was the chief concern of life.

*Bona mors* was an expression we often heard. We had an opportunity of meeting a former pupil who came to the convent to make *bona mors*. She was an orphan, of independent means, and in the last stage of consumption. Midgie was allotted two sunny rooms and was tenderly nursed by Reverend Mother and the nuns. One day we were told that Midgie would visit us in the refectory. We sat in a circle at some distance from Reverend Mother who was in the centre with Midgie, propped upon pillows in an armchair. She did not speak to us, but whispered now and then to Reverend Mother.

Poor Midgie! How weak and wan she looked, how big her eyes, how claw-like her hands.

Reverend Mother spoke brightly about Midgie's coffin. It

[1]Forty years later I was told by an old schoolfellow that letters from a man had been discovered by a nun in Lucy's desk.

was to be covered with white velvet edged with silver braid. There would be a white satin pillow for Midgie's head. Midgie would be dressed in white, with the blue ribbon and medal of a Child of Mary. She would have white satin slippers on her feet and stockings of fine silk. Midgie smiled and seemed pleased.

A few days later she died. From the dormitory window we could see the convent cemetery. We used to look out at night, hoping to see Midgie's gaseous body hovering over her grave.

Mother Aloysius did not teach religion, yet it was through her that my soul was awakened. We had been reading aloud in class—in those days an important part of education—and the chosen passage was the eighteenth psalm: *The Heavens show forth the glory of God.* We were cold and listless and read badly. Mother Aloysius stopped us. 'That is enough. You do not understand what you are reading.' That night when we went up to bed, she came to my dormitory and asked the nun in charge to allow me and one or two others of the reading class, to go upstairs with her for a few minutes. We wrapped blankets round us and up the dark stairs we went to the top floor where there was a big window.

'Shut your eyes, children . . . now, open them!'

The night was frosty, the moon was away, the sky was blazing with stars.

My head was dazzled, my heart was overthrown by the glory and the wonder of the sight. 'Is this God?' I asked, trembling.

Mother Aloysius drew the blanket closely round my shivering body. She spoke softly—the psalm that we had not understood:

'*The heavens show forth the glory of God and the firmament declareth the work of His Hands.*
*Day to day uttereth speech and night to night sheweth knowledge.*
*There are no speeches nor languages where their voices are not heard.*

*Their sound hath gone forth into all the earth and their words unto the
    ends of the world.*
*The law of the Lord is unspotted, converting souls: the testimony of
    the Lord is faithful, giving wisdom to little ones.'*

Ellie Byrne was fidgetting. 'Please, mother, which is the
Great Bear? Where is the Dog star? Show me the stars that
shoot.'

Mother Aloysius answered patiently. We had our first lesson
in astronomy. God seemed to fade from the bright sky. I was
content. I had drawn near to Him as only children may. I
could never again be afraid.

In my third year I became a Child of Mary. I was promoted
to the highest table. I was allowed to give lessons on Sundays in
the Poor's School at the Convent gate. I slept in the Immacu-
late Conception dormitory, which had a small chapel at one
end. In school I was in the highest form but I was still diffident,
mistrustful of myself. Little was done by our teachers to encourage self-reliance and independence. Rather the reverse.
Those of us who were, like myself, nervous and fearful were
confirmed in our fear of life, our suspicion and dread of people.
Our timorous outlook was intensified to such an extent that
several of my schoolfellows chose to become nuns rather than
face the danger and evil of life outside the convent. No direct
effort was made to persuade the pupils to make this choice, certainly nothing was ever said to me, and though I was whole-
heartedly religious, I had no wish to be a nun.

At the end of three years mother came to take me home for
good. Many of my schoolfellows were leaving; a few were
sorry, others were glad to be going into the world. I cried when
I said goodbye to the nuns and felt as if all my props and de-
fences against danger and harm were being pulled away. I wept
at my last Mass in the chapel. Soon I should have no part in
the Kingdom of Souls. I was pale and sad when I went to say

goodbye to Reverend Mother, who kissed me and gave me her blessing.

'It is a pity that this dear child is going into the world,' she said to mother, and for a moment I feared that mother agreed, that she had wished me to be a nun, that she did not want me at home.

'Of course she needs me,' I said valiantly to myself, but I did not feel safe until we were well away from Bruff and in sight of the loved waters of Lough Gur.

## 19: THE COLT GOES TO THE PLOUGH

Clip clop went Beauty's hoofs on the homeward road while old
Paddy, imitating 'the masther', tried in vain to make the whip
whistle over her head. 'G'wan now,' he urged when she slack-
ened at a rise in the road, 'look to y'rself or ye'll never get the
misthress back by cow-time.'

'There's no hurry, Paddy,' mother said, 'let Beauty take her
time.'

'Dooley will be tired,' I reminded mother, 'she's sure to be
waiting at the gate. Last year she was there with a leaf-ful of
hairy red gooseberries.'

'Child dear,' mother said sadly, 'I hadn't the heart to write it
to you—Dooley has gone away! Gone to the children in
America.

'Gone! our Dooley gone—and without saying good-bye!
Oh mother, it can't be true!'

'She wanted to see you but we wouldn't let her go. You remember you didn't wish her to go to the convent.'

Mother's words were like a sword-thrust in my heart. They
were true. I was ashamed of Dooley . . . afraid of what my
schoolfellows would say when they knew that the old nurse of

whom I had often spoken was a peasant. I was ashamed of their seeing her in her homespun gown and thick country boots, her plaid shawl, her white frilled cap. Darling Dooley, whom I loved next best to mother, whose kind blue eyes lit up when she saw me, whose smiling lips spoke words of tenderness and comfort to her 'doty child'—faithful Dooley!

'How soon will she come back?' I asked with trembling lips.

'Never, I am afraid,' mother answered. She was suffering too.

The door of Dooley's cottage was open; her sandy cat sat on the threshold squinting at the sun. A strange woman opened the gate for us.

'This is Mrs. Collopy,' mother said. 'Collopy has taken the orchard and works for father.

'Has old Malachy gone to America too?' I asked bitterly.

'Didn't we tell you? Malachy is dead. He was chasing some boys from the orchard one day and fell headlong against a tree. His dog stood over him and wouldn't let anyone go near. By the time father came, Malachy was dead.

'Poor old Malachy! What happened to Barker?'

'Dinny-bawn took the dog and comforted him. Murnane says his stable is like Noah's ark with Dinny's creatures.'

'May I walk the rest of the way?' I asked.

The sun had gone in, the wind blew chilly as I sat in the hawthorn arbour and cried for Dooley until my sisters came to find me. Little Annie, now ten years old, offered the corner of her pinafore to wipe my eyes. 'Don't cry,' she said reprovingly, 'grown-up people don't cry.'

I stopped at once, I am now, of course, grown-up; I am nearly seventeen, a considerable age. From now on I can only shed tears in the secrecy of the night, or not at all.

'I'll race you to the house,' I cried, sniffing back my tears; 'one, two, three, off!'

Father was in the yard with Dinny-bawn; the maids, in their milking-caps, were standing, pail in hand, while Tom Hickey at the door of the byre, counted the cows as they filed in. The turkey was gobbling to his hens, and over the grass stalked the gander, followed by goslings and geese. Here, I thought with relief, there is no change!

Bessie jumped up on the mounting-block. 'The cry!' she shouted, 'the Desmond cry! In honour of Sissy's return to the world!'

We snatched off our hats and waved them round our heads. '*Sean-ait-aboo*,' we sang in our shrill girl voices, '*sean-ait-aboo*!'[1]

The cows paused at the byre door to listen and stare.

I was happy to have come home for good, but at the same time awkward and diffident. I waited until Janie and Bessie had gone to bed.

'Mother, what time shall I get up in the morning? Shall I see the milk in for you? Will you have your breakfast in bed?'

Mother looked surprised but she did not laugh at my suggestion. 'Not to-morrow. You needn't be up until seven, then you shall help me in the dairy. Thank you, child dear.'

As I went slowly upstairs I heard father's voice.

'Are you wise, Anne? Shouldn't Sissy begin to work right away . . . begin as she must go on?'

'You don't put the colt to plough the day he comes from the field, do you, John? You break him in gradually?'

'You're always right, love,' father answered, 'it's you I'm thinking of. You're tired.'

Mother let me help her in the morning and for the rest of the

[1] Hurrah for the old place.

day I was free. I was in great request. Janie, who was going to
school at the end of the holidays, asked innumerable questions
about the ways of nuns and the routine of convent-school life.
'You aren't going to a French convent, remember,' I told her
at last. 'Your convent is Irish and Reverend Mother is father's
cousin.' All the same I thought a course of *bonne tenue* would do
her no harm, so I had a class for her and Bessie and instructed
them carefully in deportment and etiquette, until father, looking over his paper, caught his daughters making court-curtseys
to the furniture. 'My God!' he said, 'what do you think you are
doing?'

'The piano is Queen Victoria, father, and grandfather-clock
is the Prince of Wales; we're pretending they have come to call,'
I explained.

'No, father,' Bessie said indignantly, 'grandfather-clock is
Mr. Parnell and the piano is Ireland-a-nation-once-again, and
*I'm* curtseying to *them*.'

'You're a lot of young donkeys,' father said good-humoured-
ly, 'you just copy your mother.'

'Very well, father,' Bessie said meekly, 'we'll only curtsey in
future to The O'Brien and The MacNamara, and if you'll put
out your hand I'll kiss it.'

' "*In kissing the queen's hand, the débutante must take the utmost
care not to touch it with her nose,*" ' I quoted naughtily, mincing
round the room and looking over my shoulder at an imaginary
court-train.

'Anne,' father called, 'come here. Set the children down to
darn their stockings. I won't have this tomfoolery in my house.'

At the end of the summer holidays Janie, my particular
friend, left us for the Brigidine convent at Montrath. She had
finished crying the night before and set forth with the resigna-
tion of a Christian martyr about to enter the arena mixed with

curiosity to meet the lions. It seemed hard that mother should
have the pain all over again of leaving a child at school, but
father was too busy with the harvest to go instead of her. When
the car had disappeared from sight, Bessie took my arm. 'Now
you must be my friend,' she said, 'and I will be Janie to you
until she comes home.' She looked so wistful that I wondered
whether Janie and I had left her out in the cold, and taken it too
much for granted that she was content to play with Annie.
'I'm bursting with things I want to ask you and tell you,' she
went on, 'and I'm longing to teach you the poetry we learnt
when you were at school and to read the books you missed
when you do, so that we can talk about them. We'll begin at
five in the morning . . . we'll begin this minute if you like.'

'Of course, Bessie, when mother is out, I have to see to things
. . . I have to be the lady of the house, but . . .'

'*The misthress!* the y'ung *misthress!*' Bessie laughed, imitating
Ellie.

I blushed. 'Well, that's what I meant. . . but if you like to say
poems while I skim, you can.'

'I should like that,' Bessie agreed, 'a dairy is a poetical place,
don't you think, except when flies get in? I'll say something by
mother's dear Lamb.' She began at once.

> '*I have had playmates, I have had companions,*
> *In my days of childhood, in my joyous schooldays,*
> *All, all are gone, the old familiar faces.*'

'Don't, Bess, not to-day! I know that poem and it's too sad;
besides it's for old people.'

'I thought it might cheer you up thinking that all our familiar
faces are alive! You've mourned enough, Sis; Janie is really a
lucky girl to be going to school for three years, instead of going
to strangers to be a maid in a print dress and clumping boots
like the poor girls at Grange school.'

Bessie was provokingly sensible. She always saw things clearly when I saw them blurred. She could straighten out tangles and could solve many of our childish perplexities. Only where her patriotism was concerned was she unreasonable and defiant.

'I don't care what you say, I won't listen,' she dared one day to say to mother, 'if you stand up for the English you are a traitor.'

Father looked at her in astonishment. 'Who's calling names? That's an ugly word for a little girl to use! Who are you calling traitor?'

'Mother!' Bessie answered angrily. 'She's always standing up for the English.'

'Your mother would give even the devil his due. She is a just woman. You are silly to be angry, Bess.'

'I can't help it, father. It's my Irish blood. It's . . . it's King Brian Boru coming out in me!'

'King Fiddlestick!' father snorted. 'Have sense, child! If you hate like that your blood will turn green! How would you like to have green cheeks?'

'I wouldn't care. Green is Ireland's colour.'

'Ireland—Ireland! Who's been putting ideas into your head?'

'I won't tell you, father. *I'm* not a traitor! You may beat me and starve me and—shave my head . . . and . . . and . . . torture me . . . but I won't be a traitor to my friends.'

Father was too much astonished to speak.

'What a great fuss!' It was little Annie who spoke emerging from under the table where she still kept a few derelict dolls. 'What a véry great fuss! It's Mr. Madden[1] who tells us to be so very Irish. It's not a secret.'

'Annie! how dare you betray him!' Bessie would have fallen upon her but for father, who said quietly, 'That's enough,' and took up his newspaper.

Annie returned to her den. Bessie wept quietly. I joined

[1] A schoolmaster.

mother in the little room, where she was taking books from the shelves. She was trembling a little and no wonder. 'It's no good scolding Bessie,' she said, turning to me, 'the only thing is to help her to see reason.'

'If she was my little girl, I should punish her well,' I said, for I hated mother to be called a traitor.

Mother didn't answer. She was standing with *Essays of Elia* in her hand, and looking out at the night and the young moon; the stars were appearing in great sprinkles over the sky.

'What are you thinking, mother? Are you praying?'

'Dear no, child! I was thinking how provoking it is that we never see the other side of the moon.'

Evidently she was not much hurt.

That night we young ones felt rather shaken. We were afraid that father might say something stern, or that mother would read a warning chapter. Nothing of the sort. Mother read *Alice in Wonderland* and when she was tired from laughing father took the book. Mr. Carroll would have been delighted if he could have heard the Hatter and the March Hare discoursing in a resonant Limerick brogue. Even the White Rabbit took on a Celtic air when he murmured, 'Och! me w-hiskers!' and seemed a finer fellow than the nervous little animal which spoke in mother's cultured voice.

Bessie asked leave to go to bed before prayers; I knew she could not bear that night to hear mother praying for those who rule over us. She kissed father, murmuring, 'I'm sorry,' but mother she ignored, partly because Ellie was taking up her attention with strange news of the Collopys. ''Tis said himself have Mrs. Collopy's Sunday bonnet snipped like it was moths at it, and herself talkin' of leavin' him.'

'I hope not, indeed,' mother said, refusing to be excited. The next minute we were on our knees for the Rosary.

It must have been a week later, at reading time, when Bessie, who had been quiet and sad, brought herself to ask mother's forgiveness. 'I haven't changed, mother,' she said, 'but I am sorry I was rude.'

Mother smiled. 'I want to help you, child dear,' she said. 'I'm going to read you and Sissy some Lamb. He went to Christ's Hospital, the Bluecoat school, in London, when he was seven years old. That was in 1782.'

Mother took *Elia* in her hand and began to read the essay on Christ's Hospital.

' "I was a hypochondriac lad; and the first sight of a boy in fetters, upon the day of my first putting on the blue clothes, was not exactly fitted to assuage the natural terrors of initiation, I was of tender years, barely turned of seven. . . . I was told he had *run away*. This was the punishment for the first offence. As a novice I was soon after taken to see the dungeons. These were little square cells, where a boy could just lie at his length upon straw and a blanket . . . with a peep of light . . . barely enough to read by. Here the poor boy was locked in by himself all day, without sight of any but the porter who brought him his bread and water—who might not speak to him—or of the beadle who came twice a week to call him out to receive his periodical chastisement, which was almost welcome, because it separated him for a brief interval from solitude; and here he was shut up by himself of nights, out of the reach of any sound, to suffer whatever horrors the weak nerves and superstition incident to his time of life, might subject him to. This was the penalty of the second offence."

'The third attempt', mother said, laying down the book, 'was expulsion, after the beadle had scourged the boy round the great hall in the presence of the whole school. These punishments were suggested—so it is said—by John Howard, a philanthropist.

'Sissy, will you take the book and read what Charles Lamb writes in "Praise of Chimney Sweepers".'

Bessie and I stared at one another, wondering at mother's choice of reading. I began, obediently,

' "I like to meet a sweep . . . one of those tender novices such as come forth with the dawn, or somewhat earlier, with their little professional notes sounding like the peep-peep of a young sparrow; or liker to the matin larks . . . in their aerial ascents not seldom anticipating the sunrise. I have a kindly yearning towards those dim specks—poor blots—innocent blacknesses.

' "When a child, what a mysterious pleasure it was to witness their operation! to see a chit no bigger than oneself enter the chimney—to pursue him in imagination as he went sounding on through so many dark stifling caverns . . . to shudder with the idea that 'Now, surely he must be lost for ever', to revive at hearing his feeble shout of discovered daylight—and then (O fulness of delight!) running out of doors to come just in time to see him emerge in safety." '

Here mother took the book and laid it down. Her face was white, her voice strangely jerky. We felt afraid.

'Little boys,' she said, 'four, five, or six years old, were sold to master-sweeps for two or three pounds. They were given a broom and ordered to climb the chimneys, sweeping as they went. It was pitch dark in the chimney which was perhaps sixty feet high or more and seldom went up straight, but bent and wound. It was often only a foot square and the child climbed—I don't know how he climbed—but sores came on his knees and heels and elbows—and he had to go on, in spite of the pain, until his tender skin grew hard. When the chimney was very dirty a sack over his head saved him from being suffocated by falling soot. If he was afraid to go up, his master burnt his feet with lighted straw. Sometimes the chimneys were smaller than twelve inches; then a tiny naked boy was sent up and told to keep his arms and the brush above his head or he would stick fast.

'When I was a child,' mother went on, 'playing happily with my brothers and sisters on the hills round Knockaney, English children were working in the coalmines for twelve or fourteen hours a day. In utter darkness little girls and boys dragged trucks or tubs by a chain fastened to a band round their bare waists, along narrow ways not two feet high. In the cotton and silk mills, from five in the morning until seven at night, small children tended the wheels. Their pay was one shilling a week. Think what poverty was in their homes when two pence a day counted for more than the agony of a child.'

'Mother!' Bessie exclaimed angrily, 'why are you telling us these dreadful things? Why must you?'

Mother looked at us and then answered Bessie with a question.

'Those run-away schoolboys Lamb wrote about—were they Irish boys?'

'I don't suppose they were.'

'The little sweeps, the children in mines and mills? Were they Irish?'

'No,' Bessie admitted.

'Yet they suffered as much or more than the Irish suffered at the hands of the English?'

'Yes, mother. Oh, the hateful, cruel English!'

'In earlier days, in every country,' mother went on, 'people, even religious people, were still more cruel, but I won't speak of that. I want you to understand that the English were cruel to the Irish because the times were cruel—and they did not realise it. You remember what our Lord said when He was suffering on the Cross at the hands of cruel men, "*Father, forgive them.*

*They know not what they do.*" Only time and civilisation can change the nations and turn their hearts from cruelty, which is often callousness, to kindness. Time and God's grace.'

Bessie said nothing but she got up and kissed mother. Then we cried for a while about the little sweeps and mother told us of stolen boys who found their long-lost parents and slept in clean sheets once more.

## 20: MOTHER AND I

The colt went to the plough and I to work.

With Janie gone to Montrath convent, Bessie and Annie at Grange school for most of the day, I had mother to myself, and by copying her I soon learnt to be of use. I was busy all the morning in dairy, house or kitchen; in time mother began to trust me and to pass on some of her work to me while she took the rest she badly needed. Rest, however, did not mean idle hands.

'Mother, will you *please* go and lie down,' I would say, after a morning of candle-making, an adventure in which I and the maids were not trusted alone.

'I will, Sissy, I'll be glad to lie down and take the chance of getting on with father's new shirts.' That was her idea of resting. Another time, 'I've put the big chair on the lawn, mother, if you would be so *kind* as to rest,' I said to her.

'I will, child dear. The air will do me good.'

But half an hour later I found her with the lid of the wooden hive on the ground, examining the comb. 'Come here, Sissy. I want to show you a fine queen-cell . . . the bees won't sting if you don't flap . . .' I had to take her word for it!

Occasionally Dr. Gubbins bribed her to rest by bringing her a new book. Clutching the treasured volume under her arm she would go to her room, I following with a hot jar and a shawl. 'Just for half an hour,' she agreed to lie down and when I took her tea an hour later, I found her absorbed in the pages with no thought of moving.

Sometimes the book had fallen down and she was asleep, resting at last.

In those days I came very near to mother. She showed me a side of her character that I had not hitherto known. The practical, strong and reserved side gave place to another, less certain, enquiring, wondering. It was Martha giving way to Mary. We read together in her quiet room, old books from the storeroom which had once belonged to Miss Baily: George Herbert, Izaak Walton, Gilbert White; old *Spectators* and *Ramblers*. We dusted the Bible which had lain long unread and learnt the way from Bethlehem to Gethsemane.


At other times we played a kind of game with the poets, bringing some problem or difficulty for them to solve. It was almost always mother who found the answer, either from the store of poetry in her head or by searching in books. We had no dictionary of quotations in those days.

Now and again I persuaded mother to tell me about old times and one day I asked her why her eyes were sad.

'It must be their shape,' she said, but I noticed that she looked towards a daguerreotype of brother hanging on the wall.

'I thought he would never leave me,' she said. 'I can't get used to his being away. There is a wound in my heart which won't heal . . . you can't understand and won't until you see your own son go away. It is as if part of one dies.'

'Was brother so very good?' I asked her.

'It wasn't that. One doesn't care for children for their goodness, for this or that, but . . . I don't know . . . we *loved* one another. If my eyes are sad,' mother went on after a silence, 'you must remember I lived in sorrowful times—the fearful years of the great famine. Father brought me here in 1844 when we were married; two years later came the Hungry Year, the beginning of the famine of '47. That was when brother was born. We had four maids in those days; Mary-the-kitchen, Mary-the-wash, Mary-the-bread and Mary-the-dairy. We did not know how to feed those faithful creatures and our two farm-boys. "What shall I do?" I asked the parish priest. "If I give the servants *enough*, my husband and I and the baby must starve outright." "You must give only just enough to keep life in them," he told me, "if you send them away it is to certain death."

'It was heart-breaking, Sissy, to see poor people tottering to the door, half-fainting, swaying on their skeleton feet as they held out little bags for the crust or the spoonful of flour—all we had to give them. One old man was found dead in the turnip-garden; too weak to pull it up, he died as he gnawed at the root in the ground. Little children died on the floor of the cabin where they slipped from the weak arms of their mother, while outside, ravenous dogs whined and sniffed under the door, ready to spring upon the dead. It wasn't only starvation: more died from typhus and other diseases brought about by want than from lack of food. Corn, which came at last, and maize-meal, sent from America, saved those who were still alive. You mustn't think the poor were left to die—priests, Protestant clergy, doctors, and many landlords and their wives worked hard to feed the starving and risked their lives in tending people sick with typhus and in burying the dead. Someone invented a trap-coffin which could be used again and again; the body fell into the grave when the hinged floor was opened. What with horror and grief and hunger—for father and I went hungry so as to help others—I thought I should have died.'

Mother was silent for a long time.

'I won't tell you more about those days,' she said at length. 'The past is past, and the present is happy, thank God.'

## 21: MAY-EVE

One of the happiest things about my home was the quiet way in which the days passed and the amount of time there seemed to be in the hours. It must have been due to mother's methodical ways for neither she nor the maids ever seemed to be hurried or flustered. The work in hand rolled smoothly on as regularly as the clock ticked. Perhaps the maids worked well and calmly because the monotony of life was interrupted by numerous holy days when all but necessary duties were excused and we flocked into the world of faith which, to Catholics, is almost as real as the earthen world in which we live. In the bright imagination of a child, the Paradise of saints and angels is a wonderful and beautiful country into which it goes, by way of the church, to keep a feast-day with the people of that land. When we were very young we did not think of the saints as spirits, because we could not imagine a spirit. We thought of them as people like father and mother, of whom we could ask favours in our prayers and to whom we could talk in our minds. We felt we could walk with them in safety in a heavenly sunshine; theirs was a place of no fear. In imagination we gathered and brought back with us, small flowers and scented leaves, golden feathers from the breasts of birds-of-paradise, a downy plume from Gabriel's wing. What matter if our treasures were invisible? We pressed them just the same in the pages of our prayer books, among the lace-edged pictures of the saints.

The maids did not get into the other world in the way we did who knew more about it. Although they were thankful for holy days and went to Mass, they were really more interested in an old Irish world where fairies, witches and banshees took the place of our angels and saints. We children were forbidden to pry into that magic place which was, mother told us, imaginary and untrue, but we could not help knowing that the maids and most of the untaught people round Lough Gur believed that a third world, fraught with danger, was going on all round them. *God be between us and harm*, was for ever on their lips— if a red-haired stranger came to the door; if a cock crowed during the day; if a heedless girl swept the floor towards the door;[1] if she lit a candle without first crossing herself[2] or forgot to 'nip the cake'.[3]

The powers of evil, always on the alert to entangle and destroy souls, being most dangerous and most powerful on May-eve, on that day the maids were apt to be uneasy and rather sullen, watching us suspiciously lest we might, through our unbelief, frustrate their precautions against danger. They strewed primroses on the threshold of front and back doors—no fairy can get over this defence—and in the cow-byres they hung branches of rowan while the head dairywoman sprinkled holy water in mangers and stalls. The milkmaids, at the end of the evening milking, stood to make the sign of the cross with froth from the pails, signing themselves and making a cross in the air towards the cows.

[1] This sends good luck from the house.
[2] To ward off evil spirits.
[3] Breaking a small piece from a newly-baked cake or loaf to avert bad luck.

While the dairymaids were safeguarding the cowsheds, Ellie stayed in the kitchen to see that no fire or ashes were carried out of the house, nor any food given at the door. As a rule no beggars showed themselves, knowing well that neither milk, bread, nor a light for a pipe would be given them by servants anywhere, not even a kindly greeting, for who could tell that they were true beggars and not witches or *Little People* in disguise, come to steal a coal of fire and to weave an evil spell round the house and its family. The final precaution against evil spells and danger was to put out the fire on the hearth to the last red ember.

Mother, who had been giving out the Rosary one May-eve —it was the first after my return from school—lingered a little on the prayer for protection and added the words from the psalms:

> *If thou sleep thou shalt not fear,*
> *Thou shalt rest and thy sleep shall be sweet.*

It was as if she wished to re-assure the nervous maids.

Father got up from his knees and forgetting it was May-eve he told Ellie to make up a good fire, for the crumley-cow[1] was sick and hot water might be needed.

Ellie and Bridgie looked at one another in consternation and went over to the hearth, where the fire was almost dead, to confer with Tom Hickey who was having supper, and to pity him for having to sit up all night beside the crumley-cow in the great danger of the byre.

"Tis a quare thing', Tom said in a low voice, 'that every cow in the byre has a bunch of primroses on her tail[2] but just the one, the crumley, and she needing it the most, the crayther! I've a mind to singe her along the back with a wisp of straw.'[2]

'Ye c'ld do so when the masther's in his bed,' Ellie said.

---

[1]Cow with crumpled horns.    [2]A potent charm against fairies.

'Will I make up a bunch for her tail?' Bridgie asked sympathetically. 'There's lashans[1] of primroses yet in the coop where Ellie have them hid agin the tramplin' of the children on the doorstep.'

'God help them,' Ellie said, 'and them so bould agin the dangers of this night.' She crossed herself anxiously.

'God between us and harm,' Bridgie whispered, doing likewise.

''Tis not the *Good People* I'd be in dread of in the dark of night,' Tom told them, 'but to hear the cry of the Ould Kings.'

The maids shivered. 'God send they rest in their graves.'

'There's them that thinks they'll be on the move once more,' Tom went on, working himself up. 'The last time was in '48. My father was on the top of Knockfennel, tendin' the Bel-fire with a score of the neighbours—where once there'd have been a hundred—when the cry of the Ould Kings struck upon them.'

'What was it like, that cry?' Bridgie asked.

'It came rolling like thunder over the mountains from south to north; from ayst to west it rolled, from sea to sea! And the ground heaved and broke, and risin' from the clay come the army of the dead. Ould warriors were there with their ould war-horses; foot soldiers and trumpeteers and drummers an' all, waitin' for the word of command! Up the Shannon it come, along the valley and over Lough Gur, loud as judgment-day, so's every one, livin' and dead, must hear the cry of the Ould Kings. Then the army give an answerin' shout, clashin' their shields and rattlin' their swords, and lettin' out the ould war-cries of the people. . . .'

'Whativer for?' asked Bridgie who was rather matter-of-fact.

'There's but the one thing,' Tom answered testily, 'and that's Ireland! 'Twas to encourage the livin' to fight for her like them ould warriors fought.'

[1] A large quantity.

'Did your father fight, so?' Bridgie asked.

'He did not,' Tom replied boastfully. 'He had more sense, bein' so weakened by the famine that he wouldn't have the strength to kill a chick'n. My father left it to *themselves* to do the best they c'ld in the short time before break of May-day, when the kings and the horsemen, the trumpeteers and the rest of the army had to be back in their graves, the great ones under the cairns and the others wherever they come from, may be the most of them from under the bogs!'

'Tom! Tom!' came father's shout from without. Tom turned pale. Ellie laughed. 'Sure, 'tis not the Ould Kings this time,' she said. 'Ye'd best see what the masther is wantin', and mind y'r feet as ye step over the primroses.'

A little later father came in. 'The crumley-cow has a lovely calf,' he told us. 'What shall we call it?'

'May-eve,' Bessie suggested, laughing, 'or Bel if it's a bull.'

'For pity's sake!' Ellie gasped.

'Is the cow all right?' mother asked.

'She's grand,' father answered. 'Tom won't have to sit up. You'll see, he'll stay with the farmboys, for nothing would make him go home alone this night! You girls,' he said to the maids, 'you can put out what's left of the fire. . . .'

''Tis out, sir.'

Father laughed. 'If you've finished your spells be off to bed. You'll be out before sun-up to wash your faces in May-dew and to look for the snail! Be sure you pick one that's tight in the shell!'[1]

The maids giggled and blushed.

'Why do you let the maids be so silly?' I asked mother when

[1] On May-day, before sunrise, girls seek for a snail, Should it be entirely in its shell, the finder will have a rich husband; if it is out, she may expect poverty and homelessness and she will be well-advised not to marry until after the next May-day, when her luck may have turned.

they were out of hearing. 'The nuns say we must never miss a
chance of curing people of pagan superstition!'

'You can try,' mother said rather coldly; she didn't like me to
quote the nuns at her in my 'superior manner'. 'I think only
time can cure superstition,' she went on. 'I don't want to make
Ellie and Bridgie unhappy or frightened, as they would be if I
were to make up the fire to-night, or if you were to sweep up
the primroses.'

'Doesn't God mind?' I asked her.

Mother smiled at my peevish face. 'I feel sure He has a sense
of humour,' she said.


'Ellie,' I said when we were alone in the dairy the next morning, 'the night passed off without anything dreadful happening?'

'Thanks be to Almighty God for His mercy.'

'That's just it, Ellie!' I cried triumphantly, 'it was God who
kept us!'

'Him, and the flowers, and putting out the fire.'

'No, Him!' I repeated. 'And nothing bad happened to the
crumley-cow.'

'Heaven preserve us! Ye've said it! Whatever'll have happened the misthress's spear! Thrown away as like as not!'

She dashed up the steps to the yard and returned with a flint
spear-head, given to mother by an antiquary long ago. ''Twas
in the bucket, thank God, but the sixpence have gone. Mebbe
the cow have it drunk.'

'What was the spear doing out there?'

'Hannah-the-dairy (the head dairywoman) borrowed it to
put in Crumley's drink, with sixpence of me own and a taste of
soot from under the bastable. 'Twas to safen the cow from
harm!'

'Oh, Ellie!'

'The way ye look at me, ye'd say I'd murdered the parish-priest! Crumley have a grand little yalla calf,' she continued good-temperedly, 'Hannah have it named Flagger!'[1]

'But Bessie has called the calf . . .'

'*Flagger's* the calf's name! I'd best put the spear back before the misthress have it missed.' Ellie hurried away before I could say another word.

''Tis a quare thing,' she began when she had settled down to skim the pan next to mine, 'the power there do be in a spear, or an arrow, or the moss off a skull—or any other small little thing! 'Tis like you'd expect of the goodness of God to give strength to a lump of stone like the misthress's spear. Who but Him'd ever think of usin' a morsel of burnt wood out of a Bel-fire, or a May-day fire if that's all, sewn in a rag round the neck of a woman to save her from plots?[2] Or to give power to the dead finger of a corp' . . .'

'Oh, Ellie, *don't*! God does not!'

Ellie stared at me over the dripping skimmer.

'Ye haven't done learnin' for all ye've been three years at the nuns' school!' she said witheringly. 'I've heard of a man that c'ldn't get any girl to marry him because he was as bald as an egg, and him growing a head like the mane of a lion by havin' the pate rubbed with the finger of a corp'. And there was the Count's cows . . .'

'What about them?'

''Twas one time when the most of them left lettin' down their milk. 'Twas the hand of a dead baby that cured them.'

'Did the Count know?'

'Not him! He had a grand cow-doctor to them from Limerick, that stud and stared at them and shook his head, and ordered powders from his own place in the city to be mixed in their

[1] The wild yellow iris.    [2] Fairy mischief.

drink and them sufferin' torments under his eyes and roarin' for help! 'Twas Four-tooth Heffernan's brother-in-law ran all the way to Bruff for the *proper one,* who met me grand cow-gentleman from Limerick on the road below, and sorra a doubt but a wink passed between them. Well, the *proper one* measured them all over, and he blew some of the drink that the dairymaid had been boilin' with the soot and ould Paddy's scraper—for that night the misthress was sittin' under the spear and we c'ldn't borrow it so, and the Count having his spears and arrows under lock and key—where was I?'

'The *proper one* blew . . .' I prompted, being interested against my will.

'He blew some of the drink over the cows' backs, and some into their ears, and then he took half a pail of milk from the one young cow that wasn't smit, and he stirred the milk with the hand of a dead baby from the keel[1] above, lashin' and dashin' the milk while the cows turned their heads and listened till they c'ld bear it no longer and they let down the milk that was hoarded in them till ye couldn't get into the byre but by swimmin'. Elf-shot, them cows was, or overlooked. There was a Sassenach visitin' at Lough Gur that same time that had the one eye evil and the other one glass.'

'Nonsense!' I said sternly. 'I will not believe it was a soot-drink or Paddy's scraper or the baby's hand that cured the Count's cows.'

'Believe it or not makes no difference! I'm surprised at you, Miss Sissy, and you not long from the nuns, to be doubtin' the power of God in them things! We'll have you doubtin' what Father O'Dwyer told us about the relics of the saints next!'

'You do shock me, Ellie.'

'There's them that says there's no healin' in the water of the

[1] An ancient pagan burial ground. Unbaptised babies were buried there.

holy wells or in the clay from a priest's grave! Mebbe ye'll be one of them ones, God help you?'

We continued skimming in an angry silence. Ellie had had the last word.

Mother, dressed for going to Mass with a white pinafore over all, came into the dairy to finish the skimming while I got ready for chapel, the first of May being the holy day of St. Philip and St. James.

Father Ryan preached a short sermon, telling us to enjoy this lovely May-day and be thankful to God for the sun, without whose glorious light and warmth we could not live. He told us that when the people of Ireland were heathen, they worshipped the sun; now we worship God, the maker and governor of the sun. 'In heathen days', he said, 'the sun was called by several names, one was Grian and another was Bel. On May-eve the people lit fires on the hills to guide the sun from the gloom of winter into the joy of spring. On Midsummer-eve they lit the fires again in honour of summer; and on Hallowe'en when summer ended, once more fires burnt on the hill-tops, this time to light the sun down into the place of gloom which we call winter. They were called the fires of peace.

'The church taught the heathen Irish the truth about the sun and the moon and the stars, and that God rules over the heavens as well as over the earth and over the people on the earth. The church said to the Irish people: there is no harm in lighting bon-fires on the hills, but let us light them now to the great glory of God, and let us remember the Holy Ones who loved and served God, and whose vigils the church keeps on the same days that the heathen Irish kept in honour of Bel, the sun. We re-member St. Philip and St. James on May-eve, St. John on Mid-summer-eve, and the Souls of the Dead on Hallow'een. On these days', Father Ryan said very earnestly, 'I bid you put away

all fear. Dance the old dances, sing the old songs, remember, if
you will, but with pity and tender laughter, the old heathen
customs and charms of your forefathers, and be thankful all the
time that Christianity has taught you to dread none of these
heathen things, and to know that Almighty God keeps you safe
by day and by night, all your life long.'

## 22: WAKES

The only time when the even cheerfulness of the household was ruffled, was when the maids wished to go to the wake of a dead neighbour and 'the misthress' refused them her permission. Then Ellie and Bridgie sulked for days and neglected their work to hang about the back-door, asking those more fortunate than themselves for details of the proceedings. A wake was one of the diversions of country life; 'the misthress' was thought to be hard and unreasonable when she prevented her maids from showing their respect for the dead.

Mother refused to give her reasons and it was only as we grew up that we heard of the drinking and noise and the strange old games which were usually part of the ceremony, and which, even if taken for granted, must often have caused distress to those relations who were worn out with nursing and bowed down with grief.

It was Bessie who told me about wakes. She had a thirst for knowledge which was not mere curiosity. 'Tell me the truth about things,' she would say to anyone who knew more than she did, '*for a little learning is a dangerous thing.*' In this way she learnt and retailed to me many things about which our mother was silent.

'I'll tell you, Sissy, what happens at a wake. First, the body is laid on a big table in the middle of the room. I daresay you've noticed that in all the cottages the kitchen table is the length and breadth of a big man—on purpose. Well, the body is dressed in the family shroud, nice and clean, which is kept for wakes, or else in a good suit, or a dress if it's a woman, with good boots and stockings, and a sixpenny bit is put in a handy pocket. That, Sissy, is very interesting, because the very old heathen Irish thought the dead had to pay a fare to get away from earth. They were sure they needed clothes and brogues in the place where they would be, and though of course *we* know clothes are of no use at all and are only wasted when they are buried, people who can afford it still go on dressing-up the dead because it is an Irish custom. I believe many of them still think that clothes will come in useful, and that St. Peter is more likely to let in a soul wearing a decent dress and good boots than one who is just wrapped in a sheet. Do you remember Kennedy (the piper) said he would be buried in the cast-off priest's clothes he wears, so that he'd "be let slip in as a priest when mebbe he'd be kept out as a musician?"'

'Well, when the body has been settled on the table, a plate of snuff and a plate of tobacco are put on its stiff chest, and usually a saucer of salt as well for anyone who likes to have a pinch, though people who remember, swallow some salt before they set out. Then they put lighted candles round the table, five or seven or more if they can afford it—that's to keep devils from hurting the body—and they put seats round the walls, and a bench at the head of the table for chief mourners, or anybody particularly grand who might look in. I don't know where they put the drink but there's always lots of that. Perhaps it's under the table.'

'Is that why mother hates wakes?'

'Partly; and she doesn't like the young men, when they've

been drinking, walking home with the maids in the dark. The next thing that happens at the wake is the arrival of the visitors. The relations bend over the body and say how pretty it looks or how death becomes it, and they cry and lament and say a prayer, but mere friends only kneel and say a short prayer, and then take snuff and tobacco and fill their pipes and glasses and sit down, and some play the first game, which is only clapping hands as people come in. After that the boys and girls play Shuffle the Brogue, which is like Hunt the Slipper, all sitting on the floor. There are others, the Rope Game and the Horse-Fair and a very wicked one called the Mock Marriage, but really, Sissy, the country people about here aren't like that. Ellie said a wake on Lough Gur is very gloomy and religious. She said the misthress herself could attend and take no harm. But Bridgie told me that it is gloomy only so long as the older people are there. When they're gone, the table with the body is pushed on one side and the wake games begin. Even then, every half-hour, or oftener, they kneel down and all pray together for the soul of the dead person. It's the live wakes[1] that are so sorrow-ful.'

It happened about this time that an old man named Cornelius Twomey died in his lonely cabin beside Lough Gur. He was no loss, the people said, for he had made himself disliked by all the neighbours, and the only relations he had, two nephews, who worked for father, he had kicked out of his house. Bridgie, who was soft-hearted about the old, shed a tear to think of the old man dying alone, with no one to run for the priest, no one to put ha'pennies on his dead eyes nor to comfort the dog who was his only friend. It was the howling of the dog that brought the nephews to the cabin where they found the dead man stretched on the floor.

[1]The farewell party before a child of the house leaves for America.

'Has he been buried?' I asked Ellie.

'There's many would have put him in the ground and have done with him,' Ellie replied, 'but them boys have readied to wake him for the sake o' the grand ould name of Twomey.' Both the maids laughed.

When father heard about the wake he was vexed. 'The old man hadn't a friend in the world!' he said to old Paddy. 'Who would go to the wake?'

'Ye'll see, sir,' Paddy replied, 'there'll be friends prayin' round the corp'. Whereiver there's a sup o' whisky goin' friends won't be wantin', faix.'

'The boys can't afford it,' father said, 'but they're good lads, and I like to see them showing respect, even to an old black-guard like Corney.'

The morning after the wake Ellie was at the back door listening to one of the farmboys who had been present and was describing what had happened. 'Ye opened the door and looked in, och! 'twas tarrible dark inside, barrin' the table and him on it. His nevvies had him sot up with a candle in each of his two hands and the light of them shining on his white face and on the staring eyes of him. And the two young fellas stud be the side o' the corp', ayst and west of him, lookin', in the dark shadder, like it might be two divils come for the sowl, and never a word said. Sorra a one come to the door that night but let a screech out of him an' made off like a hare, all but meself an' two-three of the boys that were in the game.'

Ellie seemed to be trouncing him with vigour, for he turned to go. 'Ye may be right,' he said sheepishly, 'mebbe 'twas all ye say, but seein' the most of them that come to cry tuk to their heels, there was all the more o' the craythur for them that c'ld laff!'

## 23: THE HAPPIEST HOURS OF OUR LIVES

Bessie was as good as her word and almost every morning she woke me at five. The footsteps of Ellie and Bridgie roused her as they passed our door and went creaking downstairs; she was wide awake at once and hastened to light the thick home-made candle, settling the huge saucer-like brass candlestick on the pillow before she announced 'reading-time', with a loud clap of the book. I used to groan and pray for a little more sleep.

'You're like Doctor Watt's sluggard,' she cried, 'don't you mind having lost fifteen hundred hours of mother's reading when you were at school?'

We read in turns but Bessie took the lion's share, declaring that I chanted like a Sassenach nun giving out the Rosary. It is true that my natural accent had been tampered with at the convent. Bessie considered her own style vastly superior, especially for Dickens. It was certainly funny to listen to the Wellers, or to Mrs. Gamp and Mrs. Prig, conversing in her sweet sing-song brogue.

In the next two years we read and deeply enjoyed nearly all Dickens and much Scott, Mrs. Gaskell, Fanny Burney, some Trollope, Lever and Marryat. Sometimes we re-read passages which puzzled us with mother, and as a rule her explanation satisfied us but now and then she put us off with the provoking words, 'You will understand when you are older.' This vexed Bessie. 'Oh, mother!' she would cry, 'what if I die young?'

The first hour of our reading with mother was given to essays, poetry, travel or biography, the second to fiction. We read *Lorna Doone*—I was in love with John Ridd for weeks—*The Vicar of Wakefield*, more Dickens, Thackeray, Kingsley and the Brontës, returning now and then, for little Annie's benefit, to the loved books of our first days, *Little Women, Masterman Ready, Scottish Chiefs, Gulliver's Travels* and *Mayne Reid*. Mother enjoyed Maria Edgworth more than we did, also Jane Austen; we much preferred George Eliot.

Mother used to buy new books through Miss Forde, an old friend who lived in Dublin; others she bought second-hand through father's auctioneer friend in Limerick; some were lent us by friends, or exchanged, and Mac often left a novel behind him.

We calculated that we read with mother in the evenings, at least five hundred hours a year;[1] there was, besides, much time given to learning poetry by heart—thoroughly, so that we should remember it in our old age[2]—and not only poetry but passages of prose, and speeches which we declaimed with great vigour and feeling. To please ourselves we learnt pages of

[1] Reading aloud was encouraged in many Irish homes. We are told that in the family of C. K. Bushe, Lord Chief Justice, 'reading aloud Shakespeare, Scott and other authors was a favourite practice. . . . Sons and daughters growing up around him were initiated betimes into the higher regions of thought and feeling'.

[2] In a letter to her sister, Annie wrote: 'This is my seventy-first birthday; my sight is beginning to trouble me and now I thank God for the books we read and the songs we sang. I go over them in my memory while I rest my eyes.'

Dickens and were ready with apt quotations from him and other authors.

Our tempers were tried when we were reading Sullivan's *History of Ireland* and hatred of the English flared up once more in Bessie and, less vehemently, in myself. 'Ireland', Bessie cried, 'must have her revenge.' 'No,' mother said, 'revenge is forbidden.' Bessie declared that what would be wrong in a man might be right in a nation, while mother maintained that a nation, being made up of individuals, is equally bound to obey the law of God and the commandments of Jesus Christ.

Father had at last to interfere. 'Your mother's right, children, however inconvenient such an opinion may be to politicians,' and when Bessie wanted to argue he promised her she should thresh it out with Uncle Richard, who was both priest and patriot.

We felt for once unfairly treated when mother made us read, then and there, and while we were still feeling shattered, Doctor Johnson on *Revenge*. The last paragraph she read to us herself, her blue eyes shining with unshed tears, so anxious she was that the sun should not go down on our wrath.

'Of him that hopes to be forgiven, it is indispensably required that he forgive. . . . On this great duty eternity is suspended; and to him that refuses to practise it, the throne of mercy is inaccessible, and the Saviour of the world has been born in vain.'[1]

In this way mother disturbed our souls and forced us to see that there is no half-way house between good and evil.

The hours we spent in the little room were the happiest in our lives. We sat round the table, a well-shaded lamp in the centre, taking it in turns to read while the rest made calico chemises and flannel petticoats—Christmas presents for our poorer neighbours—or pieced together patchwork for counter-

[1] *The Rambler*, No. 185.

panes, or hemmed dairy aprons, dusters and cloths for the house. When Janie came home she taught us to smock pinafores, to embroider collars and to make fine lawn *garibaldis*[1] and white Sunday-petticoats flounced with *Swiss-work*, high-necked 'petticoat bodies' and nightgowns—heavy with tucks and insertion and ribbon-bows at collar and wrist—which we thought very handsome after the elephant's *robes-de-nuit*, invented by foundresses for use in convent schools.

While our fingers sewed, our minds escaped into the world of imagination, so different from that of Lough Gur, and plunged gleefully into the lives of our book-friends.

The house was quiet at that time. Father sat in his armchair, a glass of cold water beside him, his eyes on the newspaper, one ear cocked, as a good farmer's always is, to catch untoward sounds from byre and haggard; the other ready to listen should Mr. Pickwick or Sir Pitt Crawley come forward.

By this time the farmboys had had their supper and were gone to their room in the yard, the two maids were knitting by the fireside, talking in low tones together until it would be time for prayers. Then they would bank up the great fire with wood-ashes and in a half-circle round the well-swept hearth they would set out the creepies[2] and the little rocking-chair—just in case Mammy Jug and the grandfathers might be visiting their old home during the night.

Every evening before he went to bed, father looked out at the night and consulted with moon and stars about the morrow's weather. When moon and stars were absent, he judged by the clouds on Knockfennel's crown or the mist lying low on Lough Gur. When darkness shut out the world, a rising wind or a mutter of thunder warned him of threatening storm; even in the hush of a summer night, a breath—or the voice of silence—whispered of coming rain.

[1]The predecessor of the blouse.    [2]Low stools.

Father put his head into the byre[1] where the long lines of cows turned their moonlit faces and blew hard through their nostrils. He looked in on the tired farm-horses lying in their stalls with their legs stiffly outstretched and at old Beauty who often slept standing up, rocking herself gently and flickering her long light eyelashes. He glanced at the darkened window of the farmboys' room and answered the quiet 'Good-night, sir,' of the wayfarer in the hayshed with a kindly 'God bless you. I trust you not to strike a light,' and listening for the hearty reply, 'God bless *you* kindly, sir! Sure, ye can trust me as ye'd trust the parish priest.'

At the sound of father's steps Tear'em and Ate'em opened an eye, growled softly, their tails beating on the ground, while old Turkey gave one loud, short gobble and no more.

Then father came in and bolted the door and went quietly into his and mother's room, where she would very likely be lying asleep with moonshine gilding her fair hair.

[1]Except in summer when horses and cows were in the fields.

## 24: THE AUNTS

Mother's room was downstairs and had a door opening on to the lawn, through which she sometimes crept by moonlight or at dawn, when she heard old Turkey call *fox*. He had several distinct gobbles; *fox* being different from *visitors* and from *beggars*. When mother in her light sleep heard him shout. 'Hey, the misthress, *fox*!' she slipped from her bed and was off to defend her poultry yard long before the warning had penetrated father's deeper sleep.

'Your mother was out hunting again this morning,' father would tell us at breakfast. 'Did she wake you with her tally-hoing? Isn't she the grand hunting-woman?'

'I never make a sound, John, you know I don't!'

'Did you see the red skin of the fox nailed to the barn-door? 'Twill make a coat for Baby-Bunting here. Just you run and see!'

We ran and came back crying, 'There's no fox-skin there, father . . .' and remembered too late that it was All-Fool's day. That was when we were still very young.

Another time. 'Did you hear that mother was out cubbing this morning?'

'Oh, father! Cubbing in summer!'

'You ask her! Old Turkey had hardly given the word before your mother was out and face to face with two cubs and a vixen that was showing the little fellas how to carry a dead duck.'

'A true duck, father?'

'Indeed it was, and our Sunday dinner! Ellie had left it hanging outside..Mrs. Fox jumped—and got it, small blame to her!'

'And did she get away with it?'

'She did! Off she went, the cubs streaking after her, while your mother was gone for the hounds. Would you believe it? When Tear'em and Ate'em gave tongue and your mother cried "gone awa-a-y", those cubs turned round and laughed.'

'What next, father?'

'Your mother thought it would be a sin to hunt the pretty-faced little creatures, so she called the pack off and went herself to collogue with her bees—at four o'clock in the morning!'

'It was so beautiful,' mother said apologetically, 'the moon was shining and the dawn was breaking; larks were rising out of the most silvery dew I have ever seen. I really couldn't come in at once . . . and then I heard swarming-sounds coming from the new hive, so I took the top off, thinking I might be in time to take out the young queen, cell and all, but I was too late. She and the old queen were trumpeting at one another . . .'

'Spoiling for a fight . . .'

'No, John,' mother went on serenely, 'the workers kept them apart while the managers of the hive settled which bees should stay with the new queen in the hive and which should go out with the old queen. So I put the lid on and came in.'

'As cold as a holy trout,' father said, looking quizzically at mother who looked back at him and laughed.

Nobody but father dared to tease her. She 'wouldn't allow it' from anyone else. Still more she resented criticism, especially if anyone dared to question her way of managing and educating us. Even our priests never dreamt of taking such an imprudent step, and as for Uncle Richard, though he was parish priest of a big place like Knocklong and knew a good many people, he thought our mother the wisest and cleverest of women. You could see it in his bow when he shook hands. But there were, of course, the aunts; Mary, wrinkled and grey, twenty years older than mother; Margaret, a widow and rather lame, with a large, fine face; Anstace, a tiny thing, neat as a nun. There had been others. Ellen, who only lived to be fifty, and Elizabeth, who can't have been strong for she was so tired after nursing her husband through an illness, that she lay down and died, and a sixth whom we never knew. Aunt Elizabeth's daughter, Cousin Power, took her place in coming to see us; she adored mother, but as she was always wanting us to sew or knit for her we girls didn't much care about her. This cousin and the six aunts had all married farmers. As they loved mother very much and were (except Cousin Power) considerably older, they thought it right to speak to her now and then for her good.

Then there was Cousin Julia, for whom father had made a good match with a near neighbour of ours. She was good-natured but interfering, and talked, as Bessie said, with a great show of ignorance; also Cousin Jane Purcell, great-uncle John's daughter, who held her head high because her mother was born a Synane. I remember all these relations coming one day to visit us—it must have been mother's birthday because Mac was there too, who usually came on Sundays, and he was the only man at the party for father wisely had business elsewhere. For once Mac was subdued. We children detested him, but he was beloved by mother because he was her dear kind nephew, a MacNamara, and the son of her dear brother Patrick, who, a month or two before Mac was born, died suddenly when he was having supper after being all day at a fair. It was said that 'his hands turned in with the knife and fork on his plate and he was dead'.

On mother's birthday then, Mac rode over from Bruff, and the aunts drove on a jaunting car with a fiery chestnut horse, from round and about Knockaney. Cousin Julia walked from her farm on Knockfennel—a mile in the heat—and Jane Purcell drove herself in a pony-chaise.

It was about two o'clock on a thundery day, with midges biting outside; so we awaited the visitors in the little room in a solemn mood. Janie, home for the holidays, read aloud the death of little Nell to pass the time.

Old Paddy waited at the door to help the aunts to get off their car, backwards, and taking care not to catch their fine white cotton stockings on the step or mark their elastic-sided kid visiting-boots. They had known old Paddy so long that they did not mind if he saw a little leg, but once down they expected their nieces to come running out with their dear sister to welcome them and escort them into the house. The next move was for them to take off their bonnets and gloves and put on their indoor caps at a little glass behind the door and then, when they were settled on the sofa and in Mammy Jug's rocking-chair and father's armchair, we four girls carried the bonnets and gloves to the spare room and laid them on the white counterpane with great care, rolling the strings round our fingers to get out any creases and then leaving each pair to stream behind its own bonnet over the pillows. The gloves had to be blown up and laid there too.

When we got down again, we found two more visitors had arrived so two of us had to carry up Cousin Jane's and Cousin Julia's bonnets and lay them out at the foot of the bed. After that the trial began of sitting on creepies opposite the aunts in the full glare of the window, to be noticed and commented on, while we strained every nerve to sit still and not fidget, above all not to blush.

'It's a strange thing, Anne,' Aunt Mary was saying, 'that though you are a MacNamara to look at, not one of your children, unless it might be Bessie, takes after our family in looks. They are more robust-looking—more O'Brien.'

'Do you still force the poor children to wash all over every day?' Cousin Julia asked. ''Tis enough to give them their deaths!'

All eyes turned upon our rosy faces.

'I must say they look well,' Aunt Margaret admitted, 'although a bright colour often means a decline.'

'I expect you get to bed early so as to be out to feed the fowl in the morning?' Cousin Power suggested.

'We sit up till after the Rosary at nine.'

'Too late! Altogether too late!'

'We like sitting up,' said little Annie, 'we're reading *David Copperfield* again.'

'In my young days children didn't expect to be amused the way you amuse yours, my dear Annie!' said old Aunt Mary.

'Amused?' mother asked. It was the first time she had spoken.

'With puzzle-maps,' Cousin Julia put in, 'and stories and jingle-jangles!'

Bessie looked at me. What an amusing unknown word!

'If you remember, Anne,' Aunt Margaret said, '*we* sat down to our sewing of an evening and just went on sewing until we left off at bedtime.'

'I remember,' mother said gently, 'and how much we enjoyed the books our Poor Scholar read aloud while we worked.'

'Well now! I had forgotten all about him,' Aunt Margaret admitted.

'I can remember our father telling him to leave out love-making and swearing,' Aunt Mary said. 'It comes back to me now. Maurice his name was. He was fond of an author named Fielding and I remember our father coming in one day just as Maurice was reading—and not for the first time—some shocking lines:

> *Let other hours be set apart for business,*
> *To-day it is our pleasure to be drunk.*

Strange how lines one would wish to forget remain in the memory!'

'I think,' said Aunt Margaret primly, 'we should ask Anne's pardon for repeating such lines before her children.'

'That's nothing,' Bessie said reassuringly, 'we are used to Dickens.'

'It's shocking the bad language that's learnt from books, and by innocent children, too!' Cousin Jane Purcell began. 'I heard the Reverend Lamb—that's the new Protestant clergyman—telling our parish-priest that there's one sentence in a book— I think it is called *Legations*—with twenty-nine *damnations* in it.'[1] Cousin Jane dropped her firm voice to a whisper at the bad word.

Cousin Julia had long since made up her mind that reading is a wicked waste of time. 'Books', she exclaimed, 'are the invention of sinful men! If Almighty God had approved of books He would not have created worms to destroy them. I know you think differently, Anne, but then you aren't like your dear sisters, in any way!'

The aunts laughed. 'She may be all the better for that, even though she puts dry mustard into her cream-cheese!'

'Who ever heard of such a thing?' Cousin Jane asked. 'Now the Synanes were famous for their . . .'

---

[1] *There's a great text in Galatians,*
*Once you trip on it, entails*
*Twenty-nine distinct damnations. . . .*
**Robert Browning.**

Cousin Julia waved her aside.

'I hear Bessie had a piece in a Dublin newspaper,' she said provocatively.

'It was a poem; I got a prize for it!' Bessie couldn't help saying.

'That's the way nowadays! Writing jingle-jangles when you should be helping in the kitchen or nettling for the young turkeys!'

'Well now,' interposed an aunt, kindly, 'I wonder which of you looks after the fowl?'

'Bridgie does!'

'Your poor father!' Cousin Julia attacked again. 'Obliged to keep a maid to care for the fowl! What young farmer, do you think, will want to marry a girl who's never seen a cow milked and wouldn't know the use of a thimble if he made her a present of one?'

Just then Ellie looked in. 'I have the tea wetted, ma'am,' she said.

The aunts rustled with relief at the interruption and Aunt Anstace gently patted Cousin Julia's hand to quieten her.

'They're sweet-looking girls, Anne, and I'm sure they are a credit to the way you feed them,' said Aunt Mary, while Aunt Margaret got her lame leg into position to be ready to go to tea.

'And if anyone has said anything harsh it was kindly meant—perhaps,' Aunt Mary continued. *A shot at Cousin Julia!*

'You must be good girls and help poor mother,' Aunt Anstace advised in her little voice, trying vainly to pat Annie's head.

'I do help her,' our baby answered, 'we all do. And please don't think we only like reading; we love thimbles and needles and scissors and that sharp thing for making holes that you can *kill* with.'

'She means stiletto,' Janie put in, laughing.

'They must show you their work after tea,' mother said cheerfully and not showing that she had been pricked by Cousin Julia.

'Sissy baked the potato-cakes for tea,' little Annie went on gallantly, 'and Janie made the crab-apple jelly, and Bessie . . .'

'I . . . I . . . oh—the potted duck,' our clever one said, and not one of us even whispered, 'Oh, *Bessie*!'

'Indeed!' Cousin Julia snapped, glaring at our poor youngest. 'And pray what did you do?'

'I skam the milk,' our champion said, untruly, 'I had to, for *poor mother* was lying down—*reading*!'

Tea brought harmony and a good deal of laughter. The aunts made little jokes; Mac was amusing and rather respectful—for him; we had left off being shy, and Cousin Julia was no longer in a temper from the hot walk. At four-thirty they put on their bonnets, upstairs this time, and bustled away so as to get to their homes by cow-time. Old Paddy drove Cousin Julia back on our car. Cousin Jane Purcell was rather lingering, as she had no cows, but in the end Mac scared her away because he wanted to air his views about reading and ways of education and if he could, to tangle even mother whom he loved, in her talk.

'No, Aunt Anne!' he declared, 'I can't see the advantage of Sissy and Bessie getting, as you say, into the lives of Dickens' people. Does it do them good to be in Fagin's company with Bill Sikes, a murderer, and the Artful Dodger, and a—creature like Nancy.'

'It can't hurt us so long as we come home to sleep,' Bessie said innocently.

Mac stared at her for some time, looking into her steady, candid eyes. 'If you are going to be a governess,' he asked, 'will it help you to know Becky Sharp?'

'Do you mean would I throw a dictionary at my Miss Pinkerton? I would be the opposite of Becky in everything!' She was beginning to get excited so mother remembered that she had a note and some butter for Mrs. Grogan, which she sent by Bessie and Annie to get them out of Mac's way. I went on sitting in the window, smocking.

'Well, Aunt Anne?' Mac began teasingly, 'do tell me why you think so much of education for my cousins? And why you aren't like the aunts?'

'You are thinking of my reading every day with the children? I want to give them never-failing friends who will feed them in hungry places with food for the soul as well as for the mind, and treasure for the memory. What a jumble of quotations! I looked them out on purpose.' Mother blushed like a child caught cheating. 'I want the children to be good companions and surely a mind that is a desert can't be as delightful as one that has been cultivated?'

'I should read a lot more,' Mac said meditatively, 'if I hadn't my exams on my mind.'

'You aren't *hungry* enough! The aunts were never hungry as we three youngest were, Michael and Patrick and I.'

'For knowledge?'

'Yes, and for beautiful sights and sounds, for travel and to be with people who knew about things and could fill an emptiness in us.'

'And of course there was no one to help you?'

'Mammy Mac understood. She let your uncle Michael go to Australia which satisfied his roving spirit, and she managed to give us all three a good education. I longed to travel too but I have had to do it by proxy.'

'Poor Aunt Anne! Have you ever been *anywhere*?'

'I once went to Kilkee for a week. I was so astonished when I saw the sea! I stood and stared and the next wave threw me down.'

'You once went to Blarney, mother,' I reminded her, speaking very fast for fear of interruption, 'when I was seven you took me to St. Ann's Hill and there was a lady in the baths who you told me was a gentlewoman because she said *my husband* when she spoke of him to you instead of calling him Mr. and when she asked you whether father's people came from Clare she called him Mr. O'Brien and not *your husband* and she sang "Alice, Where Art Thou" and I played with the little Bechers whose mother they said was Lady Emily and she was lovely only small and she had a new baby that didn't like noise which was why they were sent to St. Ann's Hill and Doctor Barter went to Dublin and forgot to put on a hat and the whole of Cork was shocked but he didn't care a pin!'

'For heaven's sake *stop!*' Mac said, 'there's no need to show off your good memory!' which was the horrid sort of thing he would say.

'Well, Aunt Anne, you haven't been a great traveller certainly.'

'I feel as if I had had great adventures,' mother answered, 'for I do believe I sailed with Marco Polo, and Columbus, and went by land and sea with the crusaders. I was buccaneering with Sir Walter Raleigh and went south with Captain Cook. I discovered Albert Nyanza with Baker . . . and so much more. I'm a travelled woman—by proxy! It's a curious thing, Mac, that while my hands are doing all kinds of dairy-work—fairly well, I think . . .'

'Perfectly,' Mac put in.

'. . . I myself may be Livingstone wandering in an African forest, or I may be Joan of Arc, putting on her armour for the first time and wondering if she has it on back to front? Or I am Hagar, crying in the wilderness over little Ishmael . . .'

'Not a cheerful choice that, but clearly your way of turning Martha into Mary. I'm afraid you are a shirker, Aunt Anne!'

'I don't know, Mac! I only want to make you understand how books—including poetry—have stood to me, which is why I read with the children. I suppose you believe, as I do, that the spirits of babies come from God? We should never have known that they come trailing clouds of glory, if it hadn't been for Wordsworth.'

'It's a far cry from Wordsworth to Dickens! I am surprised at your letting the children read *Oliver Twist*.'

'*Children,* indeed!' I thought.

'They must learn to know that there is a world beyond the county Limerick, don't you think? It would never do to let them be centred in one small sleepy place till they come to think that life is a dull business. They must wake up and find out how interesting the world is even if they aren't in it. Dickens is one of the awakeners. He's a great guide to life and people. One has faith in him.'

When mother seemed to have finished explaining, I said resentfully to Mac, 'You seem to think we read no one but Dickens and that we are *amused* by Fagin and Bill Sikes. Well, we aren't. They're a warning to be very wide-awake and to recognise rascals when we meet them.'

Mac laughed. 'That's right! Keep a sharp look-out for rogues! When you settle down as farmers' wives ...'

'We shan't.'

'Or as wives of rising young doctors ...' he tapped his chest.

Mother frowned. Mac hurriedly turned his back on me.

'When I'm married,' he said, 'to a good young *English* girl, brought up by Charles Dickens, I shall teach my hybrid off-spring exactly as you teach my cousins. Regularity ...'

'Of course,' mother answered seriously, 'or you get no-where.'

'I shall say to my wife, "*regularity*, my dear, and two hours a

day for six days a week", skipping . . . may she skip swear-
words, Aunt Anne?'

'We never skip *anything*!' I put in firmly.

'What a complete education! May I let my wife read maga-
zines? or funny bits out of newspapers? I thought not!' Mac
sighed. 'I'm afraid I shall have to choose an Agnes Wickfield,
with a pure, high brow when I'd rather marry a dear little silly
Dora who'd call me Doady.'

'Go away, Mac!' mother said, 'you're wasting my time.' She
got up and went out to see what father was doing, her way
when she felt ruffled.


'Sissy! I never meant to be tiresome,' Mac said.

'You weren't, you were only silly.'

'Well, silly if you like! You must admit it is rather surprising
to come on a nest of blue-tits on the shore of Lough Gur! You
with the tongue of a shrew; Bessie like a fiery rocket, though
she's a fine creature and ought to have been a boy; Annie with
a bark and a bite, for all she's so young and pretty; Janie—dear
Janie, she's lovely, but about as kind as a crocodile if you tell
her so.

'You leave us in peace then! Perhaps absence will make our
hearts grow fonder! It might teach you not to chaff mother.
She doesn't like it. You're like the aunts, thinking we ought to
be nothing but farmer-folk. *I* think mother ought to be professor of literature at Trinity College! She's such a discoverer,
and the best lover that writers ever had. Mother is turning us
into discoverers and lovers by her way of teaching us. One
time she makes us almost faint at the beauty of poetry, and then,
when she sees us limp and swoony, she turns to something that
inspires us, that's what she calls it, like *Ivanhoe* and *Talisman*
and darling old *Don Quixote*. Then, when we've grown terribly strong and knightly, she'll read us *Yeast* and *Oliver Twist*.

When we are turned into down-trodden tailors and ravenous workhouse-boys, we pass on to *genteel* Jane Austen, and after that . . .'

'Go on, Sissy.'

'. . . when mother thinks we are *seasoned* enough we go back to *beauty*.'

'And are you seasoned?'

'I never shall be. I'm . . . I'm . . . a g—g—goose.'

'Never mind, Sis. You're young yet and soft.'

'Young yourself!' I said angrily through my tears.

Mac went out to tell mother he was sorry and it must have been then that he told tales of Bessie and Purcell Grogan. He had come upon them by the lake, reciting, and on a rock was a copy of Byron's poems. I think this happened on the previous Sunday, because when I went that afternoon to call Bessie in to tea, she was standing on a rock with the water splashing in short little waves almost to her feet and her long gold-brown hair streaming in the wind. She was saying:

> '*The stars are forth, the moon above the tops*
> *Of the snow-shining mountains . . .*'

while Purcell, to whom the book belonged, was hearing her while he grubbed for bait.

I couldn't say *tea* to Bessie until she had finished and had leapt over some lappety water to dry land, because I was thrilled by the poem, also it would have been as rude to Byron, even though he is dead, as it would be to interrupt a live person. As we walked up the hill, Bessie asked me not to tell mother. 'She has a spite against Lord Byron,' she explained, 'and keeps him shut up in the storeroom. When I told her I had been reading him up there, she didn't *say* anything but he disappeared at once. Mrs. Grogan lets Purcell read him and she is a *person* just as mother is and she may be quite as right as mother.

I felt this was both wrong and disloyal but I agreed to be silent and often, when the candle had burnt out so that we couldn't read, Bessie repeated Byron's poetry until I too knew much of it by heart. I must say in fairness to Purcell, he warned us that most ladies thought Byron wicked and so did Queen Victoria.

'Could anyone who wrote as he did be bad?' Bessie asked me.

I could not tell. 'God bless all poets,' I prayed, 'and forgive them their sins.'

That is why, when Mac had sneaked to mother and she sent Ellie for Bessie, I went with her to the little room. We stood, hand in hand and trembling before mother and Mac and looking appealingly at the back of father's head where he sat in his armchair reading the paper.

Mother had her stern face on but she spoke very gently. 'I believe you, Bessie, have been reading Byron? Why did you do it, child dear?'

'Was hiding him the same as forbidding him?' Bessie asked quietly. 'You didn't tell me?'

'I should have explained,' mother said, and Mac frowned, thinking her weak. 'Byron wrote poems which Catholics don't read or wish to read.'

'Purcell told me not to read the long one at the end, and truly, mother, I never even glanced at it.'

'We have *both* learnt several lovely poems by heart,' I confessed, 'but there isn't one that we couldn't say to Father Ryan or even to the Dean.'

Mother smiled and father lowered his paper.

'There are my good girls! Always own up! Now run away. I want a word with Mac.'

We went out to the hayricks where we hid until Mac had gone. He looked serious and we had a suspicion that father had given him 'a hearing'.[1] Father hated tale-bearers and mischief-makers.

In the evening Bessie stood up and repeated:

> *The Assyrian came down like a wolf on the fold,*
> *And his cohorts were gleaming in purple and gold,*
> *And the sheen of their spears was like stars on the sea,*
> *When the blue wave rolls nightly on deep Galilee.'*

Father liked it so much that he let his pipe go out.

[1]A scolding.

## 25: HALLOWE'EN

'Sissy, will you listen? I'm miserable!'

'Poor Bess! Is it the mist or because it's Hallowe'en?'

'I like Hallowe'en and seeing the nuts jump and snapping apples. I'm just—wretched.'

'Can't you get something to do?'

'I want to go away, far away! summer has gone and the sun never shines nowadays. I wish I had been Christopher Columbus's daughter sailing with him in his small old ship and striding on the deck with our swords rattling and blunderbusses in our hands to shoot the crew—if necessary.'

I was just beginning to tease Bessie by saying:

> 'Man for the (sea) and woman for the hearth,
> Man for the sword and for the needle she . . .'

when mother came in and stopped me with a look; she had heard what Bessie was saying.

'I have an idea', she said in her cheerful voice which was so catching, 'that when people want anything badly, they get it, though they may have to wait for it.'

'Oh, do you think I shall ever travel—over the sea? I want to go to very old countries like Greece and Italy. Shall I—some day?'

'I feel sure you will. Why don't you practise doing travelly things? I'm told it's not easy to pack boots and fold skirts. I've not travelled myself—not to speak of.'

'You darling mother! Once to Kilkee and once to Blarney!'

'That's all! I'll lend you my wedding trunk, Bessie. You can take it to the spare room and practise packing.'

'The wedding trunk—oh, where is it?'

'In the store-room—it has a criss-cross of brass nails and it's lined with wallpaper. It's shabby and the leather is peeling because it's very old; it was Mammy Mac's mother's wedding trunk.'

'Thank you, mother.'

Bessie flew upstairs.

'It's so easy to dry Bessie's tears by changing her thoughts,' mother said as we went towards the dairy together. It was her gentle reproof for my love of teasing.

Tom Hickey was speaking to Ellie at the door. He stood against the background of mist through which there came the muffled voices of farm creatures and of old Turkey, calling to his fog-bound hens.

'Tom's readying to kill a goose,' Ellie said, turning to me, 'he says will the misthress be wantin' the blood? Will I go with a bowl, so?'

I nodded. We hated the poor goose to die a lingering death, but we did not forego goose-gravy hash, our favourite dish, on that account. I began to crumble bread in readiness while Bridgie chopped onions.

Ellie came in with her red cheeks fogged and her dark hair bright with mist-pearls. 'Please God the clouds will clear before night or the Holy Souls won't find the way home,' she said, crossing herself lightly with one hand while she balanced the brimming bowl on the other.

Bridgie sighed heavily. There was no home for her parents to return to on Hallowe'en; their cabin was now a cowshed.

'What'll happen them, Miss Sissy, with never a home to sit down in and never a child to pray for them, barrin' them in Americky, and meself?'

'They'll come here, perhaps, and take a look at you asleep.'

'They'd never be so bould . . . for all they worked for ould misthress Jug. Didn't she keep them alive in the hungry years and them but children?'

'They're sure to come, then. Mammy Jug will be looking round for them as she sits in the rocking chair.'

'I'll set a couple more creepies, so,' Bridgie said, 'would ye say me uncle, Dick Dooley, will be here with the rest or will he be back at his own house with all them Collopys?'

Before I could answer such a difficult enquiry Ellie broke in. 'Tom is after seeing Mr. Collopy. The both of them was at the live wake at Grange last night. Eight girls and boys from the one small place to be goin' to America at one time—'tis too much! There was more cryin' and prayin' than drinkin' . . . the young ones tryin' to laff, and full of big talk about the money they'd be sendin' home, but the most of them had tears washin' down their faces, God help them. To think of it! By mornin' every one of them was away on the first train for Queenstown. Tom and Mr. Collopy was lingering on at the wake overnight, waitin' for the risin' of the moon, and bein' late home Mr. Collopy slept it out this morning. When he opened his eyes, there was his four children standin' round the bed like ninepins, and never a sign of Mrs. Collopy.

' "Where's mammy?" says he wid a smile and a yawn, and sot up on his arm to see was she gettin' him a cup o' tea.

"Where's mammy?" says he once more and calls her by her name. "Mebbe she's milkin' the goat," says he.

' "She is not then, she has gone out," Maggie, the eldest little girl, told him. "Mammy kissed us and told us be good and look after Da and tell him she'll be home". . . . Maggie disremembered when it was her mammy said she'd be home—"*before long*, was it?" But the second eldest little girl said, "No then! 'twas *one o' these days*, mammy said."

' "What's that?" Mr. Collopy cries, "sure she'll be home to boil the praties for dinner?"

' "She will not then," says Paddy, the eldest, and anger was on his face for he loves his mammy. "She won't come home to a man that cuts her clothes into *mince*. 'Twas *mince* mammy said, right enough."

' "Och! wirra!" the poor man moaned, shakin' like a wet dog as he turned his face to Maggie, "tell me this! What had mammy on her for clothes and what had she on her head?"

'The little girls laffed and Maggie cried, "Mammy had a sart of a bunnet . . ."

' "No then, 'twas a hat."

' ". . . and a new dress, and a shawl Mrs. Dooley left after her . . ."

' "Mammy had them a-hide in the loft!" and they laffed again.

' "Me God above!" cried Mr. Collopy, and hitchin' up his trousers, he runs out of the door, cryin' her name, seekin' and seekin' . . .'

Just then father came in looking grave. 'I've sent Paddy to the station to find out if Mrs. Collopy was on the Queenstown train. It's as well to know one way or the other.'

Mother turned very pale. 'Oh, John,' she faltered, 'I should have foreseen this when she told me her trouble. She had threatened to leave Collopy, so he cut up her Sunday dress and her bonnet, thinking to keep her, for she'd never go away in her working clothes.'

'Don't cry, love,' father said kindly, 'you could not tell what was in the woman's mind.'

'I should have guessed when she told me of a present from America of twenty-five pounds.'

Paddy came back later in the day with the news. 'Deed and bedad, Mrs. Collopy have made off with herself by the emigrant train, with all the girls and boys from the country round. Heartening them she was, with her boastin' talk of Americky, and the fine things she done when she was there before she married Collopy! 'Twas Jimmy-the-Tickuts saw the last of her, leanin' out o' the windy, laffin' to herself, and sorra a tear for them she was forsakin' . . .'

Bessie was upstairs for a long time. Mother, Annie and I visited her in turn to inspect the trunk which had been packed and re-packed and labelled with a card neatly tacked on the lid.

*Mrs. Priam*
*passenger to*
*The Isles of Greece*

'Why Mrs. Priam?' I asked, laughing.

'I pretended at first that I was starting for Athens, but then the Isles of Greece came into my head—don't the words look lovely written? I shall never get there unless I marry a Greek so I chose a name to suit.'

I felt secretly envious. Bessie thinking of marrying and visiting Greece—which we knew well, from mother's *Ancient History*—while I should be making butter beside Lough Gur for the rest of my life! Thinking of butter reminded me of bog-butter and Peter, and I blushed in my turn, seeing, in my mind's eye, him and myself in wedding-clothes, driving away in a pre-historic cart. . . .

'But why Priam? He was a Trojan.'

Bessie answered in a small voice. 'I thought his christian name might be Orpheus. O. Priam was the nearest I could think of to O'Brien. That's why.'


At last she came down, looking secret and important.

'Sissy,' she whispered, 'before anyone comes I want to show you what I've found in the store-room. It's one of Miss Baily's old books—*The General History of Ireland* by Dermod O'Connor. It was printed in 1723 *in London, at The Bible in Jermyn St., St. James's.*'

'Pretty old,' I said, 'I expect it smells nice!'

'It does—like old corks! Well, it's full of wonderful stories about kings and lords and soldiers and musicians and pirates, and near the end is *our* pedigree, "*The royal line of the most Noble and warlike Family of the O'Bryens*"—you can read about them later. Now, look here, "*The lineall Pedigree of the Noble and PRINCELY Family of the Macnemarras.*" Farther on are pages of coats of arms and crests: of the O'Briens and of "*the ancient and noble family of the Macnemarras and of the honourable family of the Pursells*"—who came from England so long ago that they count as Irish; Mammy Jug was one of them. Both the O'Briens and the MacNamaras were descended from King Cas. Sissy, do you feel great?'

'Not particularly. Do you?'

'No, but I feel . . . responsible.'

'Well, you aren't. What for?'

'Their sins.'

'You can't be. Their sins are visited on us. I don't know what that means, do you?'

'I think it means if they didn't make amends, we must.'

'It does not! It means that if they ate sour grapes our teeth are set on edge. The Dean preached about it.'

'There's no sense in it.'

'Anyhow, mother says the O'Briens were *no good*.'

'It's a pity, for they began well—Brian Boru you remember. Mr. Madden told me that the long-ago O'Briens were crueller to one another than the English were to the Irish. They put out the eyes of all the chiefs they conquered even when they were their own brothers.'

'I always feel more of a MacNamara,' I said, 'they were a better lot. Mother told me people used to make promises "by God and His Angels and the MacNamara". They built churches and tombs so they must have been religious. Read this, "Sheda Cam MacNamara founded Quin Abbey in 1402."'

'You can't go by that. That often happens when people have been particularly wicked and have to save their souls at all costs. Anyhow the O'Briens and the MacNamaras were the two most powerful families in Thomond, now Clare. They began in glory before the time of St. Patrick! Aren't we *ancient*, Sis? Here's a funny thing! The O'Briens never stirred out without an O'Hickey[1] at hand because the O'Hickeys were hereditary doctors to the O'Briens, so father having Tom Hickey at hand is just as it should be.'

'And when father thought he had shingles Tom walked miles to get some blood from a very old Mr. Keogh[2] to rub on the spots, which were only harvester bumps after all. Don't you remember Tom said the old gentleman was very pale from so often giving his blood.

[1] Irish, o'h Icidhe, 'descendant of the healer.'

[2] The men of the Keoghs are said to have a healing power in their blood, given by Providence as a reward for the heroism of a Keogh who gave his life to save a hunted priest. The blood is not to be taken by a prick or a cut but has to ooze from a finger tightly compressed by a cord.

'That was heredity coming out in Tom. He never knew that father threw old Mr. Keogh's blood, bottle and all, in the fire as well as the blood from the comb of the black cock[1] which Peg Quirke "borrowed" from Madam O'Grady's chicken-woman.'

'Let's go on with the book, Bess.'

'There's only time to skip about it. I'll tell you in my own words. For thirteen hundred years the MacNamaras were rich and powerful; then they were brought low by that wretch Cromwell. The O'Briens were destroyed by their own chief, who sold himself to King Henry VIII and cunningly got hold of the clan's land. He and lots more O'Briens turned Protestant —they were the ones mother said were no good, and nineteen of your religious MacNamaras turned at the same time! They're surely all in hell. I wonder would it be any good if Uncle Richard said some Masses for them?'

'What's all that?' said a voice at the door and there was Uncle Richard walking in. He usually came home on Hallowe'en; we used to hear him and father talking about Mammy Jug.

'There'd be no harm at all,' he said when he had heard what Bessie had to tell him, but he didn't care to talk about the badness of his family, and when Bessie asked him whether women can be doctors, he said he hoped to God they could not, for they wouldn't be able for it. 'Why?' he asked, rather fiercely.

Bessie blushed. 'I would like to be an eye-doctor and give sight to lots of dark people, so as to make up for the eyes the bad O'Briens blinded.'

Uncle Richard patted her hand. 'God will use you, never fear,' he said kindly. 'Yes, child, we will pray for those old ruffians. They lived in cruel days.'

---

[1] A less efficacious cure for shingles is to rub the spots with blood from the comb of a cock.

Bessie and I looked at one another. Had father asked Uncle Richard to talk to us?

'That's what mother says about the English in Ireland,' I began timidly.

'There's such a thing as justice,' Uncle Richard began, 'and that's been owing to Ireland for a long time and mustn't be overlooked. Your dear mother thinks more of mercy and forgiveness than of justice. There's God's justice, and there's God's vengeance, which is very terrible. *Revenge is mine. I will repay*, saith the Lord.

We trembled in silence while Uncle Richard mused.

'What is it you want, little Bess?' he asked at last.

'Oh, so many things—for Ireland,' Bessie began. 'Father said you would talk to us *as a patriot*.'

'As well as a priest,' I added conscientiously and fearing the priest in him might be hurt.

'And what would you call a patriot?' he asked.

Bessie hesitated. 'A person who loves his country enough to fight and die for it.'

'Shall we say, one who desires his country's highest good?'

'That's rather—tame, Uncle Richard.'

'Must you have bloodshed? If it's vengeance you want you can't have it. I've just told you why.'

'Why can't we have our revenge?'

'Have you ever heard the proverb, "to forget a wrong is the best revenge"?'

'England deserves to be punished!'

'Think it over! If Angel Gabriel . . .'

'Oh, Uncle Richard! Patriots first!'

'This isn't a case for patriots, but have it your own way. Supposing young Mr. Tim Healy came to the door and shouted, "A tooth for a tooth! An eye for an eye! Because the O'Briens in the Middle Ages blinded their conquered foes, Father

Richard and Mr. John O'Brien must have their eyes whipped
out to-day!" What would you say to that?—you, Sissy?'

'I should say, "What good would that be to the dead, Mr.
Healy? Two wrongs don't make a right!"'

'And you, Bess?'

Bessie shook her head. She was crying.

'As a patriot,' Uncle Richard went on, 'I should say, "Let
bygones be bygones; let the dead bury their dead; have done
with the past. Let us get on and consider what is best, *and possible*, for to-day and to-morrow."'

Bessie wiped her eyes. 'I see I shall have to give up revenge
and punishment, but I want—I terribly want—Ireland to be
free and glorious once more!'

'Was she ever free and glorious except in story?' Uncle
Richard asked us. 'Wasn't she cut up like a puzzle-map into
hundreds of little bits, and quarrelled over by a number of petty
chiefs who called themselves kings! Can't you see King This, or
King That, the grand gentleman, cantering on a rough little
pony at the head of his army of bare-legged gossoons to fight
the king over the river, or the king on the other side of the hill,
or him beyond the bog . . .'

'Uncle Richard! I'm ashamed of you!' Bessie cried, scarlet
with anger, 'have you forgotten Brian Boru and Malachi and
. . . and . . . oh! think of the old songs!'

'There you are, my girl! That's where you go for the glory!
I know what you want—an Irish king and queen in Dublin
Castle. . . .'

'Oh yes! and any number of princes and princesses and poets
and minstrels and bands and officers in cocked-hats and fancy
swords. But I want most of all a happy country where no one
would have to pay rent or taxes and no one would be poor.'

'You'd have a parliament, of course, lords and commons, and
judges . . .'

'And grand juries,' Bessie went on, 'because father is always on the grand jury, and I'd have an army in green and silver armour, and a navy and ships . . .'

'Would you keep up the railways and the roads and the constabulary?' *

'Yes, yes, all that,' Bessie cried, 'and Punchestown and colleges and theatres—all free—and splendid churches in every village, and the horse-show.'

Uncle Richard looked at her flushed face and put his hand lightly on her head as if he was blessing her.

'Well, well,' he said, 'I wonder where we'll get the money for all these fine things?'

I felt sorry for poor Bessie. 'I hadn't thought, Uncle Richard,' she faltered. 'W—wouldn't England keep us up?'

Uncle Richard's lips twitched but he didn't laugh. 'She'll likely deny herself that pleasure!'

'Oh dear, oh dear!' Bessie wailed, 'is there no hope for Ireland?'

'Surely there's hope, my child, but not for a romantic Ireland of kings and queens, of glory and riches, of all play and no work, no rent and no taxes. Give up that idea; lay it away with your little sword, for there'll be none of that. Instead of your play-boys, I pray there may be raised up men of sound sense and sincerity, steadfast and patient, who will face facts and build on them a foundation for a responsible, reasonable Ireland who shall, please God, arise and take her rightful place among the nations. These men will seek no praise and no reward, they will work unseen and unheard. The blathering of the politicians will not disturb them, nor the shouting of worn-out slogans, nor the penny-whistle din of the corner-boys. They will bide their time—and it may be a long time—to daybreak.'

The little room was dark with falling night so that we had not noticed mother, sitting near the door, until she spoke.

'And you really believe that, Richard?

'I do, woman dear, I do. May God forgive my unbelief.'

Mother's quiet voice came through the darkness like an echo of Uncle Richard's words of hope. 'I too believe in an Ireland good and great.

> *For while the tired waves vainly breaking,*
> *Seem here no painful inch to gain,*
> *Far back, through creeks and inlets making,*
> *Comes silent, flooding in, the main.*
>
> *And not by eastern windows only,*
> *When daylight comes, comes in the light,*
> *In front the sun climbs slow, how slowly,*
> *But westward, look, the land is bright.*'

Bridgie brought in the lamp, apologising for having left us in the dark while she and Ellie were upstairs, tidying for snap-apple-e'en. Ellie followed her with tea for Uncle Richard, who looked old and tired in the sudden light.

'Tom Hickey', said Ellie, 'is after askin' would he put the saddle on the mare, and to tell his Reverence the night is clear and a grand moon risin'.'

This was a broad hint that it was time for Hallowe'en games to begin. Bessie ran to the storeroom for a bag of nuts as father came into the little room, in his Sunday coat; small drops of water shone like jewels in his beard and made him seem a stranger to me, and those around me became as people seen in a dream. From far away I heard father and mother persuading Uncle Richard to stay for the night. I heard him refuse because there was no way of letting his housekeeper know, and because his curate would be all night on the road seeking him or his dead body.

We trooped to the door where the fresh air brought me out of my dream. Father had to help Uncle Richard to mount. 'Are you all right, brother? Shall I drive you home on the car?' he asked, looking anxiously at him.

'All well, John! God bless you all.'

Away he went, a bent form on his gaunt grey mare, to ride to Knocklong by the light of the hunter's moon.

'Come inside, Tom,' Ellie called, 'sure what delay is on you this night?' Into the brightness and warmth of the kitchen came Tom and a wandering fiddler from the hayshed, followed by Murnane, and Dinny-bawn who slipped in like his own shadow. The farmboys were already on their knees beside the tub of bobbing apples and soon the games were in full swing but the laughter which accompanied them was subdued on account of the holy day, and the screams, as the elusive apples dipped away from the little snaps of the maids' mouths and from the attack of the boys' strong teeth.

'Come now, Miss Sissy, and see the nuts lep.' We followed Ellie to look at two nuts, set far apart on the hearth, which represented the Collopys. Ellie and Bridgie, on their knees, watched breathlessly.

'Will she come home? Will she lep to "Mr. Collopy?"'

'Will himself lep to meet her?'

'She's movin'!'

'She is not.'

'Himself is warmin'. . . . Och, God help us! If he haven't rolled into the ashes. . . . Holy Mother!' Both maids shrieked as 'Mrs. Collopy' leapt into the fire.

Father looked at the clock. 'Have you lads snapped the last of the apples?'

'We have not, sir,' the boys spluttered as they dipped their heads in the tub.

'A few more minutes, please sir,' from Ellie and Bridgie who were jealously watching 'Tom Hickey' lepping towards a coy, unnamed little nut, while 'Bridgie' lay unnoticed in the ashes and 'Ellie' followed 'Mrs. Collopy' into the fire.

Then father drew his chair and mother's into the middle of the kitchen, for this was the one night of the year when we did not say the Rosary; we children moved near to them and Dinny-bawn sat on the floor at father's feet; the servants drew out the forms and knelt against them with the fiddler and Murnane.

When the shuffling of feet quietened and the room was still, father read the Litany for the Dead. Very solemn and lonely it was. We made the responses in hushed voices as if we were listening for the rustling of home-faring souls.

Father prayed for his own dead and for mother's by name . . . 'my father, Michael, Thy servant, . . . Mammy Mac and Mammy Jug, Thy servants, Catherine and Joanna'; for 'the lord' and other departed friends. He did not forget Ellie's and Bridgie's parents, nor Murnane's wife. He prayed for 'Dick Dooley, my faithful friend and helper', and for Tom Hickey's father, and for those whom the wandering fiddler had loved and lost. Last of all we prayed for Dinny-bawn's Mary.

> *Eternal rest grant to them, O Lord,*
> *And may perpetual light shine upon them.*

## 26: UNCLE RICHARD IS CALLED AWAY

A few days after Hallowe'en Bessie came to me on the lawn where I was beating and pummelling feather pillows. She took the bat out of my hand. 'Sissy, I believe Uncle Richard's right. I've put up my sword as he told me and you'll never again hear the din of the penny-whistle from me. In future I'm one of the Sane, Silent Patriots. But I've got to see Uncle Richard; I must ask him if there's any secret about them before I try to get Mr. Madden and Mr. O'Herlihy to join us.'

'You mustn't, they aren't the sort!' I answered firmly. 'If they didn't make a noise no one would know if they were dead or alive, and they'd hate that. They're the ones who'll keep on blowing their whistles while the Sane, Silent Ones are thinking. Besides, if you begin talking you'll spoil everything!'

'I'd like to see Uncle Richard all the same,' Bessie persisted, so we asked leave to borrow old Paddy and Beauty and leaving the pillows to freshen on the lawn, we hurried to put on our second best frocks and hats. But before we could start, a telegram came to say Uncle Richard had been taken ill. Father and mother went at once to see him.

A few days later mother sent me to help Martha Clancy, his

205

housekeeper, who had her hands full with nursing him. 'I am glad you are going, child dear,' mother said, 'old priests are often very lonely.'

Uncle Richard had to be kept very quiet, yet the sick-room would have been invaded by well-wishers had not Martha Clancy guarded it well, with the help of Morissy, Uncle Richard's old coachman. It was my duty to answer the door, and oh! the number of times the house was shaken by the knocker! It seemed as if everyone in Knocklong came daily to enquire, to squeeze in, if they could, by the chink of the door through which I spoke, and to sit down in the parlour to have a good look round and to ask endless questions which mother had already warned me not to answer. Finding me as stupid as an owl they went away, repeating their names over and over, ordering me 'to be sure to tell his Reverence that they were on their knees praying for him'. As if, I thought wearily, there were not enough of us O'Briens to do that for him. When I said this to Father Michael, Father Richard's curate, he looked seriously at me, so I added, 'but I suppose the more the merrier,' when I truly meant the more the better. So he only laughed and said I was tired out by all these well-wishers and straightway he wrote a notice and pasted it on the front door. I thought it very tactful.

### PLEASE DO NOT KNOCK
Father O'Brien is better but
must not be disturbed.
His Reverence is grateful
for your remembrance of him.

After that we had some peace! The well-wishers had no excuse to knock and the beggars—those who could afford it— thoughtfully passed us by, while those whom hunger obliged to call, tiptoed to the back door and sat there, mumbling prayers, until I chanced to open it. Even then they asked anxiously after his Reverence and forebore to beg, nor did they boast of their prayers. I used to spread jam on their bread until Martha Clancy locked the store cupboard with mutters, and the back door with what sounded like a curse. She too must have been tired out.

When Uncle Richard felt a little better he liked to talk to me, chiefly about all of us and especially Bessie. It seemed to be on his mind that he had shattered her dreams by giving the sordid reason that their fulfilment would cost too much money.

'I'll tell you what's troubling me, Sissy, and you must tell Bess—you'd better write down my words; when you are older you'll understand them.'

'We understood quite well when you were talking to us as a patriot—the new sort. . . . We knew you would have talked next as a priest if Tom Hickey hadn't hurried you away because of snap-apple night!'

'That's true. I'd like you to write down a message. I might . . . I might be called away.'

When I came back with paper and pencil I thought Uncle Richard looked very ill. He spoke slowly, weighing every word.

'I would say to Bessie that the glory and grandeur she covets for our dear country, the ease and pampering she desires for those who to-day are honest working men and women, would kill the soul of the nation. If she had her way, who could bear to leave Ireland to go to Heaven? Who would quit her fine broad roads to take the narrow way of the Cross? Would not the Cross be forgotten and the words of Him Who died on it?

'Did you ever think, child,' he said, turning towards me and speaking with more life in his voice, 'that the place chosen for the Holy Nativity was a bit of a country barely a quarter the size of Ireland? It was under the heel of a foreign power and

our Lord grew up knowing the humiliation suffered by a conquered people, for He was one of themselves. He was no rebel;
He would not tolerate revenge, nor the use of force. He knew
that empires, kingdoms, republics, come and go: to-day they are
rich, glorious, honoured; to-morrow poverty and contempt
are their lot. *Such is the way of the world.* Our Lord was concerned with heavenly matters. He held out no hope to the
people of a future of grandeur and success; He promised them
no farms, no exemption from taxes. He told them the truth. As
long as the world lasts, He said, there will be tribulation; people
will often be weary and heavy laden—kings and governors,
parents and children, farmers, fishermen, priests—it doesn't
matter who they are—at times they will be tired and full of
care, lonely, forsaken, needing help. He promised to all who
come to Him strength and comfort . . .   His rest . . . His peace.'

Uncle Richard shut his eyes and seemed to sleep although he
was talking in a low voice. Perhaps he dreamt that he was saying Mass, for here and there I caught a word. *Emitte lucem
tuam . . . Deus, Deus meus . . . spero in Deo . . . salutare. . . .*

It is curious how heavenly and earthly things get mixed together in a presbytery. That evening Uncle Richard called me
to his bedside and said very solemnly, 'I want you to do an important errand for me to-morrow. Morissy will drive you to
the station to catch the early train to Tipperary. You'll take a
second class return ticket—here's the money—and you'll go to
Cousin James's house with this letter. He or his wife will go to
the bank and bring back a sealed packet in which will be money,
a lot of money.' I was proud and excited for I had never been
alone in a train.

The parcel was given me in a bag, with minute directions for
my behaviour on the homeward journey. I was to keep a good
hold of the handle, to keep my eyes fixed on the bag, at the

same time to give a cold stare should anyone speak to me, and if the bag was taken out of my hand, even with seeming kindness, as I got out of the train, I was to 'let out a screech that'd reach the ears of the constabulary that'd sure be pacing the platform.' Although the journey was uneventful, the sight of Morissy and the grey mare at the station was a glad relief to my mind.

Father was sitting beside Uncle Richard. They praised me for my competence and allowed me to count the four hundred sovereigns which made the counterpane glitter like a buttercup meadow. Father seemed down-hearted as he pushed the money into the bag.

'I'm glad, John, to see the last of that,' Uncle Richard said to him, 'you know my wishes. Take it back with you, God bless you.'

I was told I should go home with father, so I went to my room to get ready and there, to my surprise, was mother, quietly sitting in an armchair with her hands in her lap.

'I'm staying with Uncle Richard,' she said, 'he is not so well. He wants me to be with him . . . when. . . .'

'When he's called away,' I said, unconsciously quoting his own words.

## 27: BESSIE LEAVES HOME. MOTHER'S ILLNESS AND AN EXPENSIVE CABLE

'In an hour', mother reminded us, 'Janie will be at home for good'.

'Will she be changed?' little Annie asked. 'Sissy was.'

'I wasn't! I was improved.'

'You were a little different at first,' Bessie said hurriedly for she hated Annie and me to argue. 'You thought Ellie and Bridgie familiar in their talk, and you turned pale if you saw a gravy spot on the table-cloth, but that soon wore off.'

'Janie was a little changed last holidays,' Annie went on, 'her waist was squizzen and she washed her face in buttermilk.'

'You're changed, Baby,' Bessie said to her, laughing, 'once upon a time Mac and his friends used to call you "the lovely child". Now you're nowhere, Freckles.'

'I'm not freckled, only sunburnt.'

'Buttermilk takes away freckles,' I said provocatively.

'Only mother never changes,' Annie said, refusing to be drawn. We laid down our work to examine the beloved face.

'I'm thinner,' mother said, 'and I'm always cold.'

We put it down to the trouble she had had over Uncle Richard's funeral, for he was buried with what the newspaper called 'sincere tokens of respect'. Mother had to arrange with Coffey, the caterer, to provide luncheon for the great number of priests who went with him the short distance to his grave at Knocklong. They would willingly have followed him all the way to St. Patrick's Well if mother had had her wish and laid him in the grave with Mammy Jug. Mother went in spirit with Uncle Richard farther than the grave and it was hard for her *from that distance* to have to instruct Coffey about beef and ham and to remind father about ordering J.J. or whatever was drunk at funeral luncheons, and to think of black clothes for us all. It made her tired to have to keep turning back to earth when, in spirit, she was holding Uncle Richard's hand as he stood within Peter's Gate, in the wonderment of Paradise, as truly as she had held it in the valley of death. That, at least, is what I imagine happened, until at last he let go her hand and said, 'You must go home now, woman dear.'

I was still thinking about this when father came in followed by Janie, sweet as a rose with her brown hair and dark eyes, her swan-like neck and—yes—a laced-in waist—and her absurdly small feet in high-heeled boots which she must have bought on the way home, for no convent would allow them. We were so occupied with her appearance that we forgot to cheer, or give the Desmond cry. Perhaps we were chilled by the anxious way she looked at mother and asked her if she felt well.

Janie was glad to come home. 'I suppose I ought to have stayed and become a postulant,' she said. 'Reverend Mother was disappointed in me. I was her favourite—all my own fault for being so good! I was told off to sleep at the hotel, *for a treat*, to be company for her aunt who came to Montrath on a visit.

Oh, such a bald, cold, toothless old aunt—and in the same bed! Don't you be a favourite, Bess. It's a poor life.'

After tea Janie put on a pinafore and did the work which Bessie had taken over from her as a matter of course, so Bessie, her nose out of joint, took to following mother round the house or wandering by herself, book in hand, about the lawn. Often in the succeeding days she sat alone in the beech arbour, gazing at Lough Gur and the green hills that stand about it as if she were painting the lovely scene upon her memory in colours which would never fade. Janie and I took up our old friendship; Bessie withdrew from us and seemed once more to be out in the cold. The early morning readings came to an end; Janie slept on and I, between dozing and waking, saw little Bess in her narrow bed against the wall, reading to herself and learning heart-rending poems of farewell.

I saw her standing at the wicket gate on the lawn, looking through a sudden shower at a stormy sunset. 'Why do you waste your last day at home all alone? Come in Bess, your hair is wet, your hands are red with rain!'

'I'm not wasting it. I'm saying a little poetry that fits my last day at home.'

'Come in and we'll play *Consequences*. Can't you let poetry alone for a bit?'

'*Let it alone*—as if it was a wasp! That's so like you, Sis! You keep poetry in a cage like your old bullfinch and let it hop out now and then. I've got it in my inside—all over me—and it comes out and in like breathing. It's—it's comforting when I'm mis-mis-miserable.'

More tears! I did not know how to help her and I hated the rain to hiss on my head. 'Let's go to mother,' I said, gripping her wet hand. 'Couldn't you make use of *Lead, Kindly Light?* It's a help.'

Bessie laughed through her tears. 'You darling Sis! I will make use of it. I'm sure the nuns will quench my light and empty me as they did you?'

'Empty you of what?'

'My me-ness. Where's your lively old you-ness?'

'They taught me a lot all the same,' I answered thinking of my dear nuns with quick affection.

'They'll teach me too—French and geography and history ... Sis, I'm going to work like a fury ... I'm not going to school to smock, like Janie.'

'You'll do just what you're told.'

'You'll see. I shall keep my teachers teaching till they're like squeezed lemons! They càn't expel me for wanting to learn! "What! expel Miss Elizabeth O'Brien! our Show Pupil!"'

'Oh, Bess! *Pride rules your will!*'

Bessie laughed at my shocked face. 'Mine's the good sort of pride. No one shall uproot it. It's not the garish sort—what is garish?'

'Mother will know.'

So, with forced laughter and desperate weeping, Bessie left us, ignoring the group of dairymaids who had gathered to wish her well, barely noticing her sisters, but clinging to father like a frightened child, so that at last he had to lift her on the car, where mother, already perched on the further side, was looking sadly dejected in her velvet bonnet and otter-skin cape. In the open well of the car was Bessie's bag and a basket containing the usual offerings for Reverend Mother—butter and honeycomb and flowers.

Father blew his nose. 'God keep her,' he muttered, 'God keep my little fiery Bess.' Then he caught my tearful eye and led me aside. 'Sissy,' he whispered, 'I wish I had let you take Bessie to school. I don't like the look of your mother; I'll bring her with me to Limerick next week to see Doctor Gelston. You spare her all the work you can.'

He went slowly across the yard where the maids were still talking together until, seeing 'the masther' coming their way, they dispersed. Ellie and Bridgie wiped their eyes on their aprons and made for the hearth, 'parched for a cup o' tea.' Janie and I drifted to the outermost hayrick which mother called the Wailing Wall. Here we drooped and sniffed a little, but our tears were already dry.

Father returned from Limerick alone.

'Where's mother?' we asked in sudden fear.

'They're keeping her for three days. Please God the doctors will find nothing amiss . . . you girls must take all the work off her.'

'We'll do that, father,' we answered.

'Mother will maybe have to lie a-bed for a bit . . . Sissy, tell Ellie . . . get her to wash the blankets, and you make up some real good pillows. . . .'

Father had never before talked like this; clearly he was anxious and felt the need for action.

'I'll get Tom and a pail of limewash to do down the walls and ceiling,' he went on. 'Would there be anything to put in the water to colour it?'

'There's the blue-bag,' Janie suggested while Annie thought beetroot juice might make a good pink only we hadn't any, and Ellie offered to boil lichen for 'a sort of yaller'. By the time we had decided to send Peg Quirke to Mary-Ellen, the weaving-woman, for some flax-blue dye, father and Tom Hickey had turned the furniture on to the lawn and were busy with pails and brushes, having decided that 'the misthress' would like her room kept white.

'You two can go to Bruff to-morrow and get a basin and jug, pretty, with flowers on them, and something light to lay over her . . . would you say she'd need a shawl for her shoulders? I'd like her to have the best of everything.'

In three days mother came home, escorted by Mac who was to look after 'the case' for Doctor Gelston. Janie was to nurse her. I was to do the housekeeping, and with Ellie's help to carry on the dairy work. Little Annie, who was still going to school at Grange, would make herself useful when she came home.

Mother was apologetic and upset. It would take a little time, she said, to break herself in! She wasn't used to lying as useless as a felled tree. But she laughed at Mac's grave face. 'I *know*, my dear,' she said to him, 'I made Dr. Gelston tell me the truth. If the cyst dries up, I shall live; if it doesn't, I shall die—you see I'm not afraid of that word. Whatever way it is, welcome be the will of God.'

'You'll be obedient, won't you, Aunt Anne?' You won't put a foot on the ground?' Mac, who loved her, was very serious.

'I promise! Not even when old Turkey shouts *fox*.'

The days went by, but mother did not get better; she was restless and often sad.

'What is it she lacks, Sis?' Father asked me. 'You'd think she'd be happy with all of us round her!'

'Not all of us aren't!' little Annie said. 'Bessie's away for one, but mother wouldn't like her to miss her lessons. It's brother.'

Brother! No one had remembered him!

Father went to her at once. They talked for some time and when he came out he asked for pencil and paper to write a cable. Mother spoke from her room. 'Say, "*Mother ill come if convenient*" '—that was so like her consideration—' "*no need cable*". The poor boy mustn't have that expense.'

How sure she was that he would come.

Father and I went together to send the cable. As Beauty ambled along, I looked at his unhappy face. He was unusually silent; I knew he felt worried about bringing brother home when he had settled down to farming and seemed to be getting on. 'He'll have to sell out to pay the passage home,' father said, and from the sadness of his face I wondered if he feared that mother might not live to see Michael.

Mrs. Twomey, the post-mistress, was ironing an apron when we went in, and using the counter for a table. 'Come in then, Mr. O'Brien, and welcome! Will ye excuse me one minute to smooth me apern-strings? If 'tis stamps, ye can help y'rself from the packut in the drawer. There, that's done and all,' she exclaimed, flinging the iron into the weighing scales. 'A telegram is it? Wouldn't ye have a few stamps while ye're here? Sure, it never rains but it pours! 'Tis the third telegram I've had handed me this week and to-day but Tuesday. The way the y'ung Count do be throwin' his money about! "Come to lunch," says he by telegraph to O'Grady, with never a please or a thank. And the second was but three words longer for all 'twas goin' to London, and says I to the Count, "Sure, me lard, ye can have eighteen words to the shilling, and seein' 'tis to *Lord* Fermoy, wouldn't we give his lordship his due?" Ye'll scarce believe it— if the Count hadn't wrote *Fermoy*, as he might write O'Brien to a plain man like yourself, Mr. O'Brien, and sech a message he sent. . . .'

'I don't want to hear the Count's telegrams any more than I want mine to be passed round.'

"Tis no harm, at all . . . Och, me God! a cable is it? Would Herself be dead?'

Father snorted furiously.

"Tis not the worst then, thanks be to God. Sure, sir, I meant no offence! A cable, me God, and to Australia! If 'twas to

America I'd be more familiar with it. Sissy, ask y'r Da have patience or he'll have me moidhered and senseless. Will ye see for y'rself what's in the handbook . . . what's that? Two and seven a letter! Glory to Goodness, it's not that much! No cable'd be worth it. Ye'll send it at that price, sir? Sure, 'tis you are the warm man! Have ye the letters counted, Sissy? *Michael O'Brien* —couldn't ye make it *Mike*? Ye c'd not? *Cootamundra* . . . we c'd let drop one o' them o's? Och, have it y'r own way, I'll send it so with the two, but 'tis too long altogether! Have ye figured out the price, Sissy? Eleven pounds? Holy Virgin! 'Tis the way Queen Victoria have the blood sucked out of us! And be the powers, here's Father Daly advancin' on us! Eleven pounds! An' ye have the money *in y'r pockut*, Mr. O'Brien! To be carryin' the price of a young cow and her calf as aisy as a pennorth o' baccy! There isn't another in these parts, not the Count, not Lord Fermoy himself, that'd have such a fortun' rattlin' in the pockut of his trousers. Well now, here's his Reverence. Have ye the news, Father? Mr. O'Brien is after sending for Michael from Australia.'

## 28: MAC FINDS US SOME 'BEAUX'

Tom Hickey came through the yard under a great carriage-umbrella, rain pouring from every rib-point so that he looked like a moving waterfall. He had been to the post office at Grange to fetch the letters, which were not delivered in those days in country districts.

'Two letters and the masther's news,' he said, producing them from the front of his shirt, 'and dry as ould hay, thanks be to God.'

One was for father from Reverend Mother and the other from Bessie for me.

'Dear Sissy,' she wrote, '*the lemons are squeezed* and I am to go to France. Hurrah!'

Reverend Mother was unsparing of paper and ink and long words! Bessie, she informed father, was of quite exceptional ability; she had intelligence of a very high order, phenomenal industry, and a thirst for learning which astonished her teachers. . . . A vacancy had unexpectedly occurred for a pupil in the Ursuline convent at Gravelines, in France, where the education was of the highest order. If father would telegraph his consent and send a cheque for travelling expenses by return of post,

Bessie should be the chosen pupil. She would travel with a party of postulants in the care of two nuns leaving in three days time.

Father, looking worried, went to consult mother who straightway decided that Bessie must take this fine chance, even though there was no time to bid her farewell.

'Are you sure the child wishes to go?' father asked anxiously.

'Quite sure, father. Bessie says, "I am to go to France! *Hurrah!*"'

Father shook his head and went sadly away.

Mother asked for her *Universal Geography* to look up Grave-lines. '"A fortified sea-port in the department of Nord,"' she read aloud. 'The dear child won't be so far away.'

'Not this time,' I answered, thinking of O. Priam and the Isles of Greece as I bent over mother to look for Gravelines. She had already turned to the map of the world.

'Where do you think brother's ship is now?' she asked me. 'How near is he?'

How could I answer? We did not know how he was coming, by what route, nor when he had started, not even whether he was coming at all.

'Of course he is coming home,' she said valiantly, 'my heart tells me so . . . I have not the smallest doubt.'

Brother! it was always brother of whom she spoke and thought and for whom she was getting well. Mac, even, believed she was getting well and that she might be out of bed by the time Michael's ship would be in. 'Another few weeks of perfect rest. . . .'

In spite of jealousy I began to dream about Michael. He would be a tall, fair, handsome MacNamara, a fine rider, a good shot. He would help in the management of the farm and call father sir, and be a comfort to him in his old age. He would be brotherly and would sometimes loll with us on a hayrick, telling us stories of the wild bush; he would be a champion to defend us from Mac of whom we girls were all afraid, and indoors he would read with us in the little room and laugh at out patchwork and nurse Annie's lily-black kitten, and jump up to open the door when mother went out. Our lovely brother!

'When brother is at home,' Janie said, 'you and I will be in great request. . . .'

'He will love me best,' I told her, 'because he knew me long ago! You and the others weren't born.'

'That's not what I meant. We shall be made up to by all the girls we know and by their mothers, who will want to catch brother. Father will give him the Castle farm now that the Grogans have gone, and stock it for him . . . you'll see what a honey-pot this place will be.'

'Don't be so worldly! Marriages are made in heaven.'

'Not Irish marriages aren't,' Annie said, 'but *Bessie* won't let brother be caught. . . .'

Annie had come in from school in time to hear what Janie said. She was out of breath from running, and her face was wet with tears.

'It isn't true about Bessie, is it? Father will never let her go! Peg Quirke is a hell-bound liar, isn't she?'

Peg Quirke had given her the devastating news on the Grange road.

'We can't spare Bess,' Annie stormed, 'the best of us all. . . .'

'Och, the flower of the flock,' Bridgie wailed from the kitchen, loud enough for us to know that she was sharing our trouble.

'They'll force her to be a nun over there . . . and never a friend to save her. . . .' Annie flung herself into my arms and cried down my neck.

'Wirra, wirra,' the maids lamented, crying aloud every term of grief and endearment that they knew until the kitchen filled

up with sympathising dairywomen and farm-men who for
once ignored both Janie and me when we sternly ordered them
to be quiet. If mother's bell had not tinkled, we should have
been plunged into a *live wake* for Bessie as for any of their own
departing emigrants.

'Och, the misthress!' Ellie cried and instantly silence fell upon
them all.

'Is it a cable?' mother asked Janie, adding hurriedly, 'I knew
it wasn't.'

Annie spoke more truly than we realised at first when she
said Bessie could not be spared. Bessie had for a long time been
our backbone; she had kept Annie and me up to the mark, and
Janie too in the holidays, in order, punctuality and discipline.
It was not that she nagged us, but she was so alert and punctual
herself that we could not lag behind.

With Bessie in a foreign land—for who could say how long?
—Janie and I quickly grew mentally lazy. We left off learning
poetry, thinking we knew quite enough; our reading hours
suddenly seemed to be of less importance and were too often
shirked. It may have been that we were genuinely tired by our
strenuous work in house and dairy, by visiting the sick for
mother and continually looking after the callers at the door—
fiddlers, pipers, old people wanting letters read or written, besides the daily beggars. We had too to give time to entertaining
the aunts and cousins and neighbours who came to enquire after
mother and had to be asked to sit down and given tea. Even so,
at times we pretended that mother preferred to read to herself
and that having read perhaps a hundred-thousand hours with
us already, it was only right she should please herself now that
she was laid up. Annie, clear-sighted and downright, refused to
deceive herself, and often manoeuvred us to mother's bedside,
muttering under her breath, 'I told you so! She does want us!'

as she triumphantly produced a book from under her pinafore. Once there we enjoyed ourselves as of old.

In our room Janie and I read the innocent novels of Mrs. Hungerford, Helen Mathers and Rhoda Broughton. We talked as we worked of *beaux*, proposals and weddings. Sometimes we wondered how girls like ourselves, who were neither of the county nor of the peasantry, would find husbands or be found of them. We were 'getting on'; Janie was now eighteen, I was almost twenty, a horrible age. No matchmaker lifted presumptuous eyes in our direction unless Mac had secretly appointed himself the family love-broker. It is possible that mother had consulted him, for the number of visitors who came on Sunday to early dinner and to spend the rest of the day greatly increased. In the place of the old relations who had died off, came young men, friends of Mac who seemed proud to bring them to Drumlaigh.

One of the visitors, Dan Browne, interested me because he was the brother of my adored Mother Berchmans. He was going to be a lawyer and seemed to enjoy talking to me about law and about his sister who had died of the long-standing cough which she used to stifle and smother when teaching us *bonne tenue*. Consumption of the lungs, the doctor called it. My lovely, beloved *Mother* made *bona mors* surrounded by the community, while Dan awaited the end in the parlour below. He and I mingled our tears one bleak afternoon on the shore of Lough Gur while the rest of the party were inspecting the bull in his paddock hard by.

We always walked out in a pack and usually went to Ash Point on Knockadoon, to watch Mac's friend, Giant Daly, making ducks and drakes on the water. He was a young medical student who at twenty-one weighed twenty-one stones, and was famous for ducks and drakes and for many feats of strength such as taking a neat bite out of a thick plate or glass. Mac used to watch Janie and me while the giant performed his strange tricks, wondering whether we should fall in love with his bulk and strength. Being the only child of rich people young Daly was an eligible *beau*. Our acquaintance was cut short by his early death; giants, Mac told us, have a way of dying young. Neither Janie nor I would have cared to be a giant's widow with perhaps one or two very large children to bring up.

After the stone-throwing we used to climb Knockadoon to the Rock of the Eagle and there we sat down, Janie and Annie and I in a bunch together, the young men sprawling at our feet, while Mac played Irish melodies on his cornet which were echoed back from distant rocky hills. At these romantic moments all dislike of our cousin died down and for the sake of music we forgave him much unkindness.

At tea-time more young men arrived, mostly medical students who made themselves useful whatever was going on, perticularly one day when Mac pierced our ears, in the light of the great kitchen window, with a boiled darning-needle and a cork, and inserted gold 'sleepers', made from a nugget which mother's brother in Australia sent her years ago and which had been lying in the dovetailed chest until Mac went to college and wanted to wear a ring. Mother gave him the nugget to have a ring and our little sleeper earrings made from it. The medical students stood round with unnecessary basins, towels, jugs of hot water, old linen, scissors and sticking plaster; one or two wanted to hold our hands in case we felt faint or became violent from pain. Only little Annie yelled, being too young to know that in the presence of young men all girls should be heroic.

The medical students, to their credit, showed almost equal solicitude when they arrived one afternoon to find Mac calmly playing croquet, while a poor angler was rocking in agony at the gate with a fish-hook embedded in his nose.

'For shame, Mac,' they cried, as they bustled about for the

same paraphernalia as before and a chair in which they supported the fainting man while Mac cut out the hook and we hovered in the background, feeling sick.

After tea we had music in the little room. Janie played *The Maiden's Prayer* and I accompanied the songs, for an unaccompanied voice has always seemed to me a painfully naked thing and lonesome as the hollow calling of a bittern in a bog. Dan Browne generally sang, *I've a dear, dear love on a distant shore*, and *She is far from the land*; he was proud when mother had her door left open to listen and sent father to ask for *Oft in the stilly night*. Mac annoyed us by shouting *John Peel* and the *British Grenadiers* with Sassenach gusto and a Limerick brogue. His rather grand friend, James Lynch, of Trinity College, Dublin, recited *The Charge of the Light Brigade*, while our blood thrilled and curdled. On one occasion he intoned rather than sang, *Young Ben he was a nice young man, a carpenter by trade*, with a supercilious air, as if he thought carpenters were more in our line than Trinity men; I, equally supercilious, found the accompaniment too difficult and left him in mid-air, after which a medical student with a lovely tenor voice beguiled us with *Nymphs and Shepherds*.

At nine o'clock the company went away and we knelt in our places in the kitchen while mother said the Rosary through the open door.

## 29: ME-JOHN'S MOTHER

Ellie and I were skimming in the dairy with the door barred against the tempest which filled the air and ravaged the land. The dairywomen, unable to balance the pails on their heads, had carried them from the byres in their arms, the wind-whipped milk spilling over their necks and breasts as they staggered across the yard.

'Tom have the cows shut in the byres,' Ellie said, 'the wind'd sure blow the tails off them in the fields. Ye should have seen ould Paddy come cra'lin' up the hill, holdin' to the thistles that the masther said was to be cut only last week. 'Twas the will o' God Tom disremembered or ould Paddy would have been swept through the air into the lake. He's settin' now in the stall with old Beauty, pickin' the prickles out of his hand and rub-bin' in the misthress's goose-grease, what's left of it. Sech a year for rheumatics and sickness as never was! There's ould Biddy'll be an'inted before night if the priest can keep his legs to the ground to get there in time and there's Dinny-bawn. . . .'

'What about him?' I asked.

'He have the chin-cough like the rest of the childer only worse, for he've been out with the cough on him, takin'

225

Murnane's aged old ass round the country and helpin' to pass the sick childer three times under and over the donkey to cure them of the sickness.[1] Ye should see the mothers layin' their babies in Dinny-bawn's arms and him takin' them so careful and passin' them under the belly of the ass so's its hairs wouldn't fright them by ticklin' their little noses. The way he holds them tight to him when the chokin' fit comes over them, tellin' them, *Whist, now, 'tis all right*, and *not to be afear'd*. "Och, pray for them, Dinny alanna," the mothers whisper in his ear, for there isn't one person round Lough Gur but knows Dinny-bawn is God's darlin' Innocent, which is next thing to a saint. "I'll ask God," he says, smilin' up at them—when he isn't too tired altogether or smit with the cough that's on him this long while.'

Ellie stopped skimming to brush away a tear, and I left off too, remembering how Dinny-bawn had been coming, dragging tired legs, night after night at prayer-time to kneel beside father and whisper, 'Please, sir, the children, they're mostly very sick.' And mother from her room had called to me, 'Sissy, that child's cough sounds like whooping-cough; give him some carrigeen syrup.'

That was two days before and I hadn't seen Dinny-bawn since, nor done anything about it.

'Oh Ellie, what can I do?'

'Mebbe the wind'll go down a bit and ye c'ld go see after the little fella, and ye might call in at ould Biddy. Mebbe ye'll find her a corp!' Ellie crossed herself. '*The misthress* would have been to see the poor woman days ago and her dyin'....'

'What of, Ellie? She seemed quite well a week ago.'

'Maybe so!'

'And so happy with Me-John coming home to her!'

'Ah!' Ellie said darkly and went on skimming. I waited, for I knew her silence boded an outburst.

[1]An old Irish remedy for whooping-cough.

'Did ye hear Mr. Collopy have taken the childer to a new house on the Knocklong road? There's them that says 'tis to save Mrs. Collopy a mile's walkin' when she comes home.'

'Oh, Ellie, is she coming back then?'

'I d'know,' Ellie answered and relapsed into silence for a time.

'Mrs. Collins have gone into the Collopy's house that was Mrs. Dooley's.'

'Has she? I hope she'll mind the gate better than Maggie Collopy did.'

'Mrs. Collins have an eye for what's goin' on. 'Tis she went for the priest to ould Biddy, and none too soon, considerin' she knew what'd happened her.'

I went on skimming. Ellie emptied her pan of skimmed milk into the calves' bucket and rinsed the skimmer. While she was drying it with vigour on a cloth the storm broke.

'Wasn't it yourself, Miss Sissy, read the letter Me-John wrote his mother?' she asked fiercely.

'Yes, I read it to her. She shook so when she heard he was coming home on a visit, bringing his little boy to see her and the old place, that you gave her a chair, you remember. . . .'

'I did so, and put down the kettle to make her a cup of tea and she lookin' like she'd wither away in a blight, the crayther. Did ye hear the end of it, Miss Sissy, or was y'r head so full o' the nonsense them young Sunday fellas was after talkin'—and ye wid the ears bleedin' under the gold rings Mr. Mac sot in them —that ye had no heart and no hearin' for the throubles of ould Biddy. . . .'

Ellie paused for breath and went on more gently.

'Maybe 'tis the way you're cryin?[1] There's no need. Isn't it the will of God and Him helpless when the young ones gets too far from Him, as they are apt to do once they get to Americky.'

[1] Maybe you are crying?

'No, Ellie. . . .'

Ellie tossed her head and settled her hair, using the bright skimmer for a mirror.

'Anyway, you'd best know what Mrs. Collins saw and her a sharp, noticin' woman, when all's said. Biddy, says she, knowin' by the letter that her son'd be arrivin' early, was up at dawn— Mrs. Collins saw her from her bed above in the loft—and Biddy was out watchin' the road for the car, disrememberin' entirely to blow the fire and set down the kettle, or to set the comb to her hair or a lick o' water to her face. Ye may be sure she had not one thought for herself, but all for Me-John and the doty boy he'd have trottin' at his heels.

'Starin' and waitin' and longin' she was, and when at last the dust of horse and car riz from the road, the ould woman must needs sit down till her heart quit thumpin'. From where she sot, she saw the car drivin' back empty. Sure, she thinks, Me-John will be nearin' me be the field path—seein' the road comes no nearer than the stile. The path is steep and twisty, but Me-John will make light of it and come runnin' to his mammy. So she waits a bit and then she laughs. She thinks, of coorse, 'tis the doty boy that's holding Me-John back, and him with the short little legs. So she waits a bit longer and then she sot out to meet him, flutterin' this way and that like a partridge that pretends to be wounded, thinkin' only of her young ones. When Biddy got to the stile, with the kiss ready on her lips, was her son comin' runnin'? Not at all! On the far side of the road he'd come by, she saw him, down by the edge of the water, a fine stout man in a cloth overcoat and one o' them hard round black hats and shinin' black boots. He was pointin' with a grand umberella to the hills and the islands, showin' them off to the little fella, stout and smart like himself.

'Ould Biddy stood in the same place always, holdin' on to the stile, ragged and in her bare feet and her hair all of a wisp

and a tangle. She stood there for as long as it takes an ould
woman's heart to break. Mrs. Collins, watchin' from her door,
heard her cry, "*Me-John, och Me-John!*" as me grand gentleman
turned, rememberin' he had a mother.'

'When was this?' I asked Ellie.

"'Twas a ten days ago,' Ellie answered. 'Wasn't I tryin' to tell
Miss Janie the day the both of you was cuttin' up the misthress's
ould silk shawl out of the dovetailed chest, to hang round the
picturs. I d'know did the misthress give ye leave to cut up her
shawl that was big enough to cover the roof of this house and
fine enough to be drar'd through her wedding ring? Sure
'twas sinful!'

I blushed. Janie had brought back the idea and the 'proper-
ties' from Limerick one day, cheap plates and Japanese fans for
the walls, a painted tambourine, an artificial sunflower and a
lily for the two vases; the pictures were there and only needed
draping with wisps of silk. I thought the effect *new* and *striking*,
but rather silly. Janie was charmed with it, but father! How
angry he was! He made us take down all our aesthetic decorations and remove every tin tack in a given time. Annie looked
on; she had been against the scheme all through, but instead of
exulting she was gentle and kind and helped us to hide the re-
mains in her den under the table.

"'Twas the masther comin' in swearin'-mad' (which was untrue) 'that druv the words down my throat,' Ellie went on, 'or
ye would have known that when Mrs. Collins, pryin' and pok-
in', follered them to Biddy's cabin to see *was there anything she
could do for them*, there stood the three of them, and the child
askin' *through his nose* where would he sleep and where was the
stairs and would the old beggar-woman show him—savin'
your presence—to the—you know, Miss Sissy. The ould woman was starin' down at the ten pound note in her hand and
sayin' nothin' for it meant no more to her than a bit of paper;

her mouth was open and dribblin' and above her stood her son, 'shamed of her before the child and lookin' at her with his red angry face. Only the ould cat got up from the ashes and rubbed himself agin her legs, while the child began to cry and the hens pecked at the buttons on his boots.

'How wretched, Ellie! I suppose they didn't stay, Me-John and his boy?'

'They stayed a two-three *days*, certainly,' Ellie went on. 'The little fella played he was campin', and nothin' would please him but to ride on the sow and hunt the hens into the lake. He and his Da slept the *nights* at Bruff. Me-John thought to do his duty by his mother and there's a good bit to be said for him when ye remember the fashion that's goin' these days to hide y'r nat'ral feelin's under a ha-ha, bow-wow kind of an air. Me-John certainly gave his mother two-three days of his company— her that had given him his life and all of her love. Then he went off to London to show the little fella the sights, and by now he's on the sea, bound for America. 'Tis a quare thing, Miss Sissy, Mrs. Collins says Me-John was cryin' as he went down the path to where the car was waitin' below on the road, and the little fella suddenly turned back, fast as his short legs would take him, and give his grandmother a kiss, the first and the last, and was off like a bird! God bless him.'

'And what about Biddy?'

'Och, her, the poor good woman! When ye're older ye'll know that there's no mendin' a mother's heart once 'tis broke.'

The storm grew ever wilder and noisier. Not a dairywoman could get to the evening milking which had to be done at length by our maids and the farmboys and Tom, who intended to stay the night with the frightened horses and cows.

There was no question of my going to see old Biddy, but we prayed for her and for all the sick children after the Rosary. In our bedroom the noise was terrifying; the oak tree tapped and thumped on the window, wet leaves stuck and squeaked on the glass, acorns knocked with unearthly menace. At midnight the wind fell suddenly and the rain ceased. It was as if a healing hand had been laid upon the world. We were all asleep before the waning moon rose among tattered rags of cloud. About four, old Turkey gave a short surprised gobble which was answered by a donkey's voice, 'he-haw . . . he-haw.'

Mother opened her eyes and laughed. 'It must be Murnane's old ass sheltering among the ricks,' she said and went to sleep again for the storm had stolen her beauty sleep and she was tired.

Father listened, thinking he heard a faint knocking; slipping on his clothes, he opened the back door quietly, carefully. There under the wayfarer's porch was Murnane's ass and motionless on the doorsill lay Dinny-bawn.

Father lifted him up and carried him in.

Dinny-bawn opened his eyes and smiled for joy to find him-self where he strove to be.

'*Sir*,' he whispered, '*Father*.'


The donkey was still standing under the porch when Tom Hickey came to the door at dawn. Father was dozing in the rocking-chair before the hearth where white wood-ashes had gathered and hidden the glowing heart of fire beneath. Whiter than wood-ashes was the face of the child in his arms who also slept, but in a deeper, dreamless sleep.

## 30: BROTHER

'*Nymphs and shepherds come away . . .*' I trilled as I joined Janie
and Annie, who were having a moth hunt in the storeroom
where Bridgie was collecting bundles of fleece for Mary-Ellen
to spin, and Ellie was oiling and polishing the spinning-wheel.
In the long room where the maids slept, Mary-Ellen, newly
arrived, was making up one of the spare beds 'to suit me shape',
as she said, although—to my eyes—her shape was nothing out
of the common.

'The way you do be singin',' she called to me as I emerged at
the stair-head, 'I'd say 'tis thread for weddin' clothes ye'd have
me spin!'

Her long nose came round the door followed by her face.

'You'd say wrong then,' I replied in rapid demi-semi-quavers
so as not to interrupt my warbling. '*Nymphs and shepherds. . . .*'

'All right, all right, we're all here!' Annie sang, trying to
drown me. 'What's up?'

'A telegram. It has only just come, but Doctor Gubbins
heard it read out an hour ago to the market-goers at the post-
office door. He brought the news to mother, and Janie—she's
waiting to be dressed.'

'And she shall be dressed, the love, in all her best! Is it brother?'

'It is. He telegraphed from Dublin—*eighteen words to the shilling, faix,*' I said, imitating our unconfidential postmistress. '*Mrs. O'Brien, Drumlaigh* and so on, *arriving to-day.* That's all that matters to us, the rest is private to mother. Hurry, Janie.'

'What is the private?' Annie asked anxiously. 'Is brother married? Is she coming too? Am I an aunt?'

'The private was out of Shakespeare, lover's stuff—*I think,*' I said in a whisper.

'Holy Saints!' Ellie ejaculated, whirling the spinning-wheel till it buzzed angrily, 'will I go tell Tom kill a goose?'

'Will I make up the spare room, so?' Bridgie enquired, dropping her bales and hanks all over the floor while outside Mary-Ellen scurried to the spare room to replace a pillow she had just borrowed to suit her head.

'There's no time to lose,' I said, 'but you must keep your heads and not get moidhered. Ellie, there's roast lamb for our dinner—at four as usual. . . .'

'The crayther! fallin' from the rocks the way it did to break its neck,[1] and it neither a lamb nor a sheep.'

'With mint sauce it is lamb,' I said firmly. 'Make a good fire and have it on the spit in plenty of time.'

'I d'know how will I roast it with the key of the spit lost on me? 'Tis gone since last Friday when ye'd have me roast the hare . . . sure, isn't it the bad luck an' all to meddle with the like of them?'[2]

Annie got red. 'I know where it is. I threw it in the flour-bin to punish Ellie for scalding my lily-black cat.'

[1] Except when a sheep or lamb fell and had to be killed, we never had mutton.

[2] An old superstition.

'Well, find it for Ellie, darling,' I said soothingly, 'and then run to the eel-stream for a double-handful of mint. If Paddy's there and has an eel skinned, bring it up in a dock leaf to be jelled for brother's breakfast. Ellie, you. . . .'

The maids, however, had gone about their business. I could hear them in the kitchen, telling the great news to Peg Quirke who had been minding the fire in their absence and regulating the daily beggars. Old Kennedy's voice joined in. He had looked in to ask after mother; he had a mind to stay the night; he would be proud to play for Michael, God bless him . . . the *Fox-Trot*, to honour him and the y'ung girls. . . .

In our bedroom all was quiet, even the oak tree had stopped its tapping. I changed my cotton dress for a dark blue skirt and white *garibaldi*. With a blue ribbon round my waist—which Annie erroneously believed to be 'squizzen'—and my thick brown hair well brushed and shining, I felt myself trim and tidy enough to please the most fastidious of men, the sort of sister a long-lost, bush-ranging brother would inevitably like.

Mother was in an armchair in her room, very fragile and fair, in a blue shawl over her grey dress. In her hand she held the telegram but her eyes were on the road below her window.

'Sissy, I saw the car come to the gate and now it is lost under the hill; run out and see is brother on it.'

I ran out by the back-door and saw Beauty and Paddy coming in, but no one else! How could I tell her?

I went slowly indoors and opened her door. He had come running by the short cut, past the arbours, over the lawn, in at her window and was in her arms. I shut the door softly and came away. Father was walking up and down the yard outside. 'We must give them a few minutes,' he said, taking my arm and to my surprise he was shaking a little and his face was drawn and grey. Before I could speak brother came out and gripped father's hand.

'Is this Sissy?' he asked and pecked my cheek. 'Do the wild geese still fly across the moon?'

So he hadn't forgotten!

I liked the look of him. He was not very tall; his hair was brown and his eyes blue. He had a sad almost sullen expression and a rare smile which was like mother's. Tired and rather shabby, he looked, but his pockets bulged with books. He was clearly one of us and mother's child.

'Can I use your shower, father?' he asked, 'I'll carry the water-can up and Sissy can tip it through the grating! I came off the ship in a hurry. . .' he added, looking at his frayed shirtcuff.

'Never mind, brother,' I said, 'we are great stitchers here, and there are Christmas-present shirts and socks all ready,' but he wasn't listening, for Janie and Annïe, the lovely young creatures, stood shyly at the door waiting to greet him.

'I have a pretty bunch of sisters,' he said to father, as he pecked them in turn, 'now I have only Bessie to see. . . .' He seemed re-lieved to hear she was in France. After all it was mother he loved and for whom he had come home.

We were in the little room, waiting for Ellie to take the lamb off the spit, when brother came in and stood opposite father, holding a leather wallet; the table was between them.

'There's been a grudge in my heart against you, father, all these years,' brother said in his soft voice, 'because when I left you, you vowed I would never make good. I've had a hard time of it, but I *have* made good and though I had to sell my business at a loss—not that that matters—I've brought you what it fetched! It's yours, father. I'd be glad if you could take back those words. . . .'

Father looked up astonished and we could hardly believe our eyes when brother opened the wallet and poured a flood of sovereigns[1] on the table.

[1] £300.

'I worked my passage home so that you should have the lot. With mother ill I thought you might ... find it useful,' brother added after a pause in which no one spoke. Father kept his eyes lowered and at last brother laughed nervously and said, 'Are you so very rich, father?'

'How did you make it, son?' father asked at last, looking Michael in the eyes.

'I have a strong pair of hands,' he answered, 'and two or three good friends who—who believe in me. One of them let me some land. I kept a few sheep, but my business was horse-breeding. I sold two of the loveliest mares in Australia when I came away, and one I shot—lest she should fall into unkind hands. You see I loved her and she loved me.' He laughed again nervously and turned to me. 'She used to come walking into my shack at all hours and often woke me up in the morning by nuzzling my head ... she was my greatest friend ...'

'Miss Sissy, Miss Janie,' Ellie called, and we were glad to escape, taking Annie with us and leaving father alone with Michael to take back those bitter words.

Alone did I say? but not for long, for mother, who had not walked for months, came into the little room and kissing father and Michael, took an arm of each to walk to her old place. Father and Michael were beaming, and so were we all; so were the maids and the little crowd in the yard of farm-men, dairy-women and neighbours from round Lough Gur. Michael rushed from one to another shaking hands; he looked years younger now that the grudge had gone from his heart.

'Can you bear a noise, mother?' he asked her.

She nodded and we children hastened to the door to join in the old familiar cry!

*Sean-ait-aboo*, and once more, *Sean-ait-aboo*.

Tom Hickey sidled through the crowd to father. 'I have the barr'ls handy in the barn, sir,' he whispered, 'will I give out the drink?'

Father nodded. In a moment glasses, cups, mugs were whipped from pockets where they had been concealed, and enthusiastic cheering encouraged Tom as he broached the casks of Murphy's stout.

In the midst of the cheering Ellie twitched my sleeve. 'The sheep,' she announced, trying to look unconcerned, 'I have it dished and sot on the table.'

'The *lamb*, Ellie.'

''Tis not, then. May God forgive me for mis-usin' me teapot! Mary-Ellen, God help her, have the mint sauce drunk to the last leaf.'

'But what did she think it was?'

'The quarest tea ever she swallered! "A bit musty in the mouth but warmin' and nourishin' to the inside." '

## 31: BESSIE GOES TO POLAND

Brother's return to live at Drumlaigh unsettled everyone except mother, who grew young in looks and tranquil of heart. Very soon, she declared, she would be well enough to take up her work, but the days passed and still she stayed in her room, knitting or sewing while brother read to her, usually from the book he called his bible—his Shakespeare. Janie declared they were reading the plays all through and learning the sonnets by heart. Time was kinder to them than to us who had to work harder than ever as the cows gave more and more milk and orders flowed in for Drumlaigh butter and cream cheese. We left off dropping into mother's rooms with scraps of news and hesitated at the closed door which used to stand open all day, for fear of disturbing the Shakespeare readings even to ask what should be done for a beggar who seemed to be having a fit in the yard, or to tell mother that Mrs. Collopy had come home, or that Meggy-the-Eels was sitting at the kitchen fire clad in a blanket and a cloud of steam while her clothes dried, she having fallen in the weir-stream. Though she hinted that *the misthress* would give her a sup o' somethin' warmin' if she could be told what had happened her, I would not break in on

> *Here will we sit, and let the sounds of music*
> *Creep in our ears. . . .*

or shatter their *soft stillness* with a demand for J.J.

In this way our happy reckless intimacy with mother ceased. We no longer felt of first importance; we grew jealous and restive and the more so when we saw father looking lonely and tired. When one day we overheard the men talking among themselves of the misthress's *páistín fionn*[1], we decided that something must be done about it.

Janie undertook to speak to brother because he liked her best and because her tongue was smoother than mine. Michael laughed when she invited him to sit with her on the Wailing Wall—the outermost hayrick—but when he heard what she had to say he was serious and sad.

'You're quite right, Janie,' he said, 'you see I've been thinking only of mother and of making her happy. I'm very sorry. I'll go at once and ask father to let me help him.'

Father was getting up on the car to drive to Knockaney. We saw him sitting patiently with the reins in his hand while Beauty bent her head round to see who was delaying her. Michael was talking and explaining when Con-the-ploughman limped up to say there were two young beasts on the Carrigeen hill that looked sick. Tom Hickey being away, would he and the herd-boy (who was a full grown man) medicine them? Evidently brother offered his help for the last we saw was the three of them making for the hill and father driving down the road.

[1] Pronounced pawshteen fūne, literally, little fair-haired child, the 'mammy's pet' who can do no wrong in her eyes.

Janie and I were giving the afternoon to 'compunctious visiting'. Annie was left at home to wait upon mother who was restless and wondering why brother had not come in.

We got back at cow-time; the yard was full of milkers talking excitedly together, while from the byres came the lowing of uneasy cows.

Annie flew out at Janie as we went to mother's room, and scolded her for having interfered in what was not her business and for making mother cry. Rather than argue we retired to the kitchen where Ellie was cooking a belated dinner, leaving Bridgie to 'wet the tea' so that we should be strengthened to hear bad news. Michael, we gathered, had killed two of father's best bullocks, worth fifty pounds if a penny. We discounted the value and waited to hear more.

"Twas the slowness of Con's lame leg that angered the y'ung masther,' Ellie said, 'and himself always quick as a hooked salmon. "Come on, come on," says he, when they cot up with him, and them with the breath gone out of the body with the haste he put on them. "There's no need to be all night about such a simple thing!"'

"Twas but three o'clock in the afternoon,' Bridgie interrupted. She was inclined to be too literal.

'"Give me a holt of the thing and I'll show you," says the y'ung masther, and show them he did, for while Con cried to him to go aisy for the love of God and to bend the head a bit sideways—or upways it might have been—and the herd-boy all the time tryin' to get a holt of the crayther and to jerk Mr. Michael's arm up so's he'd do no harm, sure the mischief was done and down went the bull'ck, dead as a stone.'

Ellie stopped to glare all round her and Bridgie inappropriately crossed herself.

'Wouldn't ye think that would have taught Mr. Michael

a lesson? Sorra a bit! "Better luck next time," says he, growin' red with shame before the men, and quick as a thunderflash he'd got the *machinery* into the crayther and poured in the stuff—and down the second bull'ck dropped, ayqually dead.'

Janie and I looked at one another. The catastrophe was due to our meddling! If Janie hadn't spoken to brother he would have been peacefully reading; Con would have dosed the bullocks, father would not have lost their value.

'Oh, poor Michael!' we cried together.

'Poor beasts,' Ellie put in with anger in her voice.

'Poor mother!' Annie cried from the door. 'She's going to faint, I shouldn't wonder, and all because I said I should drown myself if I were brother.' ·

'Where is he?'

Ellie answered sourly, 'Chasin' after the masther to ax his pardon—and safe to get it too.'

A pale unhappy Michael flung into the little room an hour later where we were sitting with mother reading *Alice in Wonderland* once more, and hoping to distract our minds. No one laughed; we should have preferred to recite *Out of the depths* or any other penitential psalm, so unhappy did we feel. Being a farmer's daughters we could not fail to mourn the tragedy as well as Michael's misery.

'Did you see father?' mother asked.

Michael nodded.

'What did he say?'

'Nothing. Not a word.'

If we had not been there brother might have given way and mother would have comforted him and stroked his hair. As we were there, we all sat and stared at the table for ages.

'Do you know why he went to Bruree?' brother asked at last in a miserable voice. 'He went to see Jack Gubbins about a hunter for me. It—it makes no difference . . . the mare will be here in the morning all the same. Oh! damn it all.'

He rushed away and we went on staring at the table.


Father came in with a letter in his hand and called to us all to discuss the contents as we dined. Michael had not come down so father went to the foot of the stairs and called him. 'Come on down, son. I want your advice.'

'Reverend Mother again, I suppose,' Annie said with a loud sigh which made us all laugh and feel comfortable.

Father nodded. 'It's from Montrath. Reverend Mother there has had a letter from Reverend Mother in France, to say. . . .'

'The lemons are squeezed again,' I said irreverently and we laughed once more.

Father looked at me over his spectacles.

'Right as usual! Bessie's education is complete and she is to. . . .'

'No, no, father,' Annie cried, turning pale, 'not that . . . not to be a nun!'

'Who said nun? Be quiet, Annie, *at once*,' for our youngest was inclining towards hysterics. 'Bessie has the chance of a good position as a governess with a Madame Swinarski in Poland. Where exactly is Poland?'

We all spoke at once. Michael went for the atlas and mother found the place with trembling hands. In the hubbub no one heard me say that Poland is on the way to the Isles of Greece.

'Has she gone?' mother asked anxiously.

'Certainly not,' father answered her, 'nothing can be settled without my consent. You speak first, love—or last, if you would rather. You next, son.' We young ones were all for the

adventure and after much talk and private conversation between the parents and after they had slept on it and I know
prayed about it, it was decided that Bessie should go, if escorted,
if the Polish employer's references were of the highest quality,
in short, if our Bessie would be safe.[1]

[1]See Appendix for Bessie's letter describing her new life and surroundings.

## 32: MOTHER RETURNS TO THE WORLD

'Those bullocks haven't died in vain,' Annie said as we were dressing the next morning. 'Brother was out at five with father and I think I hear mother getting herself up. She certainly is,' Annie added after listening to sounds from the room below.

'Never!' Janie exclaimed and dashed down to see what her patient was about.

'Low-spirited but determined to re-enter the world!' she reported. 'Dressed and demanding her thick dairy-boots! What is to be done?'

'They're covered with green mould!' Annie assured us. 'I'll run and tell her 'tis the will of God that she waits till they are dried and blacked. I'll persuade her to wait an hour or two and then sit in the sun and regulate the beggars, or just sit and give audiences like Queen Victoria.' Little sister ran off. She had imagination and a way with her which amused mother and made her manageable.

A capital plan it proved! The misthress was enthroned in her big chair in the yard, wrapped in her woollen Paisley shawl and a rug, when Mrs. Collopy called to report her return, to tell her adventures and recount the hundreds of dollars she had earned. She complained, too, of the strange attitude of her family who, instead of welcoming her with open arms, assured her that they had got on very well without her. Only *himself* was glad to see her; he seemed a bit downtrodden and in need of protection from Maggie, grown a bold girl, and his son, 'a big, threatening sort of a fellow ... who was once a clinging little mammy's boy.'

A look of understanding passed between the two mothers.

Peggy-the-Caps was the next visitor. She was bent double with rheumatism, too feeble and old to carry a load of bread any more, but the devil, she well knew, still took a lift on her back and him heavy with sin, and drivin' pins into her joints as she came up the hill. 'All the same,' she chuckled, 'me gentleman'll get a surprise one o' these days, for by the way he has me back doublin' over with his weight, 'twill not be long before he'll go shootin' over me head and I'll be done with him, thank God.'

While Peggy was drinking tea with one or two cronies at the wayfarer's table, her place was taken by a thin, young-old woman, dressed in a neat darned grey dress and a black crêpe bonnet. For a moment mother did not recognise her, but I knew her to be our little Moll of Grange School days.

'I've come to tell you, ma'am, that my husband is dead.'

Poor little Moll had been married at sixteen to a foxy, undersized stranger from Limerick who had paid a matchmaker ten shillings to find him a healthy, young, country bride. Her parents were poor and obstinate. ''Tis the will of God,' they told her, as she stood shrinking at the door of the chapel, misliking the look of the half-sober husband who took her away on a car, already loaded with his drunken friends, to live in a cabin in one of Limerick's worst slums. Now *himself* was dead —ill one day and gone the next, the way drunkards are apt to go. I wondered what her feelings were when she closed his eyes, weighting them with two small stones because she had not two pence in the world.

Little Moll was only twenty-four, but she looked forty. Mother comforted and helped her and promised to send clothes for herself and four little foxy children whom she had left below at her mother's. When Moll had gone to the kitchen for her dinner, mother turned to me.

'Never again, Sissy, never again, will I read poetry before six o'clock in the evening.'

Father persuaded mother to go to the lawn, promising her a surprise. In our family we all loved surprises except Bessie who had a morbid fear of anything unexpected. At the front door stood Jack Gubbins beside his horse, deep in conversation with brother, while proud Paddy walked a lovely mare up and down. She was father's present for Michael. Mother's MacNamara blood made her cheeks flush and her eyes brighten as Kangaroo was led up for her inspection.

'I've talked things over with Michael,' father said as they strolled towards the bee-hives. 'He'll never make a farmer; horses are all he cares about. He could have the Castle farm to-morrow, but it's not suitable for horse breeding and not safe.'

Father looked depressed. 'I'm hoping Jack Gubbins will put something in his way,' he added.

That is what happened. From that time until three years later, when he married and went back to Australia, Michael was more often away than at home, handling and breaking young horses, finding hunters, brood-mares and likely foals for hunting men, farmers and dealers, who recognised his good judgment and skill. He might have become a rich man but for his scrupulous honesty, a quality which caused some to call him a fool and others, like father and mother, to thank God.

## 33: A BOLT FROM THE BLUE

Father's hair was beginning to whiten; he stooped a little as he walked; many things which he once would do himself, he now left to Tom Hickey. A sequence of fine seasons had prospered the farm; barns and byres were full, and judging by the way the bank manager *respected* father, we girls imagined there must be a good balance at the bank. With his workpeople contented and comfortable in their homes, and brother well-occupied, above all with mother grown strong once more, father declared himself a happy man without a care in the world.

It was then that there came a bolt from the blue. Bessie wrote to say she was engaged to be married to Lubomir Christitch, a Serbian, captain in a Russian cavalry regiment stationed at Posen. He was a frequent visitor and friend of the Swinarskis; of the Orthodox Church, therefore almost a Catholic and the wedding would take place in the Catholic church at Posen. Bessie was practical, but also romantic; the rest of her letter dwelt on Lubomir's perfection and their great love for one another and ended by a request for father's consent and blessing '*as soon as convenient*, as mother would say.'

Two letters were enclosed, one from Captain Christitch in French, with a translation in his own writing. 'I will not say I am worthy of your daughter for that would be impossible, nor will I say that I am altogether unworthy, for then you would not give her to me,' which we thought a clever way of propitiating father. The second was from Madame Swinarski in French.

'Read it,' father said, looking quizzically at Janie and me, 'and tell me what it means.'

Oh me! Oh Mère Philomène! My French was not equal to Madame Swinarski's flowery periods. Nor was Janie's. With shame, and remembering how much our education had cost father, we handed the letter back to him. He put it in his pocket, saying nothing, and sent Bridgie to order the car.

'Countess de Salis will read it for me. She will know the right thing to do; I shall go by what she says.'

Countess de Salis was interested and kind, and the Count, our young landlord, seemed to know a great deal about Poles and Serbs. Madame Swinarski's letter, he said, translating it, was full of enthusiasm. She and her husband would have been proud to give young Christitch their own daughter. She trusted the parents of darling Bessie would give their consent and that they would allow her to arrange everything connected with the marriage as she would for her own child. Nothing could be more satisfactory, but Countess de Salis advised father not to answer these letters until she herself had made a few private enquiries from friends in the diplomatic service.

Father was glad of the reprieve. Even when the Count brought him good reports of the character and prospects of Lubomir Christitch, who was the son of a distinguished statesman at Belgrade, father and mother still hesitated. In the end they gave their consent.

Bessie was married in the Catholic church at Posen surrounded by her Polish friends, and later set off on a three months
honeymoon with her *beau garçon*—as Madame Swinarski called
Lubomir.

'We are coming home, soon,' Bessie wrote from Paris. 'This
is a most exciting town. When I have learnt it by heart we shall
start for Ireland. No lingering in London, you may be sure!'

Janie and I made new curtains for the spare room, but nothing else was touched because Bessie had a morbid dislike of
changes and surprises. We were wearing our usual dresses, too,
when at last she arrived, running over the lawn hand in hand
with her tall husband, to throw herself into father's arms.

Lubomir fitted into Drumlaigh as if he had always belonged
to us. He shouted *sean-ait-aboo* with the rest, shook every hand
that was stretched out to him, helped Tom to broach a cask and
filled glasses to overflowing. Then he went back to the door and
stood with Bessie, very splendid in the uniform he always
wore—white jacket and silver buttons—to acknowledge the
cheering.

Every fine morning he and Bessie sat in the beech arbour
learning Serbian and English very diligently. They talked to
one another in French. Later in the day they rode about the
hills; brother lent Lubomir his lovely Kangaroo and Bessie rode
a brood mare which refused to move unless her foal went too.

Father was delighted with the new son who accompanied
him to market and fair, making friends wherever he went, and
when word went round that the bullet dangling from his
watchchain had been shot into his chest in a real battle, so that
he became an object of great interest, father liked him more
than ever for his good-natured patience. People walked miles

to see the bullet; beggars called out of turn for fear of missing the chance of stroking so lucky a charm. Always 'Miss Bessie's furrin' capt'n' exhibited it with untiring friendliness.

Bessie sometimes delivered him from his admirers, calling, '*Łubo, Lubo.*'

'Goo'bye, God bless . . .' he said, disentangling himself quickly. '*Beshka, Beshka,* I come.'

## 34: MY ROMANCE BEGINS IN A GREAT FROST

No wonder that father's hair turned grey when his children shot like meteors about the world—Australia, France, Poland, Serbia—now Janie, who had never even seen a ship, was starting for Belgrade by herself under the surveillance of a man named Thomas Cook, of whose character father knew nothing and was in consequence highly suspicious.

Bessie had appealed for a sister to be sent out to Belgrade, where she was living with Lubomir's parents while Lubo, now in the Serbian army, had gone to the front in the Serbo-Bulgarian War. Bessie must be near at hand in case of his being wounded. The anxiety was hard to bear, and it was lonely being the only Catholic in an orthodox family. The family insisted on her first child being born under their roof. Everyone was very kind, especially Lubo's father who was now prime-minister—a very enlightened and progressive statesman, with whom she had long and interesting talks. Janie would like him and his daughters. It would be best to have her as she knew something of nursing from having taken care of mother, and would probably travel better than Sissy.

Father saw how my face fell and spoke kindly.

'Your mother can't spare you,' he said, 'she could never get through the day's work without her right hand.'

Dreary discontent crept over me. Must I for ever oversee the maids, regulate the wayfarers, visit the sick, make butter? Could this be called *living*? I asked myself if I should ever marry and if not, why—a question I dared not ask mother, for to speak of one's own marriage or husband was considered indelicate and the subject tacitly avoided by us both. To myself I said, 'Will they ever let go of me? If a John Ridd or a David Copperfield asks to marry me, or a teasing young antiquary, will they let their *right hand* leave them?' Janie thought they would if the suitor had land, that safe investment, but—do antiquaries trouble about owning land when they can have the run of other peoples' bogs and hills?'

Antiquaries, singly or in societies, were often to be seen on the bog where father cut turf over which I had long kept secret watch. This was once the lesser Lough Gur, and was partially drained by Mr. Baily long ago. The antiquaries seldom went empty away, for the stone and bronze people who once lived in crannogs[1] like Garret Island in the big lake, seem to have been famous for losing weapons and tools, even combs and gold ornaments. The pair of antiquaries for whom I watched never came. Mr. Tilecote couldn't come any more because he was dead; Father Ryan showed me newspaper praises of him. I left off watching. Peter may have died too, although for me he was alive in a niche of my memory. I had kept him there for years, treasured and unfaded. I compared other young men with his image; however polite and lively they seemed when Mac brought them to see us, directly I stood their images below Peter in his niche I knew they were skimble-skamble stuff.

*All but one.*

This was Richard Fogarty who in height and slenderness was

[1] Lake-dwellings.

not unlike Peter. Like him he had a low laugh and a pleasant voice. If he had not Peter's gaiety, imagination and acquaintance with fairies and long-nosed pigs, he was not so prone to tease, nor would he ever dream of ordering me to eat swallow-meat or to fall into a squinting trance. Unlike Peter he was cautious, and had the true Irish contempt for haste; whether these are good or bad qualities I cannot say. At the time I agreed with Bessie that

> *Blessed is the wooing*
> *That is not long a-doing.*

I was not in love with Richard, but I was interested in him, and as time passed by I began to resent his taking three years to make up his mind. Our romance, such as it was, began in the winter of 1879-80, when I was almost twenty-two and Richard one year older. Lough Gur was frozen from end to end for three weeks. Such a thing had not happened within the memory of the most ancient dwellers on its shore; the strange event set them remembering tales of previous frosts told by their own ancient folk.

' 'Twould be Fer Fi, the red-haired dwarf, at his tricks again,' they agreed. Fer Fi, we knew, was brother of Ainë, the Woman of Wailing, lover of poets and learned men. the Banshee who comforts their last hours with *Ceolsidhe*,[1] the playing of harps, wood wind and muffled drums.

Fer Fi played *Suantraighe*[2] on his three-stringed harp till the deep springs froze and stood like tall trees of stone to hold up the icy surface of the lake.

It is lucky to hear Fer Fi's music, luckier still to hear him laugh as he looks to where dark waters have been and sees a field of whiteness shining under the small sun of winter. Gran'da Spillane heard Fer Fi laff to split his sides when he saw Mr. O'Brien

[1]Fairy-music.     [2]Sleep-music.

and Tom Hickey thumpin' and batterin' on the ice with cud-
gels, to see will it be safe for the three y'ung girls, with Mr.
Michael and Doctor MacNamara (Mac) holdin' them be the
ribs while their legs go shootin' from under them. . . . The
gran'das double up with merriment and trot recklessly on the
very edge of the ice where frozen rushes and cresses make the
going safe for old legs.

When Fer Fi is happy he plays *Gentraighe*,[1] his second tune—
he only knows three—and draws people to Lough Gur from
far and near. 'County, country and town' met and swooped
about together in the friendliest way. One would have said the
millennium had come, for lion skated with lamb, ox and ass ate
sandwiches together. Landlords and fenians played hockey in
love and fellowship and in their lightheartedness one and all behaved as if Lough Gur was their own, instead of belonging to
Ainë and Fer Fi and Count de Salis and the old gran'das—and
the young O'Briens. *Sean-ait-aboo!*

Among the throng were Alfie and the medical students, some
now blossoming into doctors, who were most obliging in prop-
ping us up and propelling us until we had learnt to keep our
balance and to control our wayward feet. It was after Janie had
set off at the head of a train of admirers, and Annie had skilfully
extricated brother from the flock of girls whose minds were set
on marrying *Drumlaigh*, that Richard Fogarty took my hand
with shy friendliness and skated with me to watch Jack Gubbins,
graceful in spite of his girth, cutting beautiful figures where the
ice was smoothest, or to see little Lady Fermoy flitting like a
swallow about the lake, or to cheer the Dean's coachman as he
rode his master's mare from side to side, or to visit old Paddy
at the far deserted lake-end, where baffled wild fowl stood about

[1]Laughter-music.

in an unhappy huddle, taking little notice of the old man who was keeping open the holes which father had had made to give them water. Or we skated slowly alongside the bull's meadow —Richard, as a farmer, being interested in cattle—and saw his great head nodding over the half-door of his shed. Father had had him shut in so that he should not take a run among the company on the ice.

Later Richard helped me to give out the good things which mother sent down for us and our friends, coffee and tea in boilers which perched on perforated buckets of fire, baskets of bread and butter, sandwiches, cake and apples, which were in great request.

Richard was not exactly a stranger to us. Father, who had known his father and uncles well, often met him at fairs. His sisters had been at the convent with me; sometimes they took me to tea with his mother at their farm.

'Do you remember,' I asked him, 'how you used to bolt when I arrived? I saw nothing of you but your coat tails!'

Richard blushed. 'I remember walking back with you and my sisters to the convent door. You were the only girl I'd ever seen who wasn't frightening.'

'Oh! Am I frightening now?'

'You are not, thank God,' he answered fervently. 'I think you're nice . . . I like your face. I'd like to write to you if I may?'

We had been writing for nearly three years, unromantic, matter-of-fact letters; occasionally and by chance we met and found that we still liked one another; we talked about everyday things, parted and wrote some more unromantic letters. Richard came to the dance which father and mother gave for us in the unoccupied Castle farm, where the Grogans once lived. The stars shone, romantic Japanese lanterns hung from trees in the garden and up the drive, yet the charming scene failed to make him sentimental, nor did the wax-candles which lighted the room in which we danced enhance my looks in his eyes to a distracting point. He watched me dance with other men without jealousy, and remained calm when other youths shouted with enthusiasm over the fine violin playing of old Mr. Regan and Thady, his fiddler son, accompanied by a grandson who 'worked' the triangle with delirious zeal when grandfather nodded, and another who thumped bravely on the old Erard which had been brought from home for the occasion in a float.[1] Almost all the young men wore evening clothes, much to father's amusement and to Janie's satisfaction and mine, but to the withering contempt of Mr. Lavery, the little dancing-master, grown very old, whom mother had invited to look on, and who stood in a corner in his velvet breeches and buckle shoes, despising trousers and boiled shirts.

Janie was the loveliest, and I the happiest of the girls who were there; father and mother were proud of us, and so was Lavery, although he deplored his old pupils *demeaning* to round dances. He was pacified when I chose him for my partner in *Sir Roger de Coverley* at the end of the dance in preference to Richard and all others. We bowed and chassé'd, gave the high hand and rounded elbow to opposite partners, led off to right and left with two magnificent turns, meeting again with deep bow and deeper curtsey. Equally splendid was the icy disdain with which we treated the applause of our inferiors. My convent schoolfellows declared that Mr. Lavery and I were models of *bonne tenue*.

'Bravo!' Richard whispered in my ear as he said goodbye, 'now I am sure you have a kind heart. You're a clever little monkey too. I—I'll be writing again before long.'

[1] A low cart used for carrying animals.

As time went on father grew impatient and thought Richard was playing with me. He liked him and none the less because he was a substantial farmer and the heir of two prosperous uncles.

'Shall I have a word with the young fellow, love?' he asked mother ōne day. I heard her quietly advising him to say nothing and let things take their own course.

After the dance our *beaux* took to calling regularly on Sunday afternoons. Father discouraged those who had no land and, on one occasion when two medical students drove rather boisterously to the door, father turned the horse's head round, bade them begone and let them never again insult his family by arriving in such a state. Ellie who saw the episode, told us that 'the y'ung fellas were not drunk, but had drink taken. They was sober enough when they went,' she added pityingly, 'after meetin' the Day o' Judgment in the masthter's face.'

Among the sober and well-behaved was a new young man whom Alfie had brought to the dance and who called persistently ever since.

'After Janie, as usual, I suppose!' poor father said, rather annoyed, because her admirers seldom had land behind them and were often what we privately called city gents.

'I think he admires Sissy,' I heard mother say gently, 'he seems to follow her about with his eyes.'

'Sheep's eyes,' father grunted crossly.

This was news to me. I looked Mr. Coppinger over and found his sheep's eyes fixed on me. Compared with him-in-the-niche, he was but a puppet.

'Why doesn't Richard Fogarty look in on Sundays?' father went on, looking aggrieved, and well he might with a pack of youths frustrating his Sunday rest. As mother didn't answer he took his hat and went out to see the bull where, by the lake, he met young Mr. Willie Stewart, Lord Carbery's agent, who stopped to talk. Whether they plotted to decide my future I cannot say, but father returned in high good humour and Richard heard the next day that Miss Sissy O'Brien had a promising new suitor! Who would be more likely to tell him that story than his landlord's agent, Mr. Willie Stewart?

## 35: COURTSHIP

It was the last day of harvest, a splendid day, the heat tempered
by a brisk breeze. Father and his men were in the cornfield,
loading the last of the golden stooks. In the rickyard great John
Heffernan and Four-tooth, his son, were shaping sheaves to
their liking on the stack in readiness for the last loads. The maids
were sitting with old Peggy-the-Caps on the wayfarers' bench
playing weird mousey notes on Jews' harps. In the kitchen Peg
Quirke minded the singing kettle.

There was a stillness over the place. Janie and Annie were
away; mother was resting after attending the wedding of a
neighbour's daughter, who did not know which of two brothers she was to marry until she stood before the altar and saw
*the wrong one* by her side.

I was in a sad and pessimistic mood unworthy of the lovely
day; with Tennyson under my arm I was making for the hawthorn arbour thinking to read *Mariana,* when Ellie came in
search of me.

'There's a horse in the yard with a letter for you, Miss Sissy,'
she said with a broad grin on her homely face. 'The ould
stable-lad will give it to no one but yourself, not if Holy

Father himself sent word from Rome, would he give it to anyone else.'

'Thank you, Ellie,' I said coldly, and leaving *Mariana* face
downward on the grass, I went towards the low-bowing
groom.

"Tis from Mr. Richard,' he whispered. 'He told me get back
wid the speed of the Black Mare o' Lough Gur[1] that died from
a puff of run.'

I took the letter to the little room. It was a plain, straightfor-
ward offer of marriage, unadorned by any word of love or line
of poetry. I answered equally simply, accepting the offer. Then
I went to mother.

'*Mr. Fogarty's groom*,' Ellie announced meaningly, 'will not
wait another minute for the answer. He is stravaiguin' up and
down the yard in his little ornymental spurs like a fightin'-cock
in a pit.'

'You had better see him, Sissy,' mother said.

'Will I get the answer now for Mr. Richard?' the old man
asked piteously, gathering the reins in his hand.

'No,' I told him in a matter of fact voice. 'The answer will go
by post.'

'Och! how will I say him that, God help him! Wouldn't
there be *anny* sort of a word I c'd tell him? If ye c'd but see him
fidgeting about the yard, onaisy as a weaned foal . . .'

'Tell him I will write.'

The old man's face fell. He said no more but rode away,
drooping and dejected.

Mother was not surprised to hear my news. She read Richard's letter and approved my answer which Tom Hickey, how-

[1]A famous chaser of the past which was never beaten in a race and died
from galloping too fast.

ever tired from harvesting, must take to the post after father had given his consent. It would not have been proper to send an answer by the groom. It would have seemed like leaping into Richard's arms.

I wandered about while mother's quill squeaked as she wrote to inform the aunts of my engagement. Another of them had lately died and been buried in the deep grave at Knockaney, where, according to their solemn promise to one another, all seven sisters would lie together.[1] No husbands were to come between them.

Father came in and gave me his blessing. He cared a great deal for my happiness and thought Richard and I were well suited to one another; besides which Richard's land and prospects were on a par with the dowry he would give with me. He sat down to write to Mrs. Fogarty, the father being dead, and to Father Ryan and to Jack Gubbins and to Cousin Jane Purcell, while Janie, all smiles and excitement, wrote the news to Bessie in Belgrade and brother in the county Meath. The maids hovered wistfully in the background. They were told nothing; perhaps they understood that the aunts and the priest must hear before anyone else for later they changed their manner and behaved as they did when mother's Fenian nephews were *in keeping* in the little room years before, pretending ignorance, knowing all.

It is funny being engaged: one feels like plain gingerbread suddenly gilt; parents are pleased, as if one had won a race; sisters assume an unusual respect. One does not quite know how an engaged girl ought to behave.

The aunts arrived with Cousin Power next morning to bestow blessings and advice; Cousin Jane Purcell likewise, who

[1]The promise was kept.

congratulated me with the unnatural heartiness common to spinsters, which I have since thought is like the patter of a quack at a fair who highly recommends medicine he would scorn to swallow. Jack Gubbins rode over to slap father on the back and drink our healths in *J.J.*, and Doctor Gubbins called on a solemn errand—to warn mother that there was consumption in the Fogarty family—Lily, my schoolfellow, was very ill with it. When mother said, 'We are all in God's hand,' he turned a pitying eye in my direction.

Cousin Julia came by chance the same afternoon. We looked guiltily at one another for no one had written the news to her.

'Look at you now, the three of you!' she began indignantly as she tossed back her bonnet strings, 'sitting down to read three separate books *in the afternoon.*'

'We don't read a book in pairs,' Annie said, 'it's bad for the eyes.'

'Show me the young farmer that wants a wife who sits about with a book when she ought to be churning or feeding the fowl!' Cousin Julia stopped and drew a deep breath.

'We churn very early in warm weather,' Janie told her. 'Sissy and I were in the dairy at five this morning.'

'The hens are up as soon as it is light,' Annie said. 'We don't have to feed them often on a farm. Father invented a way-out for them by which foxes can't get in, so they're up early when the grass is full of worms and slugs . . .'

'Hens need meat-food if they're to lay rich eggs.'

'Slugs and worms are very meaty,' Annie retorted, the glint of battle in her eye. We looked apprehensively at our bold baby and tried to propitiate the visitor.

'It was good of you to come over in this heat, cousin. Won't you lie on the sofa while Ellie gets you some tea?'

'Sofa indeed! *I* wasn't brought up soft as all that. Who plays on that piano, I should like to know?'

'I do,' I answered with spirit. 'We all do, one or two at a time. Father loves to hear us.'

'He seems to want to keep his daughters with him till they're as withered as old peas in a pod.'

'We're fairly young,' Janie said meekly.

'Sissy's getting on, but she's a fine handsome girl still and all, with her brown eyes, and brown hair thick enough for a sparrow to nest in. How tall are you, child?'

'Five feet eight.'

'I'll keep an eye out for a tall husband for you. . . .'

Just then mother came in. 'Have you told Cousin Julia your news?'

I blushed furiously and prepared to bolt. 'I couldn't . . . you tell her . . . I'll see about tea.'

'Sissy is going to marry Richard Fogarty.'

'For God's sake! That thin young fellow! Why wasn't I told?'

'You are being told,' Annie said laughing.

'I might have been consulted! That overgrown young man with a sister dying in a decline! Well, well! I'm glad one of you is getting off and making a good match. Not but what you'll miss her, Anne,' she added, turning to mother.

'I shall. I am losing my right hand.'

In the kitchen Ellie and Bridgie were giggling hysterically.

'The ould news-picker! *Why wasn't I told?* says she, frothin' at the mouth! *Why wasn't I consulted?*'

'What *that one* knows at cow-time the country-side'll be repeatin' before moonrise.'

'Och, Miss Sissy, will the misthress leave me and Bridgie run with the news to the neighbours? She will? Now? Glory to God! You can wet the tea, so? God bless you, Miss Sissy and *himself* and may you have a fine long family.'

How extraordinary, I thought it to have a *himself* of my own.

That night the kitchen was packed with well-wishers who all talked at once. The air hummed with blessings. I felt as if flowers were falling on me. I was very happy. It seemed as if the neighbours did not dislike me; they even loved me.

At nine they went away having eaten and drunk; reluctantly they went, still talking, disturbing the sleeping creatures of the farm. Old Turkey gobbled for a long time so that some of those descending the hill believed they heard Fer Fi laughing.

Hectic days followed. Father Ryan called and was very kind; with his white hair he reminded me of Uncle Richard whose curate he had been.

'Your uncle would have approved,' he said, 'he liked all the Fogartys. I think he would have asked you are you sure you love young Richard? We priests see too much of loveless marriages.'

'Yes, Father. I love him.'

'You have waited so long. . . . I thought perhaps you were thinking of someone else, waiting . . . I mean . . .'

'No, Father. Yes, Father?'

'That's right, then. I once thought you had a fancy for that young fellow who came with Tilecote——'

'P-P-Peter?'

'A clever young lad—he's written a capital monograph on the Indigenous Long-nosed Pig.'

I looked at the ceiling to keep my tears from overflowing. Father Ryan went to the window. With his back turned to me he said gently, 'You have put him out of your heart?'

'Long ago, Father. It was a childish fancy, not l-l-love.'

'And you love Richard?'

'I do, Father. I do love Richard.'

'I wish all girls had your sense, my child.'

I began to laugh. *My sense,* I thought, *my willy-nilly sense!*

To keep myself in control I began to mutter under my breath, thinking of Richard,

> *How do I love thee? Let me count the ways.*
> *I love thee to the level of every day's*
> *Most quiet need, by sun and candle-light . . .*

Richard came over the following day driving himself on a spick and span jaunting-car. He invited me to go for a turn with him. It was understood that Janie would be our chaperon and that when she could not come Annie or mother would take her place. We drove in almost complete silence; the fiery horse needed all Richard's attention. After a pleasant drive of ten miles without a stop or an accident we returned to Drumlaigh. Janie and I ran to our room to take off our jackets while Richard went with Paddy to rub the hot horse down. With the door shut, we laughed until we cried, and Annie thumped us on the back and thrust a wet sponge in our faces.

'Stop laughing, stop crying,' she ordered, 'or I shall go for mother.' So we stopped at last. Neither Janie nor I had any idea that being engaged is so funny.

When Richard went away that evening at prayer time he shook hands all round and looked at me. I went obediently to help him on with his coat. Father was wrapt in his paper, mother reading, Janie and Annie sewing with downcast eyes. I left the door wide open, fearing my family would think that Richard might kiss me good-bye. I need not have been afraid. He took my hands, kissed them warmly and was gone, exactly like Mr. Browning in E.B.B.'s Sonnet xxxviii.

I read this to Janie in bed and we laughed all over again, until father's voice boomed through the grating, 'Be quiet, children.'

'I adore Richard,' Janie whispered.

'I'm glad you do. I feel quite fond of him myself.'

Richard and I were allowed by mother to visit his aunt, Mrs.
Fogarty, by ourselves, because father had business in Bruff and
would drive with us to the door of the *Carbery Arms*[1] and call
for us again. It was a most exciting moment arriving with
Richard at the heavy, iron-lined door of our future home,
where Betty Butt, a short fat old servant was waiting 'to alarm
the mistress', who came promptly to welcome us. She was a
fine, imposing woman whom I loved at sight as she received
me in a vast embrace. In the background, hugging Richard,
was Mrs. Kane O'Dowd, a visiting aunt of his, who for good
nature and loquacity might have been twin-sister of her immortal namesake. I learnt, over a glass of cowslip wine, that she
was originally the wife of Colonel Kane of Ballycotton, whom
she buried; finding widowhood oppressive she married Mr.
O'Dowd, solicitor to the Customs in London. From experience
of life in Ballycotton and stations abroad and in London, in the
army and the law, she had become, she assured us, a thorough
woman of the world. There was some mystery about her step-
son who had a post at Buckingham Palace, of what nature no
one ever heard, but we learnt that a royal carr'ge was sent to
bring him to the palace.

'You're going to London for your honeymoon, I hear,' she
said to Richard, 'so if you hang about the gate you'll maybe see
Jimmy driving in. God bless the man, he'll not be too proud to
give you a nod of the head.'

Aunt Elizabeth led us over the house, beginning with the
sunny rooms known as Lord Carbery's end; the bedroom, with
a carved four-post bed, plain club-footed tables and chairs which,
Mrs. Fogarty told us, were genuine Queen Anne; speckle-pattern
Spode basins and jugs and a carved looking-glass on the wall,

[1]The hotel was let with the farm of which Richard became tenant on the
death of his uncle.

'Chippendale, as you may know by the leaves and the doves,' before which successive visiting lords arranged their wigs. In the sitting-room where they used to interview tenants, and which was to be our sanctum, were two red velvet armchairs. Richard moved them to the hearth-rug and behind his aunt's back, showed me how we should sit in them—uncommonly close together, I thought.

'Your poor uncle died in that bed,' his widow remarked, 'and so shall I, please God, and you two, too, in your turn. Major Evans, old Lord Carbery's brother, slept in it on and off for years before he died. Now the judge has these rooms for three weeks on end, when he comes for the sessions. He pays a pound a day. Colonel Fenton Freke came now and again in past years and had to lie from corner to corner of the bed, he's so tall, but Mr. William Freke, his brother, is just the reverse and declared he got lost every night. A lively little gentleman he was then, with beautiful soft curls on his head, and whiskers like two big golden sausage-ringlets. He used to make your poor uncle. shoot with him all day and sit up half the night, telling stories and singing songs. *At the Court of Carass* was one, about one of his own relations, a lady, for love of whom a Protestant clergyman hanged himself. When Mr. Freke sang *Och! 'Twas Dermot O'Rowland MacFigg,* people outside came crowding into the bar-parlour to hear his fine voice and jolly laugh, and to drink his health. That was long ago. None of the family comes nowadays.'

When we reached the kitchen we sat down to hear about the black cook from William the Fourth's kitchen who was brought to Bruff by Major Evans as his servant, and chose to stay as *chef* in the hotel. He was a character besides being an artist at his job. His coffee and Indian curry brought numbers of gentlemen and officers to the hotel, who would send for him after dinner and tip him well. He stayed with Aunt Elizabeth until he died.

"'Twas a strange thing,' Betty Butt told me when I went to admire the old delf she was washing, 'but the hair of the black cook turned as white as flour, and for all his skin was dark, it could show pale when he was ill. There wasn't one in Bruff but pitied poor Darkey for dying so far from his own country. He lies quiet enough in the churchyard yonder, God rest his soul, but once or twice, at nightfall, he's been seen sitting in the chimney corner, basting the roast on the spit like any humble old follower of the family.'

Aunt Elizabeth stood up and said 'Nonsense' in a loud, decided voice, before leading the way to the parlour where Aunt O'Dowd was already sitting in her place at the well-spread table.

'Do you like our home?' Richard whispered in my ear behind the door.

'It's *perfect*,' I murmured, 'it's too good to be true! I shall love to live here and help Aunt Elizabeth.'

'Oh,' Richard said, disappointed, '*Aunt Elizabeth*.'

'No, you.' As his ear was so near I kissed it lightly. He told me afterwards it was like a gun going off.

## 36: MARRIAGE

October came and went with its mists and sunshine, its warm dark evenings when Richard and I sat in the beech arbour watching the moon rise and now and then exchanging shy kisses.

Hallowe'en came again; apples bobbed, nuts hopped and skipped. Once more father read the Litany for the Dead and we prayed for her who had joined the great company of faithful departed, darling Dooley.

And at last, when November was going out in dreary darkness, came the day of my marriage. The sky was dark when I woke, except for a few stars; a cold wind flicked oak-galls and twigs against the window pane, breaking the silence, while I lay thinking, wondering if I were sorry or glad. Soon a faint light shone through the grating and faintly rose the voices of father and mother talking together. Then the maids stole downstairs to blow up the fire and make tea which we might not share, for we were to receive the Holy Communion and must go fasting to church.

'Sissy,' mother said at the door, 'you have an hour to dress.'

'I am all fingers and thumbs,' I complained to Janie, 'will you help me? Will you do my hair?'

In my petticoats, white stockings and satin slippers, I went to mother in the spare-room to put on the dress which Bessie had worn at her wedding, white, soft and lacey, and her narrow wreath of orange-blossom, and the Limerick-lace veil lent me by Mr. Todd of Limerick. I took my gloves in my hand and let mother wrap my shivering body in a shawl and a fluffy new blanket.

Father and brother drove away on the car as Ellie hurried up to announce 'the *landoo* for Miss Sissy'. Aunt Elizabeth had sent the wedding landau from the *Carbery Arms*, with a pair of greys and Dan, her smiling coachman, bedecked with chrysanthemums.

'God bless you, dear Miss Sissy and send you happy,' Ellie cried at the door.

'God be on the road,' Bridgie sobbed; she had meant to say something less ordinary but forgot it.

'Good luck, oh, good luck!'

Loud cheers rose in the yard; dogs barked, the greys pranced, the coachman cursed.

We are safely past the sandpit, the alley, old Malachi's orchard and Dooley's cottage. The wind is buffeting the lake and throwing spray at the carriage. Two or three old gran'das stand by the roadside, curtseying as old men did in those days. They cheer shrilly and the coachman pulls in the horses. The gran'das laugh and point to east and west.

'Fer Fi is laffin'!' they shout, 'that's good luck for ye! Good luck.'

How they came crowding round me, the spirits of the magic lake—Ainë, Fer Fi, the Old Kings in diadem and torque. As in a dream I see stone men worshipping within stone circles whose monoliths are crusted with copper and gold; bronze men are running incredibly swiftly after elk and boar; on the hillside a giant is being buried, his golden sword beside him, by a tribe of giants who sing hymns to a Sacred Pig; a company of dwarfs, Fer Fi's men, are manning the ship of the banshee's music-makers who carry comfort to the dying on Gur's shore, as to Mary Deasy, sewing her shroud; old Biddy, crying for Me-John; Dick Dooley, rattling in his throat, the youngest Miss Baily. Here come fairy folk in turquoise jackets, riding piebald horses the size of cats, hunting weasel. Ten times more alive than mortals they are, keen-eyed, shouting as they hurl their tiny spears. . . . 'Got him, that time! Not yet . . . he's off . . . yoi, yoi, yoi, gone away!'

Sissy O'Brien has gone away from her home—for ever. Her coach is drawn by the Black Mare of Lough Gur and Lord Desmond's silver-shod horse. They are driven by old Miss Baily, her rings slipping over her fingers.

'Wake up, Sissy! we're getting to Knockaney!'

Father Ryan is still in his house next the church for it is not yet half-past eight. The sacristan runs to knock on his door. The priest is getting old; for his sake the wedding is here instead of at St. Patrick's Well. He comes clutching his cassock, bending his head to the wind. Father is at the door—the darling man, how can I leave him? Mother is going away from me, walking up the aisle in her grey dress and lace fichu. She is a lovely MacNamara! And how unselfish to let her *right hand* go.

Janie unblankets me and arranges my veil. She looks rosy and warm in her silvery woollen poplin. Am I not foolish to be dressed in gossamer?

'Can't I keep on the blanket?' I ask her feebly. She stares. 'Wake up, Sissy, you're wool-gathering! Attend to your wedding!'

'Come along,' says father briskly, 'step out.'

Three ghosts step out alongside. One has a lovely face in a nun's veil. 'Walk naturally,' she breathes, suppressing a cough ... 'the Foundress ... *bonne tenue* ...'

'One two, one two,' the second murmurs, 'hold up the head, chin in, one two, one—two ...'

'That's my doty child,' says the third, 'God bless her.'

Richard and I are married. We stare at one another in astonishment. Father slips the marriage fee, twenty-five pounds, into the priest's hand and gives gratuities to the sacristan and others. Several people kiss me. Brother first and out of his turn; Corney Fogarty, the best man; Minnie, my sister-in-law, who is going to be a Faithful Companion of Jesus, and my own dears. There are no guests, for Lily Fogarty is dying.

Richard and I drive away in the landau. We are going to Knocklong because of catching the Dublin train. I refuse to wear the blanket or *be said* by anyone. I am a married woman. Richard remembers that he did not kiss me in church, so he does it now, carefully, because of my wreath. It was like Mr. Browning's second—E.B.B.'s Sonnet xxxviii. I say, 'Isn't it cold?' and Richard says he is warm because his mother made him put on a thick vest. 'She cried dreadfully,' he adds. 'It really is cold,' I say after a pause, 'it's sleeting.' Richard wishes we were sitting in the red velvet armchairs before our own sitting-room fire. I wish I was having hot tea with Ellie in the warmth of the hearth at home.

We arrive at Harris's hotel, Knocklong, and step into a throng of beggars, not our own, but pushing, vociferous crea-

tures from Limerick. Richard throws them coppers which the
waiter has in readiness at the door; he knows the etiquette of
weddings. Mrs. Harris kisses me, and shows me where the
bride's chair is set opposite the wedding-cake. It is ten o'clock.
Father Ryan sits on my left, father is opposite with Mrs. Harris,
mother next to Richard. I can reach her hand behind Richard's
back. I hold it fast while the maids are taking off the white
ribbons which deceivingly hold previously carved chickens in
shape. A waiter is carving ham and cold beef. The celery is
frozen but there are hot baked potatoes, thank God. Cold apple
tart, jelly—you'd think we were at a summer picnic.

'Sissy—the wedding cake, cut it.'

I try. Richard sees how I fumble and strengthens my hand
with his own, warm, strong, friendly. I look at him and then
hurriedly away. Was I making sheep's eyes? God forbid.

There are to be no speeches because of Lily but father stands
up and says, *'My dear children, God bless them;'* Father Ryan
echoes, *'God bless you both,'* and everyone drinks and chokes
because of the icy bubbling of the champagne.

After that I go to Mrs. Harris's hot bedroom where Janie lets
me out of my finery, talking about keeping it for her own
wedding one of these days. Mother, with trembling hands,
helps me into a warm woollen dress which matches my hair
and into the sealskin coat which is her present to me. Mrs.
Harris sits on the hearthrug to put on my toasted stockings and
boots while Janie settles my hat and turns its elastic under my
hair. I am putting on my gloves, hiding my wedding-ring with
reluctance, when Richard comes to the door. 'Time to go,' he
says, smiling at me. He looks like St. John in his brown frieze
overcoat.

'Good-bye, father *darling*. Good-bye, mother, oh *mother* . . .'

'Come along, come along!' brother shouts, fairly throwing

us into the carriage and banging the door. 'Right, Dan! Drive like Billy-o or they'll miss the train. Good-bye, Sis.'

Whizz, comes the rice, whizz, whizz! Oh, the wretches!

'Good luck,' brother shouts, jumping about so that no one has time for tears. 'Now then the O'Briens, all together for the old cry—Lough Gur for ever! *Sean-ait-aboo.*'

# APPENDIX

## A LETTER FROM BESSIE

The posts from Poland were slow and it seemed a long time before we had word of Bessie's arrival; longer still before we heard about her new home, but at last a letter came, meant for us all.

*. . . I must tell you about my new home. There is one suite of rooms that delights me to look at: four or five little salons, one opening into the other, and so prettily furnished; when all the doors are open you can look to the end which crowns all—a greenhouse full of splendid flowers and a beautiful view over the country enlivened by the sails of boats going up and down the river. The garden with its parterres is exquisite; the fruit garden is immense and full of splendid fruit trees. Over the porch of the house there is a wide balcony where one can sit and read or walk up and down. In our schoolroom there are two large windows looking into the garden.*

*Now I must describe the persons with whom I have to do. Well, to begin with the nominal head of the house, Monsieur Swinarski. He is small and not remarkable in any way. He admires Madame and listens most attentively to everything she says. Sometimes she talks like this:—'Mademoiselle O'Brien, no one could have a better husband than mine! I assure you he is a treasure, but whatever my affection may be for him I do not wish you a husband like him; no, a woman ought to look up to and be in fact a little afraid of her husband. Now, I can't do that, positively no; however much I may love and respect Monsieur Swinarski I do not fear him. No, impossible! He always refers to me if any question of importance is to be decided.*

*Respect, admire him—yes, but fear him—no. Joseph!—Impossible!'*
*Monsieur Swinarski, who has been looking round the room, de-*
*lighted, during this declaration, gives a last parting glance of triumph*
*at the assembled company as if to say 'Does anyone pretend to say he*
*ever saw a cleverer woman than my wife?' and then turns to thank*
*Madame for her eulogy of his virtues and kisses her hands five or six*
*times with extraordinary fervour. Number 2, who is really Number 1*
*as you can guess, Madame Swinarski, is beyond my description. I*
*seldom felt so attracted towards anyone; she is intelligent, well-in-*
*formed and noble-hearted, above all so patriotic; you cannot imagine*
*the extent to which she carries the love of her country, and so we are*
*well met. She cries sometimes in speaking of the wrongs they all suffer;*
*we compare our stories and what a resemblance we find between the*
*two nations! Just listen to one or two homely examples:—the Poles*
*are accused, like the Irish, of being dirty, of sleeping nine or ten in one*
*room with the pig, of getting drunk at fairs, of being always divided*
*and quarrelling among themselves. They, like us, are remarkable for*
*their wit, their family attachment and generosity, their hospitality,*
*their great awe of and devotion to their priests. The peasants salute*
*each other like ours, saying, God bless you, or May the name of Christ*
*be praised. They are inclined to superstition and mistaken piety, such*
*as making the sign of the cross and saying devout prayers before setting*
*out on a stealing expedition. They are accused, of course by their op-*
*pressors, of disguising their real sentiments, palavering, etc., and are*
*noted for their quick temper. They share our devotion to the Blessed*
*Virgin Mary. The Poles' manner of praying aloud in the chapel, of*
*moaning and beating their breast at the Mass, reminds me forcibly of*
*what we read of the old Irish customs. As for their houses, they are*
*exactly like those in the row near Ned Dineen's house beyond the*
*Chapel, on the way to Knocklong, and there is always either a dung-*
*hill or a lough of water outside the door. The people are always gay*
*even in their greatest distress. I could go on for hours proving to you*
*that oppression is the cause of their and our faults, otherwise how*

*could there be such a striking resemblance between the two nations, so far apart, having no communication and of different race?*

*I must continue to describe Madame. You should see her when she talks of her country! She always finishes in tears. Her mother died saying, 'My God, I never did anything wrong; I always gave to the poor; I practised faithfully my duties as a Christian and a good Catholic. I never so much as harmed a fly, but I cannot forgive the enemies of my country! No, never! and I pray in this solemn moment when I go to appear before the great Judge, that the most terrible misfortune may fall on the head of whoever of my children forgets the misfortunes of Poland! To you, my sons, I leave it to avenge her! You, my daughters, never dare to rejoice in your family or in solitude; never be happy—I forbid it to you—till Poland is free!' Her sons, both before and after her death, were in every insurrection of the country. Once, after a battle in the depths of winter, she went over the battlefield with a lantern in her hand looking for the corpses of her husband and two sons; she was accompanied by Madame Swinarski (then only 15 years old). Every body lying there she lifted, peering into the dead face. 'Is it Casimir? Is it Stanislaus? Is that Thaddeus?' What courage, and what a scene for a young girl, especially when she found her brother, 16 years old, dead not from wounds so much as from the cold which penetrated and congealed them. They carried him home between them, and had a rejoicing for the neighbourhood in his honour. 'This is the dearest of my children,' said his mother, 'he has given me more happiness to-day than all the rest of you put together. I can only say that I hope to see each of you share the same glorious fate! For what is a Polish noble born if not to die when the enemies conquer?' Madame Swinarski is the counterpart of her admirable mother, yet her brothers and sisters say, 'Our Valerie has not a grain of patriotism!' When I heard this I cried out, 'Oh, then, if that is the way, may God defend us from the others!' She assures me that with them it is shame and disgrace to a family that has not lost some member fighting against the Germans or the Russians. The contempt they have for a young man* who has never been imprisoned, or lost an eye or an arm, or cannot show that he has taken an active part in the rebellions, is unbearably cutting.

Now Number 3, this is Madame Wagner, sister of Madame, who has lived here since her husband died. She is the tallest woman I ever saw; her right arm being paralysed I often find an opportunity to do little things for her; she is grateful for the smallest attention. She is Sophie's Mamma and has another daughter who is at school in Paris. Just think what she pays every quarter! Twenty-four pounds without extras, washing, etc.! Is it not very expensive?

Now Number 4, Mademoiselle Antoinette, who came to meet me at Strzalkowo. She is gay and pretty and is nearly always here. I like her very much; she pretends to teach me Polish and I teach her French; we get on very well together. You must know everyone here speaks French. Polish is the language of the people, and all speak it, but French is used in good society. It is a good thing that the Poles keep alive their old tongue, but, as is always the case with a conquered nation, people seem to despise it. After all, what were they to do?—speak the conqueror's tongue as we Irish unfortunates have done? Perish the thought! Neither German nor Russian will ever be the tongue of Poland. No! They took to the language of France, that glorious defender and protector of the oppressed. Thus we find people living hundreds of miles from France, speaking and writing the French language as if it were their own! Oh, that we Irish had done the same! The Germans have forbidden Polish in all the schools but of course, however it may vex them to leave things as they are, they dare not meddle with the French language.

Numbers 5 and 6, Constance (Madame's daughter) and Sophie (Wagner) her niece, who was to have gone to Paris with her sister but, as I happened to be here, her Mamma desired she would remain; therefore Madame Swinarski presented her to me as my second pupil with many excuses and hopes that I would not believe she had intended it from the first or that she had wilfully cheated me. I am glad to have her; the more the merrier! I do not think it will make any difference in my salary but I am satisfied, for teaching is in itself a re-compense. Sophie is more of a child than Constance, she is pretty and a fine character, and she has fun in her too. I believe she has talent for music; both of them can play simple pieces; at present I am wading through Just before the Battle, Mother with Constance—she finds it rather difficult. I have an hour's music lesson with each child every day and an hour for my own practice.

Monsieur Swinarski, who never has anything to do, comes in and sits down near the great stove to listen, for he delights in my playing; he walks up and down when I play a march, and waltzes round the table with Mysia—ah! that brings me to Number 7, and surely such an important personage cannot be left out of my category. She is Mademoiselle Swinarski, everyone's pet, especially her own. I must say I pity Monsieur Swinarski. See what it is to be a gentleman! He can't always go out hunting, he does not care for reading, and a Polish noble never dreams of undertaking business or farming. As for me, I would do gardening sooner than spend my life with my hands in my pockets! I wonder he never thinks of it.

Number 8 is Monsieur Ostmanrwski—I don't know how to spell his name—he is the overseer and as he only speaks Polish and German our conversation never goes farther than two or three phrases, for I am afraid to talk German here where everyone is so conversant with that language, besides as I already told you they do not like speaking it. There is nothing particular to say of Number 8; he is low-sized, with dark whiskers, black eyes and is quite unpretending. We only see him at meals; we salute and that's all. We often meet him on horseback about the grounds—he raises his hat, the demoiselles nod. Behold the extent of the acquaintance!

Number 9 is—the governess; she and Number 8 are the only ones who are not members of the family. I have nothing particular to say about her; she is serious and much occupied with her duties; she comes from France, but is a native of Ireland and seems to be very proud of it!

*I forget her name, they cannot pronounce it here. Perhaps you could
give me some information about her? She is rather a commonplace
individual, never seems to notice anyone or anything; she spends much
of her time in writing long letters to which she generally receives a
short reply. Poor thing! Is she not silly? I am sure you think so.
Well, so much for the family. Now it would not be fair if I didn't give
you a peep downstairs. There is the housekeeper; she orders everyone
about, even Madame, and fulfils her duties perfectly, but she is old,
and has had great sorrow, and having lost her only child she has no
one to love. She is weary of living, silent and sullen, and does not
know how to speak a civil word to anyone. I often hear her in the
kitchen growling at the servants.*

*Dickens would have delighted in the solemn boy who is butler and
footman in one. I have never seen such a stock-still face! He goes
about offering the dishes as if he were made of stone—you must know
that here a plate is put before each person, the solemn boy holds the
dish on his arm and offers you a fork to help yourself. If you refuse, he
shuts his eyes in despair and goes on to the next. When we laugh, as
we often do at Monsieur Swinarski's jokes, the boy writhes as if in
agony and hurriedly leaves the room rather than be so disrespectful as
to join in the merriment. The maid who does our rooms wakes me
every morning by kissing my knees through the coverlet! She is such a
good poor thing, quick, humble and diligent. These are all the servants
with whom I have anything to do. There are besides the coachman,
cook and housemaid.*

*Now that I've done with persons, I must tell you a little about the
customs here. First, that you may know on what footing I am, let me
assure you that governesses are not at all looked down on as in the
British Isles—on the contrary, they are looked up to and treated with
the greatest respect; this I find not only with regard to myself but with
other families in the neighbourhood, above all when the governess is
French or English, which latter includes Irish, cursed arrangement! I
find, if I want to be agreeable; I must go a great deal into society,*

*which you are well aware is not to my liking. It is sometimes annoying when I am writing and the children are studying and all is quiet and silent, a carriage drives up to the door and we are overwhelmed with visitors. It would be greatly to my mind to remain in my room at my ease, but till now I have made the sacrifice on every occasion and complied immediately with Madame's request that I should present myself. She treats me with even extra attention and kindness when there are visitors. She never calls me anything but* Ma fille *or* Cher enfant, *and the young ones too have dropped the formal* Mademoiselle O'Brien *for* Mademoiselle Bessie, *which is become my regular name. I believe the people to whom I am introduced think it is my surname, at least, it is the only way I can account for the question a lady put to me soon after my arrival. 'Are you an only daughter, Mademoiselle? or are there still more demoiselles Bessies?' Everyone is very kind to me, they almost always speak French on account of me, and if one forgets and relaxes into Polish, another is sure to remind her how tiresome it must be for me when I can understand nothing. I have met no one as yet who speaks English. They like my playing immensely because I play with feeling—so they say. I am invited everywhere, but as yet I have not gone to parties except once, for I asked permission to remain at home. Since I really desired it, Madame did not press me. I hope I need not go. You must know they are all dancing mad; it is dance, dance, till I am perfectly sick of it. It is a year since I danced—you remember how strictly it was forbidden at the Convent— besides here they jump about in a way I can not. The national dance of Poland is very pretty, they call it the mazurka. It is like a galop, mixed with figures as in the quadrille, after which the principal lady throws a kerchief in the air and whoever of the gentlemen catches it waltzes with her twice round the room. Madame Swinarski plays for us to dance. Sometimes she plays the prayer of Poland for her liberty. I never heard anything so religious, solemn and sad; it drew tears from the eyes of Montalembert when he heard it. He came here, I am told, after an unsuccessful insurrection, and found the nation in mourning;*

*all the women wore black, and in the churches nothing was heard but the most sorrowful music. Did I tell you that it is the peasants who sing in church? Everyone sings, young and old, the organ is scarcely heard. The name of our church is Mishlybusla. Is there not something Irish in that sound?*

*Do not be surprised at any irregularity about my letters, as the post is very uncertain; there is difficulty in bringing the letters across the frontier. These stupid Russians are all along the boundary, every second man on foot and on horseback with a settled distance between them, always watching lest anyone passes who has not a legal permission to show. I forgot to tell you of my passport. I had it, of course, at Gravelines. France being a Republic it begins in the name of the French people.* We, the constituted authorities, pray that the states and countries allied or in friendly relations with France, let pass freely and without question or hindrance Mademoiselle Bessie O'Brien, residing at Gravelines, native of Ireland, born at Lough Gur, Co. Limerick, and passing in Belgium, Germany and Russia, and also to give her aid and protection in case of need. *Then comes signalement: eyes, hair, colour, complexion, height, etc. (it flatters me so much I do not think you would recognise me). Do you remember how Harry Lorrequer changed his passport by mistake and was paid all the honours due to Meyerbeer? It is time that I should bring this letter to a close, perhaps it is already much too long for your patience. Remember, Sissy, I expect you will reply to it—and show by your remarks that you take some interest in me and my new surroundings.*

# Irish Country People

## Kevin Danaher

*Irish Country People* is simply one fascinating glorious feast of folklore and interesting sidelights of history recorded without a fraction of a false note or a grain of sentimentality. The topics covered in the twenty essays range over a wide field of history, folklore, mythology and archaeology. There are discussions about cures, curses and charms; lords, labourers and wakes; names, games and ghosts; prayers and fairy tales. Nowadays we find it hard to visualise the dark winter evenings of those times when there was no electric light, radio, television or cinemas. We find it harder to realise that such evenings were not usually long enough for the games, singing, card-playing, music, dancing and story-telling that went on.

We can read about a six-mile traffic jam near Tailteann in the year 1168, just before the Norman invasion, and the incident is authenticated by a reference to the *Annals of the Four Masters.* The whole book is tinged with quiet humour: 'You should always talk to a dog in a friendly, mannerly way, but you should never ask him a question directly, for what would you do if he answered you, as well he might?'

# Folktales of the Irish Countryside

## Kevin Danaher

Nowadays there is a whole generation growing up who cannot remember a time when there was no television; and whose parents cannot remember a time when there was no radio and cinema. It is not, therefore, surprising that many of them wonder what people in country places found to do with their time in the winters of long ago.

People may blink in astonishment when reminded of the fact that the night was too often too short for those past generations of country people, whose own entertainment with singing, music, dancing, cards, indoor games, and storytelling spanned the evenings and into morning light.

Kevin Danaher remembers forty of the stories that enlivened those past days. Some are stories told by members of his own family; others he took down in his own countryside from the last of the traditional storytellers. Included are stories of giants, of ghosts, of wondrous deeds, queer happening, of the fairies and the great kings of Ireland who had beautiful daughters and many problems.

A homely, heartwarming collection of tales that spring naturally from the heart of the Irish countryside.

## 'That's How It Was'
### Kevin Danaher

Irish folk tradition is a wonderful mixture of fact and fancy. Many people believe that our forefathers were so simple and credulous that they believed everything they heard. This is not true and although there were people who would swallow any tall story just as there are many people today who believe every word in television advertisements the average person long ago knew the difference between the fact and fiction that abounded in folk tradition.

Stories believed to be true, especially tales of past happenings were always certified by the saying 'That's how it was', indicating that the *seanchaí* believed it and you had better believe it too, at least within his hearing!

With Kevin Danaher |we travel the roads with the farmers and drovers on the way to the fairs and we meet the *spailpíns*, tramps, tinkers and the travelling musicians and listen to them swap greetings and gossip. We travel the roads our forefathers walked, we rest under the trees that shaded them and we pass the walls that heard their songs and their laughter.

## In Ireland Long Ago
### Kevin Danaher

Those who have only the most hazy ideas about how our ancestors lived in Ireland will find enlightenment in these essays which range widely over the field of Irish folklife. Kevin Danaher describes life in Ireland before the 'brave new world' crept into the quiet countryside. Or perhaps 'describe' is not the right word. He rather invites the reader to call on the elderly people at their homes, to listen to their tales and gossip and taste their food and drink; to step outside and marvel at their pots and pans, ploughs and flails; to meet a water diviner; to join a faction fight; hurry to a wedding and bow down in remembrance of the dead.

Not only does the author write about people with reverence, but those people are reverently introduced to the reader by their own words, as when the Kerryman replied to the Dublin man who asked him if he could take a photograph of his donkey with the baskets: 'You never saw one before? Oh man, you must be from a very backward part of the country!' In this book Kevin Danaher has not only given us a well balanced picture of life in Ireland, but has also gone far to capture the magic of the written word.

# The Year in Ireland – Irish Calendar Customs
## Kevin Danaher

If one were to ask which brand of folk tradition most widely reveals the panorama of the whole, the answer would undoubtedly be 'Calendar Custom'.

Calendar Custom is deeply influenced by climate, fertility of the soil, by sea and river, lake and mountain; it is connected with the daily and yearly routine of work; it embodies divination, healing, mythology and magic; abounds in tale and legend; amusement, sports and pastimes. It contains elements from all phases of Ireland's changing history – pre-Christian features and features which recall the flowering of Early Irish Christianity. Every body of people who came into Ireland have added to Calendar Custom; Scandinavian, Norman, Scots and English have left their mark on it. Above all it is embedded in the common tradition of Western Europe, so many of its features being Irish versions of practices more widely known.

This beautiful book by Kevin Danaher describes how the round of the year, with its cycle of festivals and seasonal work, was observed in the Ireland of yesterday. We follow the rhythm of the year from New Year to Easter, May Day to Harvest and Christmas along the chain of highdays and feastdays, St Brighid's Day, The Borrowed Days, Midsummer, St Swithin's Day, Lunasa, The Pattern Day, Samhain, Martinmas and Christmas. The rich and warm life of Irish folk tradition unfolds: the work of farm and fishing boat; belief and usage; feasting and merrymaking. Picturesque customs are revealed – some forgotten, some forbidden, some still familiar, such as: 'the making of St Brighid's cross; marriage divinations; watching the dancing of the sun on a hilltop on Easter morning; going to the Skelligs; cock-throwing; bullbaiting; herring processions; the swimming of the horses on Lunasa'; and many others. A multi-coloured tapestry.

Kevin Danaher has drawn on a wide variety of sources and on more than thirty years experience of research into Irish folk tradition.

# The Course of Irish History

Edited by T. W. Moody and F. X. Martin

Though many specialist books on Irish history have appeared in the past fifty years, there have been few general works broadly narrating and interpreting the course of Irish history as a whole, in the light of new research. That is what this book, first published in 1967, set out to do; and it is a measure of its success that it is still in demand, being now in its sixteenth printing.

The first of its kind in its field, the book provides a rapid short survey, with a geographical introduction, of the whole course of Ireland's history. Based on the series of television programmes first transmitted by Radio Telefís Éireann from January to June 1966, it is designed to be both popular and authoritative, concise but comprehensive, highly selective but balanced and fair-minded, critical but constructive and sympathetic. A distinctive feature is its wealth of illustrations.

The present edition is a revised and enlarged version of the original book. A new chapter has been added, bringing the narrative to the end of 1982, and the illustrations have been correspondingly augmented. The list of books for further reading has been expanded into a comprehensive bibliography of modern writings on Irish history. The chronology has been rewritten, updated, and much enlarged, so that it now amounts to a substantial supplement to the text. Finally, the index has been revised and extended both to include the new chapter and to fill gaps in the original coverage.

The book has been planned and edited by the late Dr T. W. Moody, fellow emeritus and formerly professor of modern history, Trinity College, Dublin, and Dr F. X. Martin O.S.A., professor of medieval history, University College, Dublin – an appropriate partnership for this enterprise of scholarly cooperation. Of the other 19 contributors, 17 are or were on the staffs of the universities and university colleges of Ireland and two were on those of the universities of Cambridge and of Manchester.